Emigration and Political Development

Although policy makers, international organizations, and academics are increasingly aware of the economic effects of emigration, its potential political effects remain understudied. This book maps the nature of the relationship that links emigration and political development. Jonathon W. Moses explores the nature of political development, arguing that emigration influences it. In particular, he introduces a new cross-national database of annual emigration rates and analyzes specific cases of international emigration (and out-migration within countries) under varying political and economic contexts.

Jonathon W. Moses is currently a professor of political science at the Norwegian University of Science and Technology, where he has taught since 1993. Moses has published several books including *Ways of Knowing* (2007, with Torbjørn Knutsen), *International Migration: Globalization's Last Frontier* (2006), and *Norwegian Catch-up: Development and Globalization before World War II* (2005). He is a co-editor of *European Political Science*. Among his research interests are globalization, international migration, social democracy, and the European Union. Among other places, his articles have appeared in *World Development*, *Journal of Common Market Studies*, and *Politics and Society*.

T0381673

Emigration and Political Development

JONATHON W. MOSES

Norwegian University of Science and Technology

CAMBRIDGE
UNIVERSITY PRESS

Shaftesbury Road, Cambridge CB2 8EA, United Kingdom

One Liberty Plaza, 20th Floor, New York, NY 10006, USA

477 Williamstown Road, Port Melbourne, VIC 3207, Australia

314–321, 3rd Floor, Plot 3, Splendor Forum, Jasola District Centre, New Delhi – 110025, India

103 Penang Road, #05–06/07, Visioncrest Commercial, Singapore 238467

Cambridge University Press is part of Cambridge University Press & Assessment, a department of the University of Cambridge.

We share the University's mission to contribute to society through the pursuit of education, learning and research at the highest international levels of excellence.

www.cambridge.org
Information on this title: www.cambridge.org/9780521173216

First published 2011

A catalogue record for this publication is available from the British Library

Library of Congress Cataloging-in-Publication data
Moses, Jonathon Wayne, 1962–
Emigration and political development / Jonathon W. Moses.
    p.   cm.
Includes bibliographical references and index.
ISBN 978-0-521-19543-0 (hardback) – ISBN 978-0-521-17321-6 (pbk.)
1. Emigration and immigration – Political aspects.   2. Political development.   I. Title.
JV6124.M67   2011
320.9 – dc22   2011012922

ISBN   978-0-521-19543-0   Hardback
ISBN   978-0-521-17321-6   Paperback

To Maggi

Contents

List of Tables

List of Figures

Preface

Work on this book began several years ago when I first became aware of the inadequate development options available to people in the world's poorest places. A teacher of international political economy, I had become impatient with the meager development rewards generated by trade, foreign investment, and aid (not to mention the broader structural reforms encouraged by the Washington Consensus). Frustrated, my students and I longed for more responsive, promising, and radical alternatives. It is in this context that the potential of international migration first caught my eye.

As my experiences in the developing world began to accrue, so too did my frustration over the lack of alternatives. Being an emigrant myself, I was familiar with the complicated social, political, and economic webs that migrants spin and set when we move across country or around the globe. In immigrating to Norway, I had learned of the role that pre–World War I emigration to the New World had played in that country's economic and political development. I also knew that Norway's experiences were not unique: The first stones in Europe's nascent democracies and their constituent welfare state edifices were laid at a time of substantial (and relatively free) international migration. With time, I began to wonder if Europe's political development at the turn of the nineteenth century was not facilitated by a liberal international migration environment – and whether we limit development by placing so many obstacles in the path of today's international migrants.

Aware of the significant political barriers to liberalizing international migration, I was driven to find out what potential, if any, international migration could bring to those who were born on the wrong side of

Heaven's Door (to use George Borjas's gripping title). I began my investigatory journey with small steps, as I was (and continue to be) quite concerned about the enormous personal risks that individual migrants and families often take in the process of migrating. Along the way, I found that many migrants were willing to bear these costs in exchange for the small doses of hope and opportunity that migration provides (especially when contrasted against the limited opportunities that people find at home). Even more curiously, I found emigration generating economic rewards in those countries that were casting off some of their most ambitious young sons and daughters.

My first steps were taken in the realm of economics, where a lack of data and a reliance on somewhat fanciful models are not seen as handicaps or deterrents. In particular, my work with Bjørn Letnes uncovered the astronomical economic gains the world community might expect to harvest by matching the international demand for, and supply of, labor (Moses and Letnes 2004, 2005). However, it did not take long before I began to speculate about how emigration might affect the political constellations of sending states (e.g., Moses 2005a, 2006). This work made me recognize the need to look at the effects of emigration in a more systematic and empirical fashion. After all, it is one thing to find good reasons for expecting emigration to generate political development – it is another thing to find evidence of these effects in a broad swath of human experience. My attempt at doing this now rests in your hands.

In writing this book I have incurred many debts over several years. Most of these debts are to friends and familiar faces. Indeed, in a project like this, the biggest cost is always measured in terms of time spent away from the family. I am privileged in this regard, in that Thandeka, Aurora, and Maggi have always supported me and my work. Just as important, they have never made me feel guilty about spending time with my other passion. I am likewise fortunate to work in a very accommodating environment at the Norwegian University of Science and Technology's Department of Sociology and Political Science. It is easier to write about faraway problems when nested in such supportive home environments.

This project is unusual in that I have become indebted to a number of people whom I have never met and probably never will meet. In particular, I have benefited from the help of many statistical bureau and central bank staff from around the globe. It is only because of their generous assistance and diligent responses to my queries (through phone and e-mail exchanges) that I have been able to assemble the EMIG database presented in this book. Too seldom do the collectors and purveyors of statistics receive the recognition they deserve; I am very grateful for their help.

I am also moved and astonished by their assistance. For someone old enough to remember the world before e-mail, I find comfort in learning how delightfully small the world has become (alas, this is more so for data than it is for workers). In this shrinking world, I have been helped by complete strangers who have volunteered their time and expertise to a distant project with little foreseeable return or effect on their own lives. This has been a heart-warming experience.

In the process of writing and finishing this manuscript I have gotten to know many new people and found a few new shoulders on which to lean. Foremost among these are the supporting staff and Syndicate at Cambridge University Press – especially my editor, Eric Crahan. I appreciate their help and advice along each step of this long process.

Last, but not least, I have managed to incur a number of intellectual debts, in various forms, with individual friends and colleagues. A project like this one has required me to sample from a long smorgasbord of evidence and approaches. To be successful, I have needed to rely on friends who could help me track down specialized material or provide other forms of specialized knowledge. In this regard, I would like to thank Kam Wing Chan, Thomas Halvorsen, Bjørn Letnes, Adam McKeown, Sabrina Ramet, Stian Saur, and Indra de Soysa. Other friends and colleagues have invested significant chunks of time to read through the manuscript. In particular, I would like to thank Michael Alvarez, Jo Jakobsen, Erik Jones, and the anonymous reviewers at Cambridge University Press for their very helpful comments on earlier drafts.

In the end, of course, I alone am responsible for the work before you. I have relied on these family, friends, colleagues, and strangers to help build the argument, but none of them can or should be held accountable for whatever errors and omissions remain in the text. I only hope that they are few in number.

Trondheim
18 February 2011

Acronyms

AFL/N	Workers' National Trade Organization, Norway (*Arbeidernes Faglige Landsorganisasjon*), subsequently LO
AFL/US	American Federation of Labor/US
AR1	Form of Autoregressive Statistical Model
CCF	Cross-Correlation Function
COW	Correlates of War
DNA	Norwegian Labor Party (*Det norske Arbeiderparti*)
EC	European Community
EEA	European Economic Area
EU	European Union
GDI	Gross Domestic Indicator
GDP	Gross Domestic Product
GNI	Gross National Income
GNP	Gross National Product
HDI	Human Development Index
HDR	Human Development Report
ILO	International Labor Organization
ISI	Import-Substitution Industrialization policies
IWW	Industrial Workers of the World
Ln	Natural logarithm
LO	Norwegian Confederation of Trade Unions (*Landsorganiasjonen*)
NAF	Norwegian Employers' Organization (*Norsk Arbeidsgiverforening*), subsequently NHO
NHO	Confederation of Norwegian Enterprises (*Næringslivets Hovedorganisasjon*)
NSA	Norwegian Social Democratic Labor Party (*Norges Sosialdemokratiske Arbeiderparti*)

NW   Newey-West standard errors
OECD   Organization for Economic Cooperation and Development
OEEC   Organization for European Economic Cooperation
PCSE   Panel-Corrected Standard Errors
PNR   National Revolutionary Party, Mexico (*Partido Nacional Revolucionario*)
PNS   Sinarquista National Party, Mexico (*Partido Nacional Sinarquista*)
PRI   Institutional Revolutionary Party, Mexico (*Partido Revolucionario Institucional*)
PW   Prais-Winsten regression
SLP   Social Labor Party, U.S.
SPA   Socialist Party of America, U.S.
SSRC   Social Science Research Council
TSCS   Time-Series Cross-Sectional
UK   United Kingdom
UN   United Nations
UNDP   United Nations Development Program
U.S.   United States
WWI   World War I
WWII   World War II

I

Introduction

Roughly 3 percent of the world's population lives in a country other than the one in which they were born. Of these 200 million people, about one-third moved from a developing to a developed country, another third moved from one developing nation to another, and the last third moved from the developed world to the developing world. According to the United Nations (UN 2006), the 10 largest suppliers of international emigrants in 2005 were (in decreasing order) Mexico, China, Pakistan, India, Iran, Indonesia, the Philippines, Ukraine, Kazakhstan, and Sudan.

These 10 countries are mostly poor. More to the point, the leadership in each of these countries is astutely aware of the economic returns associated with emigration; indeed, most actively promote emigration as part of their broader development strategies. This awareness is founded on their own experiences with emigration, a burgeoning academic literature that links emigration and economic development, and a growing international effort to understand the economic effects of migration.[1]

International migration is also being fueled by a growing awareness of the economic benefits it generates in the receiving countries, which are frequently at the other end of the economic spectrum from the sending countries. At the start of the second decade of a new millennium,

[1] For example, the UN Secretary-General and a number of governments launched a Global Commission on International Migration in 2003 (with a resulting report in 2005). The UN also held its first High-Level Dialogue on International Migration and Development in September 2006, resulting in the creation of the Global Migration Forum. The World Bank has also been very active on this front (World Bank 2006), initiating the International Migration and Development Research Program and its subsequent publications (Özden and Schiff 2006, 2007a). Most recently, the UNDP's 2009 Human Development Report focused on "Overcoming Barriers: Human Mobility and Development."

advocates tout the role that immigrant labor can play in satisfying critical economic functions in the developed world, whether harvesting the crops, shoring up a deficit in health care workers, staffing the technology front, or adding youth to ageing populations.

Although policy makers, international organizations, and academics are becoming increasingly aware of the economic effects of migration, we remain ignorant as to the potential political effects of rising emigrant stocks. We are beginning to understand how remittances are spent in local economies, but still have no idea about how (or even if) emigration spreads political capital. Although we are increasingly aware of the economic relevance of local hometown associations, we are oblivious as to when emigration can be a conduit for new political ideas and influences or when it serves as a venting device used to get rid of troublesome rabble-rousers. At a time when we are developing sophisticated international plans to deal with the economic costs of brain drain, we know nothing about its political equivalent. Most remarkably, in an era that celebrates "Democracy's Century" (Freedom House 2000), we do not know whether emigration facilitates or deters democratization.

Consider the 10 labor-exporting countries listed in the opening paragraph. Although this group of countries shares a legacy of economic underdevelopment, they have very different political constellations. Neither does there appear to be any clear relationship between the absolute number of emigrants and a country's level of political development. As shown in Table 1.1, the 2008 Freedom House Survey (and its component country reports) describes four of these countries (Ukraine, Mexico, India, and Indonesia) as free; the other six countries are characterized as being either partly or not free. The largest source country (Mexico) is listed as free, whereas the second largest (China) is not.

Given their economic situations, we can expect these countries to continue exporting workers in the foreseeable future.[2] The question we then need to ask is, How will emigration affect the political development of these source countries? Will continued emigration undermine or strengthen India's democratic traditions? Does emigration from Pakistan encourage the growth of a nascent democratic culture and institutions, or does it flame the fires of jihad? To date, these questions have not even been asked, let alone answered.

---

[2] Whether other countries will continue to accept them remains to be seen in a world economy in turmoil. Yet the likelihood of accepting future immigrants turns on the anticipated effects of that migration, including the sort of political effects studied in this book.

TABLE I.I. *Sources of International Emigration, 2005*

	Avg. # Annual Emigrants (2000–5)	Emigration Rate per 1,000 Population	Political Rights Score	Civil Liberties Score	Freedom Status
Ukraine	140,000	2.9	3	2	Free
Mexico	400,000	3.9	2	3	Free
India	280,000	0.3	2	3	Free
Indonesia	200,000	0.9	3	3	Free
Philippines	180,000	2.3	4	3	Partly free
Pakistan	362,000	2.4	6	5	Not free
Kazakhstan	120,000	8.0	6	5	Not free
China	390,000	0.3	7	6	Not free
Iran	276,000	4.1	6	6	Not free
Sudan	104,000	3.0	7	7	Not free

Note: Kazakhstan's Freedom House scores are for 2007.
Sources: Freedom House (2008); UN (2006).

At one level, the lack of attention to this issue is understandable. For most of the postwar period we have lived in a world in which formal limitations on international human mobility were seen to be natural and long-standing. Large-scale international migration occurred infrequently, in the wake of extraordinary events, so that questions about the effects of this migration were often bracketed off as being irrelevant for mainstream economic and political analyses.

A rising tide of globalization at the close of the 20th century changed all this, and political economists and policy makers began to consider the effects of international migration on the receiving country economies, the sending country economies, and the international economy in general.[3] What is remarkable about this expansive literature is that it remains

[3] Obviously, this literature is enormous; Moses (2005a: 56–8, 2006: chapter 6) provide summaries. The first literature is most developed in the United States and is perhaps best captured by the influential work of George Borjas (1999), but it should not be limited to him. Other examples include Simon (1989), Smith and Edmonston (1997), U.S. Department of Labor (1989), and Böhning (1984). More recently, there has been a renewed focus on the positive impacts of immigrants in the host country; for example, Legrain (2006), Riley (2008), and Pritchett (2006). Similar efforts can be easily found in most other OECD countries. The growing literature on the economic effects of emigration on sending-country economies is surveyed in Özden and Schiff (2007a), World Bank (2006), and, most recently, UNDP (2009). For the global efficiency gains associated with international migration, see Winters (2002), Moses and Letnes (2004, 2005), Iregui (2005), and World Bank (2006).

4 *Emigration and Political Development*

focused on the *economic* motives and effects of emigration, even though most international migration is heavily channeled by political constraints and influences.

After all, today's potential migrants need to negotiate a number of political hurdles. In some countries, exit restrictions still prohibit emigrants from leaving. In most of the others, residents are now free to leave. Yet even if a potential migrant lives in a country that allows for free exit, not a single country is willing to accept immigrants with open arms. Instead, any potential emigrant faces a myriad of restrictions and qualifications, as richer states effectively filter out all but the wealthiest, the most (politically) repressed, those with family ties or desired skill sets, or the most diligent. In the Middle East, where many of today's international migrants are now headed, other political barriers channel these migrant flows. Few other types of international exchange are more politically determined, and yet much of the literature avoids explicitly political analyses!

This is not to say that political scientists are not interested in migration issues – only that their focus, like that of the economists until recently, has been trained on the effects found in the receiving countries of the developed world. There is a substantial literature that examines variations in migration control systems and their relative effectiveness[4] and another that analyzes the political and social effects of immigrants in the developed world.[5] By contrast, however, there is remarkably little work done on the broader political effects of emigration in the countries of origin. This book aims to fill that gap in the literature.

Toward that end, this introductory chapter has four tasks, the first two of which have now been completed. I have tried to convince the reader of the need for more awareness of the political effects of emigration. As

[4] Most of this work focuses on receiving countries, where national controls regimes can be seen as part of larger nation-building projects (Torpey, 2000), the result of domestic interest group pressures (Money, 1998, 1999), the rights-based politics of liberal states (Hollifield, 1992a), state interests broadly defined (Weiner, 1995; Zolberg, 1981), or changes in the international system (Guiraudon and Lahav, 2000; Hollifield, 1992b; Sassen, 1996). There are even some, such as Hayter (2004), who argue for the abolition of such controls. Yet there is another literature that examines the way in which sending states encourage or discourage emigration. See, for example, Inglés (1963), Dowty (1987), and some of the more recent work by Nancy Green (Green 2005; Green and Weil 2007).
[5] These studies consider the effect of migration on assimilation, national identities, and conceptions of citizenship (e.g., Honig, 2001; Joppke, 1998, 2000; Soysal, 1994). There are also older studies that see migrants as a surplus pool of labor (an industrial reserve army) that is more exploitable politically, because it is unregulated, nonunionized, and cheap (Castles and Kosack, 1973; Piore, 1979).

international migration becomes a more common and visible consequence of globalization, it behooves us all – at both the receiving and sending ends of the migration chain – to have a better understanding of whether (and when) its political effects are benign or malignant. My second task has been to show that there is a curious lacuna in the migration literature around this subject. Whereas economists have become increasingly interested in the economic effects of emigration, the political effects remain largely unexamined, at least in any systematic way.

The very existence of such a gap in the literature might lead us to doubt the existence of a systematic relationship between emigration and political change. Indeed, policy makers in both sending and receiving countries do not seem to be aware of or concerned with the potential political effects of emigration. This brings me to this chapter's remaining two tasks: to show that there are sufficient grounds to expect political emigration to deliver political effects and to introduce a research design that can reveal those effects. These tasks are more difficult, requiring more elaboration, so the next two sections are committed to them.

MOTIVATIONS

I can think of three types of reasons for why we might expect emigration to affect political developments in the country of origin: The first is grounded in the role that migration has played in studies of economic migration; the second derives from an established literature that links economic and political development; and the third is evident in a couple of well-known historical events. The remainder of the book elaborates on these reasons; this section presents my motivations for embarking on this study.

Economic Arguments

Economists have long been aware that migration can play an important role in economic development: Demographic developments play a central role in explaining the conditions that can foster economic growth (e.g., the relative balance among land, capital, and labor costs), and migration can play an important role in affecting those demographic developments. Consider, for example, Robert Allen's (2009: 21) argument about why the Industrial Revolution began in Britain:

The path to the Industrial Revolution began with the Black Death. The population fall increased labour mobility by generating many vacant farms, and that mobility undermined serfdom. The low population also created a high wage economy. The benefits of high consumption were not confined to people: sheep ate better as well, and their long wool was the basis for England's early modern worsted industry – the new draperies. The enormous export of these fabrics through the port of London led to rapid growth in the city's population and the rise of the coal industry to provide the capital with fuel.

This argument does not focus on migration per se, but migration lurks in the background of the story Allen tells. It is a fascinating narrative, one that explicitly recognizes the complexity of development: how development depends on concomitant changes along several fronts, the need to focus on the variability of relative costs, and the blend of political and economic factors that combine to explain development. In this narrative, the Black Death facilitated mobility (across farms and into cities), and this mobility affected the price of labor (relative to land, energy, and capital), thereby encouraging investment in labor-saving machines.

This focus on relative costs and productivity levels is familiar to students of Arthur Lewis's dual-economy approach to development economics. In an article from 1954, Lewis asks us to think of developing economies in terms of two sectors: a small capitalist (or industrial) sector and a large traditional (or agricultural) sector. Because productivity is much lower in the traditional sector than in the capitalist sector, economic development could be facilitated by moving labor out of the traditional sector and into manufacturing, where it could be employed more productively. To the extent that it is reasonable to place the traditional sector in rural areas, and the capitalist sector in urban areas, migration (from rural to urban areas) therefore becomes a key component for encouraging economic development. From here it is just a short step to extend this sort of argument to the study of international migrants.[6]

Yet the role of migration is also evident in more broad-based approaches to development, such as the capabilities approach associated with the Nobel Laureate, Amaryta Sen. For Sen (1999: 38), "[o]ne of the biggest changes in the process of development in many economies involves the replacement of bonded labor and forced work, which characterizes

---

[6] Lewis's approach was subsequently applied in a study of international migration by Charles Kindleberger (1967) to describe the migration of surplus labor in the Maghreb countries of Northern Africa and Turkey as part of the postwar economic boom in the European Community. Although Kindleberger's focus is on the effects in Europe (the receiving area), not the effects on the (sending) Maghreb, I use it to launch an analysis of guest-worker programs in Chapter 6.

parts of many traditional agricultures, with a system of free labor contract and unrestrained physical movement." Although Sen was probably referring to internal (domestic) restrictions on mobility and labor market participation, the same argument applies just as forcefully to global labor mobility.

My initial motivation for studying the political effects of emigration was found in this consensus among otherwise disparate economists. By examining different aspects of economic development, economists have pinpointed the important role that emigration can play (and has played) in affecting the relative costs of the relevant factors of production. These relative costs have important political corollaries, as we see in the next chapter.

Political Arguments

My second source of motivation comes from a wide body of work that links economic and political factors and effects. This work can be divided into two very different research traditions. The first draws on a well-established literature that links economic to political development, in which economic well-being is shown to increase the likelihood that a country will be able to transit to and sustain democracy (e.g., Lipset 1959). If international migration facilitates broad-based economic growth in the countries of origin, and this economic development encourages the growth of an independent working or middle class, then political development might be indirectly linked to emigration. In contrast, emigration could generate lopsided economic growth in the sending countries, with more pernicious political effects as a result. Perhaps remittances are encouraging the growth of smaller enclave economies that deter the organization of independent classes that can challenge corrupt or unjust political authorities. We simply do not know which scenario is more likely. Yet the established links that connect economic to political development suggest that we can expect emigration to have an indirect (and lagged) effect on political development (working through the effect on economic development).

The work from a second group of political economists provides grounds for expecting a more direct link between emigration and political development. This group collects around the work of Charles Tiebout and Albert Hirschman. Tiebout's (1956) work examines the way in which individuals (or consumer-voters) signal their political preferences by choosing to move from one political jurisdiction to another (within a given country). Hirschman (1970) links this threat of exit with the capacity to voice support or dissent to explain how organizations can obtain important information necessary to stave off eventual deterioration. Neither one of these authors worked on international migration. Tiebout (and his followers) was skeptical of extending his argument to higher levels of analysis, and Hirschman's original work focused on firms and political parties. Yet both types of analyses can be extended to the study of international migration. As we see in Chapter 3, it is possible to employ this broad swath of political economy to establish a baseline set of expectations that link emigration – either directly or indirectly – to political development.

Historical Examples

In short, it is not unreasonable to think about the political effects of emigration as a sort of trailer to the economic growth effects that are now being documented in a burgeoning literature, and there are several good theoretical reasons to expect emigration to generate more direct effects on political development. However, there is a third reason to expect emigration to affect political development, and this reason can be seen in the lessons generated from three very different historical examples: the birth of the American Republic, the fall of East Germany, and the disintegration of Yugoslavia.

The American Magnet. When the United States declared its independence at the end of the 18th century, some of its most prominent thinkers asserted America's right to transform subjects of European monarchs into republican citizens, thereby freeing them from any allegiances and obligations to their erstwhile rulers.[7] Migration played a central role in this struggle, and its political power was evident to authorities on both sides of the Atlantic.

At issue was the question of political allegiance. At the time, both the common law doctrine of "perpetual allegiance" and the law of nations recognized that the subjects of a given realm were obliged to follow its customs, laws, and reigning monarch. If America was to hold its own, it needed to break this perpetual bond between sovereign and subject. At the same time, America needed to provide its residents (no longer subjects) with a new way of thinking about allegiance and obligations.

[7] In Moses (2009), I developed this argument in more detail.

The new state under construction could not draw on these traditional bonds.

Migration, and the recognition of a natural *right of expatriation,* was the device used to meet both these needs of the new country.[8] Although we no longer think of changing one's home at will and acquiring a new nationality as natural rights, some of early America's most influential voices – including Samuel Adams, Tom Paine, and (especially) Thomas Jefferson – did. Indeed, these thinkers used the right of expatriation as a means to justify a new type of political community, one based on individual and truly voluntary consent.

In heralding this right of expatriation, America's founding thinkers focused the world's attention on the political power of migration. This focus has usually been trained on the role that migration plays in signaling allegiance (and consent) to the immigrant's host country, but it also entails significant political consequences for the sending countries as well. After all, by choosing to leave a given political community one is clearly (if tacitly) retracting one's consent for its underlying contract (or regal bond). Just as important is the realization that not leaving a community (when one can) has the effect of amplifying an individual's tacit consent for that community.[9] Indeed, in the formative years that bracketed the American Revolution, Americans justified their own nascent political community by reference to the injustices of existing communities in Europe (a claim that was supported by the fact that people were fleeing them and thereby withdrawing their consent).

For the right of expatriation to function in practice, however, it requires the willingness of at least one state in the international community to welcome newcomers. America's willingness to play this role was evident from the very start of the new country's history. Less than two decades after independence, with the Naturalization Acts of 1790 and 1795, this right of expatriation was secured in legislation by the new Congress. For the first time in human history, a community explicitly declared that any alien can be considered a citizen of its nation.[10]

---

[8] A right of expatriation implies a right to change one's home at will and a right to acquire a new nationality. See, for example, Borchard (1931).

[9] This notion – that a sort of implicit consent lies embedded in the freedom of exit – has deep roots in Western political theory. In the closing passages of Plato's *Crito*, we find Socrates arguing eloquently for the role that freedom of exit plays in securing consent.

[10] I hasten to point out that any alien "being a free white person" was free to join the new political community. Indentured servants, slaves, and (American) Indians were not included.

There is widespread recognition of the importance of the American model in inspiring the democratic wave that swept across Europe in the century that followed. Yet it is less well known that this influence went beyond serving as a source of inspiration. The very existence of the United States – an island of republican refuge in a sea of absolutist monarchies – proved a genuine threat to the established order. For the first time, dissatisfied subjects had a real opportunity to break their bonds as subjects to a sovereign and exploit their right of expatriation.

This *real* possibility to emigrate (secured now by a state that was willing to embrace immigrants) severely circumscribed the power of existing states to exploit and mistreat their citizens. As argued by the eminent French economist and statesman, Anne-Robert-Jacques Turgot (1778: 389), states in Europe would have to improve conditions or risk losing subjects to the new country:

The asylum which [the American people] opens to the oppressed of all nations must console the earth. The ease with which it will now be possible to take advantage of this situation, and thus to escape from the consequences of a bad government, will oblige the European governments to be just and enlightened.

In short, the United States' early experience provides us with another reason to expect that migration (or just the possibility of emigration) can affect the political development of countries on both ends of the migration chain. For receiving countries, immigrants provide new political input with explicit consent. For sending countries, the threat of emigration has the power to challenge the authority of unjust states, and emigration itself offers an avenue of recourse for the dissatisfied subject. Individuals found themselves with two powerful instruments for influencing government: the threat of emigration and the real possibility of political asylum in another country.

Turgot's comment proved prescient, as Europeans flocked to the New World in the 19th century. Europe experienced its first wave of democratic reforms in the wake of this political and economic exodus.

The Fall of East Germany. A more recent example can be found beneath the rubble that was the Berlin Wall. Throughout most of the postwar period, the Soviet Union and its satellite states in Eastern Europe maintained stringent controls on the movement of their peoples. For fear of ideological contagion, the new Soviet Man (or Woman) was kept at home by means of a complicated blend of internal and external passports. For the lucky few who were allowed to travel abroad, the Secretariat of the Party Central Committee had issued "Basic Rules of Conduct." It is against this restrictive backdrop that we can marvel at the radical developments that occurred in East Germany at the close of the 1980s.

In August 1989, a flood of would-be émigrés from East Germany tried to escape to the West via Hungary (and on to Austria and then West Germany). After the Hungarian authorities stopped trying to stave off this flight, about 30,000 East Germans had escaped to the West by the end of September. What is unusual about this migration is that these people were free to employ their right of expatriation: East German citizens were welcomed as citizens in West Germany. Unlike most subjects of every modern state, East Germans were able to secure the sort of political refuge envisioned by America's founding thinkers.

Although the majority of East Germans may have desired significant political reforms, it should not surprise us that many were unwilling to leave their homes, friends, and families. Emigration is a drastic step to take, which is usually undertaken only by those who have already exhausted every other means of redress. For the others, active protest is a more convenient means of signaling dissatisfaction with unjust rule. Not surprisingly, then, massive throngs of protestors took to the streets of Leipzig, Dresden, Berlin, and other East German cities to voice their dissatisfaction with their government and to signal their intent *not* to leave. Therefore while tens of thousands of East Germans were taking flight, even larger numbers were demonstrating in their home streets – rallying under the slogan "*Wir bleiben hier!*" [We stay here!] and demanding greater input and change at home.

As we now know, this combination of emigration and protest wielded remarkable political leverage. On November 1, 1989, the East German cabinet reopened its border with Czechoslovakia. Two days later the ministers in charge of security and police resigned. After a reported one million demonstrators jammed the streets of East Berlin, the rest of the cabinet resigned. Still, people continued to leave East Germany. In the following week, some 50,000 people were said to have left before the East German government eventually threw in the towel and announced the opening of all of its border points. On November 9, the Berlin Wall fell.[11]

---

[11] For more background information on these events, see Meyer (2009), Offe (1996), Ekiert (1996), and Stokes (1993). As we see later, Albert Hirschman's (1992, 1993) work on the East German example is particularly relevant. I have also employed this example in earlier work that shows the political effects of migration. See, e.g., Moses (2005a, 2006: chapter 5).

The Berlin Wall proved to be the Achilles heel of state socialist regimes in East Germany and across Eastern Europe. A week after the borders were open, the East German secret police, the dreaded *Stasis*, was disbanded, and the leading role of the Socialist Unity Party was renounced. Within the next few months, much of Eastern Europe experienced similar revolutions.

The Flip Side. The early American and recent East German experiences illustrate the political potential of emigration. Indeed, in Chapter 3 I use experiences such as these to produce a framework for further study. For the social scientist, however, it is important not to be blinded by the allure of promising cases, because it is equally possible to find examples where repressive and unjust regimes encouraged and even facilitated emigration. Under these conditions, emigration might have a negative effect on political development.

This is the lesson one can learn from Eric Gordy's (1999) remarkable account of how Slobodan Milošević and his Socialist Party of Serbia remained in power by controlling key aspects of daily life in Serbia. In effect, Milošević buried any real alternatives to his rule and effectively silenced the voice of any and all opposition. The effectiveness of this strategy was enhanced by the flight of thousands of young and educated Serbs (and non-Serbs), an exodus that sapped the opposition of some of its more articulate and vibrant members and may have facilitated Milošević's increasingly harsh rule.

Of course, Milošević was not the first ruler to employ such tactics. The history of the Soviet Union is littered with exiled dissidents, as are the histories of other communist and totalitarian states. In these examples the sending governments actually encouraged emigration or even forced people into exile as a way to rid themselves of a pesky opposition. Thus emigration has a political effect, but one that seems to contradict the effect we can see in the U.S. and East German examples.

In short, the political effects of emigration seem to cut both ways. This realization is itself the most important motivation for further study. As the number of international migrants rises and as countries increasingly use emigration as part of their (economic) development strategies, we need to have a better understanding of the conditions under which emigration facilitates more democratic and just political developments. It is just as important, however, to know the conditions under which emigration might have the opposite effect.

Yet it is difficult to understand how emigration affects political development, because the researcher is forced to confront a whole host of conceptual, empirical, political, and ideological challenges. What is needed is a research design that is sensitive to different contexts – one that can measure the political effects of emigration (both positive and negative) to uncover the conditions that link emigration to more developed and just polities.

THE ROAD AND CHALLENGES AHEAD

Chapter 2 begins by defining and operationalizing the dependent variable: political development. At first glance, this seems like an easy task. After all, it is possible to imagine a continuum of possible states – one that goes from totalitarian states on the one end to democratic states on the other. It is then possible to describe movement along this continuum (from totalitarian to democratic) in terms of political development. The approach is facilitated by indicators derived from several good databases that measure levels and/or degrees of democratization over several countries, across time. To test for the political effect of emigration, it is then fairly easy to compare levels of emigration in a country with subsequent levels of political development (measured as increased democratization). In short, this approach is both simple and convenient, and I use it whenever possible.

The problem is that this approach and its indicators are woefully inadequate for many of the tasks at hand. The source of the problem is that the scope of the phenomenon (political development) is much broader than the scope of the indicator (democratization). More to the point, the effects of emigration apply to a much broader spectrum of cases than are captured by existing indicators for democracy. To find a more suitable (and broader) measure of political development we have to consider the scope and nature of the independent variable: emigration.

Migration is first and foremost a local affair. Migration decisions tend to be made by individuals and families, informed by friends and neighbors. Indeed, much of contemporary migration research points to the role of social networks in lowering barriers along migration pathways and channeling resources along predictable conduits.[12] These networks

---

[12] E.g., Curran and Saguay (2001), Massey (1990), Massey and Garcia-España (1987), and Massey and Zenteno (1999).

generate chainlike patterns to migration flows: Small numbers of initial migrants establish a bridgehead in a faraway place, send information back home to friends and family, and hence encourage more emigration from that original point of departure. As a consequence, it is possible for one community to experience high levels of emigration, while a neighboring (and otherwise similar) community is left unaffected by emigration.

Thus the effects of emigration can vary from community to community, depending on the spread of these networks or chains. The problem is that the democratization indicators – like most indicators employed by contemporary social scientists – are collected and aggregated at the national level.[13] Although it is possible to think of varying levels of democracy within a country (e.g., from town to town), there are no comparable indicators that stretch across countries and time. The national indicators that we use only capture the effects of emigration if a significant proportion of communities in the state experience emigration. This is a rather high threshold to cross.

A second problem derives from the very scope of the project. If we are interested in the general effects of emigration and realize that they can vary over time and across space, then we need an indicator that is sensitive to this variation. An indicator that aims to capture the degree of democratization, for example, does not capture it over time, even at the national level, because democracy is a remarkably modern concept. Consequently, reliance on this indicator would confine the study not only to national levels of analysis but also to a relatively small part of the historical record. For example, a Freedom House survey (2000) of the 20th century could not find a single state that qualified as a democracy in the year 1900. An indicator of democratization would therefore prove problematic for examining the effects of emigration on political developments in the late 1800s.

Moreover, it is quite possible for emigration to have an effect on political development in nondemocratic contexts. For example, it is not unreasonable to expect that migration within contemporary China has had some sort of political effect on the regions of out-migration: Indeed, we find evidence of this sort of effect in Chapter 8. However, it makes little sense to use a national indicator of democratic strength to try and capture these effects in nondemocratic contexts.

---

[13] The problems associated with methodological nationalism are not new. For more general references, see Beck and Sznaider (2006) and Chernilo (2006); for more on the problem as it applies to migration studies, see Wimmer and Schiller (2002a, 2002b, 2003).

For these reasons, Chapter 2 develops a more pliable measure of political development that draws on the capabilities approaches associated with (among others) Amartya Sen and Martha Nussbaum, but that can be operationalized in a way that facilitates both temporal and spatial comparisons. This measure is broad enough to capture developments in a large number of varying contexts, across time, and within countries. In my study, I thus use statistical indicators of democratization – when they are available and applicable – but turn to more context-sensitive indicators when they are more suitable.

Once the dependent variable is defined and operationalized, we can begin to consider how it might be affected by emigration. This is the task of Chapter 3, which presents a framework to examine the broad experiences of political development and emigration; this framework tells us where to look and what to look for in the empirical record. Such a framework needs to be sensitive to the possibility that emigration can have both positive and negative effects on political development and that these effects will likely vary across contexts.

In addition, it needs to reflect the fact that political development can and has occurred in the absence of emigration. The importance of this constraint should not be downplayed. We need to be sensitive to the very real likelihood that emigration can play a permissive – rather than, say, an initiating or determining – role in political development. In short, we need to contrast the effects of emigration on development with the potential for political development in the absence of emigration.

Building on the work of several prominent authors, including Albert Hirschman (1970) and Charles Tiebout (1956), Chapter 3 outlines four approaches for examining how emigration can affect political development. The first approach looks at the indirect linkage, in which emigration affects economic growth and this economic growth in turn generates political development. The remaining approaches examine more direct linkages, of both the positive and negative sort. In particular, I look at the individual-level effects associated with the emigrants themselves, the effects of emigration on the relative power of significant groups (such as peasants and workers) within the sending country, and the way that emigration forces communities to compete with one another in offering better conditions for mobile constituents. These effects can potentially work in a variety of ways: They can both facilitate and deter political development.

From the discussion in Chapter 3 a short list of variables can be generated that are important for explaining the political development effects

of emigration. To test the explanatory power of these variables, it is
necessary to use a case-selection strategy that controls for their variation. The dimensions to be controlled include overarching regime type
(i.e., relatively free, regulated, and limited human-mobility regimes); the
total population of the sending area; sending-area contexts (to control
for geography, level and nature of development, etc.); time (to ensure
proper causal sequencing); and outcome (i.e., to secure sufficient variation on both dependent and independent variables). The remainder of the
book uses an innovative blend of statistical and case-oriented studies that
are situated in time and space to control for these important forms of
variation.

Thus Chapter 4 examines the changing nature of the relationship
between international emigration and national political development over
time. We know that the number of democratic states ebbs and flows over
time; most famously, Samuel Huntington (1991) speaks of three waves
of democracy. We also know that the number of international migrants
varies significantly over time, in a similar wavelike fashion: International
migration reached record heights before WWI, fell significantly in the
interwar period, and rose again after WWII. Chapter 4 examines whether
and how these trends can be related.

A historical perspective makes it easier to see how the level of international migration and the number of democratic regimes change over
time. Chapter 4 aims to provide an overall view of their aggregate relationship from the mid-1800s to the present. To find a correspondence
between global levels of emigration and (1) the spread of democracy and
(2) the extension of political rights and civil liberties, I regress two overlapping political databases onto a newly constructed database of global
emigration flows. I then use this correspondence to establish the existence of distinct international migration regimes and to gauge the length
of the lag that links emigration and political development. I conduct this
analysis with both time-series and pooled time-series data.

The three chapters that follow examine some of the global patterns
uncovered in Chapter 4. These examples are organized as cases under
three regimes of international migration: (1) a period of relatively free
mobility before WWI, (2) a period of highly regulated temporary (or
guest-worker) flows after WWII, and (3) a period of more global yet still
highly regulated flows at the turn of the 21st century.

The first of this set of chapters, Chapter 5, examines the political
development effects of emigration at a time when there were relatively
few formal constraints on international mobility. I look at the case of

Norway, a country that experienced the second highest rate of per-capita emigration before WWI (just below Ireland a half-century earlier, but higher than in Italy a couple of decades later). In the second to the last decade of the 19th century, one-tenth of the Norwegian population was estimated to have left to the New World. At the same time, Norway introduced a number of broad-based democratic reforms that were aimed at keeping its remaining workers at home and satisfied. This chapter shows how these two patterns are intertwined with each other.

Chapter 6 examines the effects of emigration during and immediately after World War II, when special arrangements were secured to facilitate the international migration of "guest workers." In particular, this chapter contrasts the lessons of two postwar guest-worker arrangements. The Bracero Program regulated the flow of temporary contract workers between Mexico and the United States between 1942 and 1964. The second program stretched into the early 1970s and enticed workers from around the Mediterranean basin to supply the burgeoning needs of postwar economic growth in Europe. In these disparate examples we find that the international migration regime allowed sending countries significant control over the size, nature, and source of their emigrant outflows. This capacity to control – combined with underlying demographic trends – seems to determine whether emigration deterred or facilitated subsequent political development in these countries.

The ability and willingness to control international migration flows are important characteristics of the recent time period, which is the subject of study in Chapter 7. New work by the UN has resulted in a more comprehensive database of international migration, and these data reveal that very small (often island) states are most prone to very high per-capita levels of emigration. Although these states tend to be economically underdeveloped, a trait that helps explain their high-emigrant status, the analysis in this chapter shows that they actually enjoy a higher level of political development than one might otherwise expect, given their level of economic (under) development.

Given that the recent international context described in Chapter 7 has been characterized by significant political limitations on international free mobility, Chapter 8 examines the variation of political effects that result from migration within nation-states. Here too, it is possible to find both cases where internal migration has been more or less free and cases where migration has been severely restricted. This chapter examines the political development effects of the "Southern Diaspora" (Gregory 2005) – the migration of Blacks from the rural U.S. South to northern industrialized cities – to show how this substantial Black migration affected subsequent political development for those who remained.[14] Contrary to initial expectations, similar effects were found in the wake of internal migration in contemporary China. Despite significant legal restrictions on internal mobility, Chinese provinces that have experienced high levels of emigration have also experienced bigger increases in their subsequent human development. These two very different cases provide another means for controlling for regime influence by analyzing the effects of emigration within a given cultural and historical context.

The final empirical chapter, Chapter 9, examines the political effects of individual migrants in two ways. The first part analyzes the *nature* of these political effects by way of a biographical sketch of Martin Tranmæl, a Norwegian labor activist whose political and strategic perspective was influenced by his brief immigration to the United States. By examining Tranmæl's biography, we can see how the experiences of the individual migrant, in an era with relatively free mobility, can act as a political conduit linking developments around the globe. To check whether it is reasonable to generalize from Tranmæl's experiences, the second part of the chapter shows that significant foreign experience is a common attribute of revolutionary political leaders. It does so by examining the biographies included in two datasets and finds that emigrant experience is a remarkably common feature in their otherwise very different backgrounds.

Chapter 10 reflects on the journey traveled throughout this book. We find that political development is facilitated by emigration, but that the nature of the relationship is complex and contingent. Three complementary factors influence political development: (1) the relative size of the emigrant stream (as a share of the country's population); (2) the surrounding emigrant regime type (i.e., liberal or restricted); and (3) the polity's underlying demographic trends. These are not necessary conditions – but they appear to facilitate political development by shifting the class balance of the sending community in ways that spur economic and political innovation and transformation.

In effect, emigration brings about a shift in relative class power and provides some powerful rhetorical ammunition in the subsequent

---

[14] Although it is common to use out-migration, rather than emigration, when referring to internal (within-country) flows, my argument holds that the political repercussions from these flows are identical. For this reason, I buck the consensus and discuss within-country demographic movements in terms of emigration and immigration – adding "internal" as a modifier in cases where it may be necessary to clarify.

struggle. The threat of increased emigration and the attractive examples being offered from abroad force political elites to address perceived injuries. When these conditions are not in place – when the surrounding regime does not facilitate migration or when the sending region is undergoing high rates of demographic growth – it seems that political authorities can exploit the lure of emigration to siphon off trouble-makers, to release political pressure in sensitive or tense areas, and to strengthen the political position of elites in emigrant-sending regions.

2

Toward Political Development

Before we can study the political effects of emigration, we need to clarify what is meant by political development. At first glance, this seems like a fairly straightforward task. After all, there is a vibrant *development* literature in political economy, and much of the policy discourse in the developing world implies that policy makers adopt policies that can and will improve the political conditions for the country in question.

However, a closer look reveals remarkably little consensus about what constitutes political development – or even whether it is a useful concept for study. Early efforts to define and capture the concept proved largely unsuccessful, and many political scientists ended up jettisoning it for more convenient analytical surrogates, such as modernization, nation-building, democratization, political culture, or even just plain "change."[1]

At the same time, a broader development literature became enamored with the work of economists who were willing to set aside many of the political scientists' conceptual caveats and cut directly to the empirical chase. For most of the post–World War II period then, development was largely synonymous with growth in national income or production. Although these sorts of income-based measures have drawn much criticism in recent years, they enjoy one particularly favorable characteristic: They lend themselves to disaggregation and comparability. In short, it is possible to measure economic development at various levels (individual, community, state/province), across countries (employing exchange rate adjustments), and over time (employing price/inflation adjustments).

---

[1] For a recent review of the continued utility of the early literature on political development, see Pasquino (2009).

We in social science need a comparable indicator for measuring political development, one that can capture and value change in a given political context. We need a simple, linear measure of political development that can characterize change over time and across contexts in terms that are positive (political development) or negative (political decline). In addition, we need a measure of political development that is pliable enough to stretch across three types of variation: time, space, and levels of aggregation. This is no easy feat, because most social scientific indicators are collected at the national level, and few extend very far back in time. Ideally, we want an indicator that aggregates easily and that facilitates interpersonal comparisons, as income does in studies of economic development.

Unfortunately, no such indicator exists, and this is not the place to develop one. Rather, I propose an umbrella concept of political development, based on the capabilities approach associated with Amartya Sen, Martha Nussbaum, the United Nations Development Program (UNDP), and others. Not only can this umbrella concept be expanded to cover a number of particular indicators that are better suited for capturing political development in the plethora of contexts where we might expect to find the effects of emigration; it can also be collapsed down into simple indicators of democracy, when they are available.

This flexibility provides both handicap and advantage. On the one hand, employing an umbrella concept limits our ability to compare across contexts, except in very general terms. On the other hand, the very flexibility of this approach allows us to study the political effects of a given variable across an expansive range of contexts. Although we cannot compare directly across cases, we can use this broad measure to gauge political change, over time, in a given context. This pliability allows us to generalize about the political effects of emigration on the basis of a broader and (much more varied) sample. This chapter introduces such a capabilities approach to political development and uses it to justify a series of indicators that are used in the chapters that follow. Such an approach allows us to draw from already established indicators where and when they exist. At the same time, the capabilities approach can guide and inform studies in those contexts in which suitable indicators have not yet been developed.

EARLY INROADS

The first attempts to define political development were steeped in semantic confusion and resulted in several overlapping typologies. For example, in 1966, Lucian Pye catalogued ten definitions before adding his own synthesis, in which political development expanded the *equality* of individuals in relation to their political system, increased the *capacity* of the political system in relation to its environment, and increased the *differentiation* of institutions and structures within the political system. Similarly, Samuel Huntington (1965) summarized a number of competing definitions of political development in terms of their focus on rationalization, (national) integration, democratization, and participation (or mobilization). More recent efforts have only widened the definitional expanse: Fred Riggs (1981) catalogued sixty-five different definitions from forty-nine different works, and Han Park (1984) listed an additional thirteen definitions!

In light of the plentitude of conceptual vantage points, it is not surprising that many political scientists had difficulty finding useful indicators for development and even more became leery of employing the concept of political development. Instead, comparativists turned to related concepts, such as modernization, that are easier to capture empirically. This development is clearly evident in the early (1960s) work conducted at the Social Science Research Council's (SSRC) Committee on Comparative Politics, under the stewardship of Gabriel Almond.

Those political scientists who continued to work on the concept of political development adapted their analytical ambitions accordingly. Rather than try and capture a complex concept such as political development with a rough comparative indicator, these authors came to embrace the complexity of the concept and moved away from comparative empirical projects that relied on unidimensional indicators. Thus when Lucian Pye (1963: 16) argued that "no single scale can be used for measuring the degree of political development," many others followed suit.[2] The result is that political scientists have not agreed on a general or unified framework for studying political development.[3]

While political scientists became intimidated or dazed by the complexity of the development concept, economists trudged ahead unfazed by the conceptual difficulties. From its inception shortly after WWII, the field of development economics has been characterized by its "overarching preoccupation with the growth of real income per capita" (Drèze

---

[2] E.g., Almond and Powell (1966: 299ff) conceived of development along three dimensions, whereas Rustow and Ward (1964: 6–7) employed eight dimensions, Emerson (1963: 7–8) developed five categories, and Eisenstadt (1963: 99) relied on four.

[3] That is not for lack of trying. See, for example, the work of Stephen Chilton (1988, 1991).

and Sen 1995: 9). Although there are many competing ways of capturing an income-based measure of development,[4] the general tendency is clear and its influence widespread: Development is understood as economic growth, or change in well-being.

Although critics of income-based measures enjoy a long and distinguished pedigree,[5] this simple metric continues to dominate development studies, and its influence extends far beyond the realm of economics. By providing a convenient, linear, and simple measure of development, economists influenced the way that anthropologists, sociologists, political scientists, geographers, and especially policy makers came to think about the concept.

Then, in a curious and unlikely turn of events, the initial hesitation and reluctance of political scientists began to infect the neighboring discipline of economics. The crude manner in which economists came to measure (and understand) development was challenged by those who wanted to return to a notion of development that embraces its complexity and multidimensionality. These new approaches abhor simple attempts at measurement or confinement within the boundaries of a single academic discipline.

CAPABILITY APPROACHES TO DEVELOPMENT

There are three similar and very broad-based approaches to human development that can be used to cordon off a space we can call political development. These approaches are associated with a Nobel prize–winning economist, an influential political philosopher, and an institutional wing

---

[4] The most common measures include GDP/GDI and GNP/GNI. Gross domestic product/income (GDP/GDI) is the sum total of all incomes produced in a particular country in the form of wages, profits, rents, and interest (for activities carried out in that country). Gross national product/income (GNP/GNI) includes GDP/GDI plus all transfers of income from other countries (e.g., repatriation of profits on foreign investment, remittances of migrants received, foreign investment inflows) minus all transfers of income to other countries (e.g., outflows of foreign direct investment and profits of foreign direct investment, and transfers of income by migrants to families back home).

[5] See, e.g., Hicks and Streeten (1979); UNDP (1990); and Sánchez (2000). The most usual criticisms note the difficulties many developing countries have in producing dependable accounts and that national income accounts only register monetary exchanges; include commodities such as nuclear weapons (that hardly count as "goods") and the costs of cleaning up "bads" (such as oil spills); treat natural resources as both free and limitless; and ignore the value of leisure time and the labor exerted at home and in the informal economy, freedom and human rights, equality, and distribution issues (within a given country).

of the United Nations: Amartya Sen, Martha Nussbaum, and the UNDP, respectively. Although these approaches' objectives are broader and more ambitious than mine, each approach implicitly recognizes the important role that political development must play in securing broad-based human development.

Amartya Sen

Perhaps nobody has done more than Amartya Sen to challenge the narrow way in which economists have conceived of and measured development. Criticizing simple commodity or welfarist measures of well-being, Sen argues that agency and human capabilities (in addition to more traditional measures of utility and welfare) must play a central role in securing development. This emphasis on agency is best summarized by the title of his influential 1999 book, *Development as Freedom*.[6]

For Sen, development is about removing the constraints and providing the opportunities necessary for individuals to exercise their reasoned agency. Development is not just about maximizing economic growth; it is also about removing "poverty as well as tyranny, poor economic opportunities as well as systematic social deprivation, neglect of public facilities as well as intolerance or overactivity of repressive states" (Sen 1999: 3).

This way of looking at development is different from traditional approaches in at least three important respects. First, it requires that we delve into the complicated ways in which freedom and development are related. Second, it requires that we broaden our conceptual horizon to include social and political (as well as economic) indicators. Finally, Sen's approach to development highlights the difficulty of making international comparisons of development and emphasizes the importance of contextual studies that allow us to situate and interpret how political, social, and economic changes affect individual perceptions of well-being.

Let me elaborate on the first of these differences, because a focus on freedom implies an interest in the more political aspects of development. Sen argues that freedom and development are associated in two interrelated ways. On the one hand, substantive freedoms (such as the right to participate in politics or the opportunity to receive a basic education) are constituent components of development (Sen 1999: 5). These freedoms are sought in themselves and are, in effect, indicators of development.

---

[6] Although the discussion that follows draws from his 1999 book, Sen's contribution to the capabilities approach is much broader. See, e.g., Sen (1979, 1984, 1985, and 2000).

Thus developed states enjoy broad-based substantive freedoms, whereas underdeveloped states do not. The existence of these freedoms is constitutive of development.

At the same time, Sen argues that freedom can contribute to development in a more instrumental way. Indeed, he devotes most of his 1999 book, *Development as Freedom*, to outlining five types of freedom and the ways in which they are instrumentally related to development. These freedoms are said to advance the general capability of a person: "Greater freedom enhances the ability of people to help themselves and also to influence the world, and these matters are central to the process of development" (Sen 1999: 18).

The first of these (instrumental) freedoms is what Sen (1999: 38) refers to as *political freedom*, or the opportunities that people have to determine who should govern and on what principles. Political freedom entails the kind of political entitlements that we broadly associate with democracy, including the civil and political rights that allow individuals to scrutinize and criticize political authority and to enjoy the freedoms of expression, association, and dissent.

Sen also recognizes the important role played by access to *economic facilities*, because a person's economic entitlements depend critically on his or her ability to secure resources. For example, the lack of access to credit restricts the development of economic agents (whether they are individuals, firms, or families), because they cannot fully use their economic entitlements for the purposes of consumption, production, or exchange. Yet the importance of this second freedom is perhaps most evident with reference to labor markets, which many of the world's most desperate inhabitants have difficulty entering:

[T]he crucial challenges of development in many developing countries today include the need for the freeing up of labor from explicit or implicit bondage that denies access to the open labor market. (Sen 1999: 7)

The last three categories of freedom can be mentioned briefly without suggesting that they are less important than the first two. Sen's third category of instrumental freedoms concerns *social opportunities*, or the arrangements that a society makes for education, health care, and the like. In the same way that social and legal restrictions inhibit people from accessing economic facilities, an individual's poor health or lack of an education can restrict access to the labor market. Sen's fourth category, *transparency guarantees*, recognizes the importance of openness: People need to be able to deal with one another under conditions of trust and with guarantees of disclosure and lucidity. Such guarantees play an important role in combating some of today's most serious development challenges, namely corruption and financial irresponsibility. Finally, Sen recognizes the importance of *protective security* as a category of freedom that is important for bringing about development. Without real protection from abject misery, starvation, and even death, individuals can find themselves vulnerable to great deprivation in the face of shifting market conditions.

By recognizing freedom as both a constituent part of development and as an instrument for bringing it about, Sen forces us to change the way in which we understand and study development. Most important is the need to move away from singular (economistic) metrics of development (which facilitate large-N comparisons across space and time) and toward using contextual interpretations of development across a broad range of indicators.[7] Sen's work

outlines the need for an integrated analysis of economic, social and political activities, involving a variety of institutions and many interactive agencies. It concentrates particularly on the roles and interconnections between certain crucial instrumental freedoms, including *economic opportunities, political freedoms, social facilities, transparency guarantees*, and *protective security* (Sen 1999: xii, italics in original).

The result is an approach to development that is unabashedly value-laden, context-specific, and political in orientation. Development is defined relative to what people can and *should* be able to do (relative to their "functionings," in Sen's language). In short, "[d]evelopment . . . is a process of expanding the real freedoms that people enjoy" (Sen 1999: 3).

Martha Nussbaum

Martha Nussbaum's approach to development derives from her background as a feminist and Aristotelian scholar. In *Women and Human Development*, Nussbaum (2000) offers a capabilities approach to

---

[7] By criticizing a single metric of development, Sen develops an argument about the difficulty of making simple interpersonal comparisons. It recognizes that the utility of a given commodity (or mix of commodities) can vary significantly across individuals and contexts. Therefore a focus on simple economic metrics is problematic, because the utility we derive as an individual varies with the good. For example, the utility I get from a swimming pool is radically different from the utility that such a pool provides a paraplegic. As individuals we have different needs, and we obtain our well-being in very different ways.

This same contextual sensitivity is evident in Sen's discussion of the capability of appearing in public without shame (e.g., Sen 1984: 28, 332–8). Sen notes how different our world is from that of Adam Smith, when Smith comments on how it was impossible to appear in public (in eighteenth-century England) without a linen shirt.

establish a series of fundamental political principles that focus on the lives of women in developing countries.[8] Given her different point of departure, it is not surprising that Nussbaum's objectives, language, and approach differ from Sen's in several important ways.[9]

Most evidently, Nussbaum's project is not limited to creating a comparative indicator for human development, based on capabilities. Although this objective is important, Nussbaum's main intent is to establish a threshold level of capabilities that can be used as a foundation for the development of central constitutional principles (Nussbaum 2000: 12). For that reason, she delves into the normative and philosophical issues involved and provides us with a concrete list of capabilities that she argues can and should be applied universally. Her ten central human functional capabilities are as follows: life; bodily health; bodily integrity; senses, imagination, and thought; emotions; practical reason; affiliation; other species; play; and control over one's environment (pp. 78–80). By providing such a list of capabilities, Nussbaum wishes to focus our attention on the two activities that are necessary for securing human development: "not only promoting appropriate development of their [individual citizens] internal powers, but also preparing the environment so that it is favorable for the exercise of practical reasons and the other major functions" (p. 85).

There is much conceptual overlap between Nussbaum's list of ten capabilities and Sen's five instrumental freedoms. Like Sen's freedoms, Nussbaum's list does not easily translate into a coding book or checklist for comparing national levels of human development. Yet one cannot study this list (or Sen's, for that matter) without recognizing the important role that basic political rights and institutions play in securing these capabilities.[10] In particular, Nussbaum's tenth capability (control over one's environment) includes "[b]eing able to participate effectively in political choices that govern one's life, having the right of political participation, protections of free speech and association" (2000: 80). Yet a strong role for politics in securing each of the other capabilities is also evident.[11]

---

[8] As with Sen, Nussbaum's work on capabilities extends far beyond this single book. See, for example, Nussbaum (1988, 1990, 1995, 2003, and 2005).

[9] For comparisons of Sen's and Nussbaum's contributions to the capabilities approach, see, e.g., Clark (2005) and Crocker (1992).

[10] Nussbaum (2000: 96ff) explicitly elaborates on the relationship between human rights and human capabilities.

[11] Consider the first capability: *life*. Nussbaum (2000: 78) elaborates on this capability by adding, "Being able to live to the end of a human life of normal length; not dying prematurely, or before one's life is so reduced as to be not worth living." To secure this

Like Sen, Nussbaum focuses on differences in opportunities across contexts. These opportunity differentials are particularly important for explaining the systematic ways in which women suffer across the globe. Although some differences result from social norms or public policy decisions, others result from natural conditions that cannot be resolved by a simple vote in the legislature. Yet public policies can be developed to provide people with the full social bases for these capabilities (Nussbaum 2000: 81–2).

Consider a person's health. Some share of illness will always result from poor luck or endowment (e.g., being hit by a car or born with a handicap). Therefore governments will never be able to ensure that all citizens will enjoy equal levels of health. However, there are aspects of health that can be influenced by public policy, and individual endowments or unlucky situations can be improved by that public policy. In recognizing this, governments can be held responsible for delivering the social bases of these capabilities: They can make up for the initial differences that result from natural endowments or bad luck.

Nussbaum (2000: 84–5) refers to these initial differences in terms of a three-part classification of capabilities. *Basic capabilities* include the innate and rudimentary equipment of individuals. Thus to exercise free speech, one needs to be able to speak – literally. *Internal capabilities* are what Nussbaum refers to as "mature conditions of readiness" (p. 84). They are the developed states that allow a person to exercise a requisite function (if allowed by the surrounding circumstances and constraints). Sometimes these states occur naturally, without much external intervention (e.g., one becomes capable of sexual functioning by simply growing older); more often internal capabilities build on preexisting basic capabilities, but they develop only with support from the surrounding environment (e.g., learning how to love).

On top of this pyramid of capabilities is what Nussbaum refers to as *combined capabilities*, in which internal capabilities are combined with suitable external conditions to enable the individual to exercise the function. Combined capabilities speak to the real opportunities available to individuals; they combine endowments, potential, and the absence of restrictions in a way that parallels Isaiah Berlin's (1969) notion of

capability, the political community has to provide access to a healthy (elaborated on in the second explicit capability) and secure environment. Of course, there are many ways to bring about a healthy and secure context for individuals, but each requires specific political institutions and norms, as well as the implied use of force.

positive freedom.[12] Thus a person living in a repressive nondemocratic regime might be born with a basic capability to speak, and she might have developed an internal capability that allows her to exercise thought and speech in accordance with her conscience, but the nature of the political regime itself inhibits her from actually doing so. In other words, a citizen in this political context does not enjoy the combined capability to exercise thought and speech in accordance with her conscience.

Nussbaum's approach, like Sen's, focuses on human equality, but it shies away from complete egalitarianism, or even a Rawlsian maxi-min–style solution.[13] For Nussbaum, this is done by keeping the approach's focus on capabilities, not functionings,[14] and allowing citizens to be as free as possible in determining their own courses of action. Although "it is perfectly true that functions, not simple capabilities, are what renders a life fully human . . . we could hardly applaud it, no matter what opportunities it contained. . . . for political purposes it is appropriate that we shoot for capabilities, and those alone. Citizens must be left free to determine their own course after that" (Nussbaum 2000: 87).

The Human Development Index

In the capabilities approaches of both Sen and Nussbaum we find a desire to focus on individual capabilities, a need to create a conceptual space where it makes sense to compare quality of life across contexts, and an often implicit criticism of the simple economistic approaches commonly used to measure development. Both authors want to generate a framework that facilitates cross-contextual comparisons of human welfare without succumbing to the shortcomings inherent in the simple welfare or commodity approaches embraced by economists. In practice, however, both approaches have a tendency to hover a great distance above the empirical ground.

---

[12] Positive freedom or liberty is understood to be the possibility of acting in such a way as to take control of one's life and realize one's fundamental purposes. Berlin contrasts this with a negative conception of liberty that is understood in terms of the absence of obstacles, barriers, or constraints.

[13] A maximum-minimum solution is one that maximizes the opportunities for society's least advantaged residents (the minimum).

[14] "Functionings" are the things people manage to do or be (e.g., living a long and healthy life, being a respected member of the community, raising a family, achieving satisfaction in sports/culture). People experience poverty when they are deprived of such basic capabilities to achieve functionings.

A third approach addresses head-on this need for explicit comparative indicators by providing a concrete empirical approach for measuring (broad-based) human development. This basic needs approach builds on the work of Paul Streeten, Frances Steward, and Mahbub ul Haq, among others; it has resulted in the UNDP's (1990) Human Development Report.

The first Human Development Report (HDR) introduced the concept of human development in terms of progress toward greater human well-being. More importantly, the HDR provided a statistical appendix filled with country-level data on a wide range of development indicators. At the most general level, this approach embodies the capabilities approaches of both Sen and Nussbaum, emphasizing the end of development (progress toward greater human well-being) over the means to that end (e.g., income per capita). In practice, its resulting index – *the Human Development Index* (HDI) – operationalizes these capabilities in terms of three development objectives: access to health, to education, and to goods.[15]

The first (1990) *HDR* analyzed the record of human development over three preceding decades and examined the experience of 14 countries in managing their economic growth and human development. Its conclusions might be summarized in three points. The first was the welcome realization that many developing countries had been making significant progress in achieving human development, with the gap between rich and poor countries narrowing considerably, and that there was no automatic link between economic growth and human progress. Second, the report showed how respectable levels of human development were possible even in countries with very modest levels of incomes. Its third (and often forgotten) conclusion was that the developing world was spending too much of its meager income on military spending.

The *HDR* then introduced a composite index for human development, the HDI, which covered 133 countries in 1987, ranging from Japan (which topped the list with an index score of 0.996) to Niger (0.116). Over the years, the *HDR* has expanded and improved its index, so that it currently includes rankings for 182 countries with component indices for a number of important indicators (such as life expectancy, literacy, school enrollment, and income) that are combined together in a single

---

[15] Sen's relationship to the HDI is complex. Sen helped draft (and consulted on) the initial *HDR*, and he saw it as an important improvement to a naive commodity or welfare approach to human development. Yet he has also been quite critical of certain aspects. See Crocker (1992) and Sen (2000).

rough index used to rank countries in terms of human development. In short, the HDI offers an improvement on base welfare or commodity indicators of development by providing a much broader measure of development.

Yet the Human Development Report and its component HDI are not without problems. Three of these are particularly evident in light of the sort of issues that concern us now. The first is its limited applicability: Because the index only stretches back to 1987, it cannot be used for studying the development effects of emigration during earlier periods. Given that the post-1987 period represents a period with substantial limitations on international migration, relying on the HDI alone would seriously constrain our ability to generalize to other periods and contexts.

Second, the HDI is collected to facilitate comparisons across nation-states. Although this is useful, the development effects of emigration are not restricted to this level of analysis and may be occurring at lower levels; for example, within nation-states. For this reason, the HDI constricts the sample not only in time but also in space and does not allow examination of the possible effects of emigration in important (within-state) contexts.[16]

Finally, and most damning from our current perspective, the HDI does not include any specifically *political* components. This lacuna has long been recognized as an important shortcoming. Indeed, already in the original (1990) report, the UNDP promised more work on the subject of democratization, noting that a democratic political and social framework was not necessarily an impediment to the attainment of relatively high levels of human development. Later, the 2002 report was dedicated to the issue of democracy and political development. In this report the UNDP explicitly considered the role that democracy could play in encouraging development and argued that "countries can promote human development for all only when they have governance systems that are fully accountable to all people – and when all people can participate in the debates and decisions that shape their lives" (UNDP 2002: 3). Like freedom for Sen, the UNDP sees democracy as an important development goal in its own right: "[E]njoying political freedom and participating in

---

[16] This situation has recently begun to change, as data are being gathered at subnational levels in several countries. For example, see the most recent *China Human Development Report 2007–8* (UNDP 2008: 139) for a province-level breakdown of HDI in that country. Indeed, I employ this subnational ranking in Chapter 8. Similar figures can be found for states on both sides of the U.S.-Mexican border, see Anderson and Gerber (2007).

the decisions that shape one's life are fundamental human rights: they are part of human development in their own right" (ibid).

Despite recognizing the importance of political development, the UNDP has not been able (or willing) to incorporate an explicit indicator for political development in its HDI. In failing to include such an indicator, it is following a long tradition of avoiding this difficult issue. Although the UNDP report notes that human development is incomplete without human freedom, it has not been able to agree on an adequate measure for this important component of development. Mahbub ul Haq himself is said to have experimented with an index to political freedom, but apparently without success (Sen 2000: 22). Indeed, Sen (2000: 23) concludes his overview of "A Decade of Human Development" by noting the need to include democracy in any broader measure of human development.

MEASURING POLITICAL DEVELOPMENT

Each of the approaches described earlier recognizes the central role played by politics in obtaining broader based development, but none offers an indicator that might allow us to compare levels of political development across varying contexts.

For Sen, political development seems to imply democracy, and democracy provides much of the freedom that is itself constitutive of development. Yet democracy also facilitates the other instrumental freedoms that Sen links to development. In particular, democracy helps protect people from political and economic catastrophes (such as famines and descents into chaos) that undermine an individual's *protective security*. Finally, democracy can empower people in ways that allow them to expand their *economic facilities* and *social opportunities*, as well as to secure *transparency guarantees*.

Likewise, in providing her list of constitutionally guaranteed minimum capabilities, Nussbaum recognizes (albeit implicitly) the central role that politics plays in her approach. Although she tends to shy away from direct references to democracy, Nussbaum's list of ten central human functional capabilities depends on a political context that can secure individual rights and on the possibility of individuals participating in, and exerting influence on, the choices that govern their lives.

Finally, and most explicitly, the UNDP has always recognized the need to introduce a political indicator for development, and its experts have often implied that this could be done with an indicator that captures different levels of democracy. So far, however, the UNDP has been unable or unwilling to do so in practice.

Conceptual Challenges

The difficulty of the task – of creating a simple comparative indicator for political development – is a function of the complexity of the underlying concept. As a concept, political development does not lend itself to being captured along a single, linear dimension, as in the way that income, for example, can measure economic development.

What, then, are the special qualities of political development that we need to address when choosing or developing an appropriate indicator? It is important to emphasize four important qualities (and their inherent challenges). First, we want an indicator that can capture the main thrust of the capability approaches – that political development can be understood as an expansion of the real freedom that people enjoy. This expansion can be measured in terms not only of the extension of formal democratic rights and freedoms but also of changes to the general environment that can facilitate the employment of these rights and freedoms.

The other three qualities are related, but introduce particular challenges of their own: Political development is path dependent and context specific; political development depends on individual capabilities that are often lost in composite (aggregate) indicators; and political development exists at several levels of society, which requires indicators that are sensitive to this variation.

To grasp the nature of the challenges we face, consider the difficulty of employing the most reasonable surrogate measure for political development: a democratization index. After all, it is now commonplace to embrace liberal democracy as the end of contemporary political development. By imagining a continuum that stretches from nondemocratic to strongly democratic states, we can create a reasonable surrogate measure for political development. Indeed, as the reader will soon see, surrogates of this type are used throughout this study.

The difficulty lies in agreeing on a single indicator for comparing and ranking the astonishing variety of democracy's institutional forms. After all, there are as many types of democracy as there are governments in the world, and we do not (nor should we) agree on a common standard for measuring the strength of a particular democracy. For example, few of us would be willing to argue that an electoral system based on proportional representation is always more democratic than one that relies on a majority system. Similarly, who is willing to claim that presidential systems are necessarily less democratic than parliamentary systems? Ranking institutional forms of democracy along a single dimension is an exercise in futility.[17]

One reason for this difficulty is that political development is path dependent; each political form has resulted from a unique political past. Even if we try and freeze time and compare political contexts of a particular time or era, it is very difficult (not to mention contentious) to try and rank contexts in the way we commonly do with economic concepts.[18] These difficulties are exacerbated when we try to extend the comparisons back in time and conceive of ways to compare political development in

[17] There is broad recognition of this among democracy scholars, as evidenced by the *Journal of Democracy*'s symposium on the quality of democracy published in their October 2004 issue. The general consensus seems to be that it is not very useful to evaluate and compare countries in terms of their democratic quality, or level of democraticness. Although Stein Ringen agrees in principle, he does believe it is possible and useful to compare democratic states in terms of their moral goodness – to compare how democracies "... do what they do, or how good they are by criteria of quality" (Ringen 2007: 41). To do this, Ringen provides a very rough quality index and uses it to compare 25 contemporary democracies at a single point in time.

[18] Consider an example. At a general level, we might ask whether recent changes in contemporary China constitute political development. In asking this question, we do not ignore the difficulties we can expect in measuring this potential development, only that it is possible to look at changes in China over time and depict them in terms of progress (or the lack of progress). Any successful measure would have to be sensitive to China's political past and receptive to what is possible and desirable to accomplish within the Chinese context.

We can then ask the same thing of the United States. Every country, regardless of its existing level of political development, can achieve greater development: This is the promise inherent to progress. As in China, the way we might measure political development in the United States should be sensitive to the United States' unique political trajectory: its colonial past, its relationship to Britain, its strong agrarian history, its Civil War, its rise as the world's political and economic hegemon, its successes and failures during the Cold War, etc.

The problem is that these countries – even though they share the same temporal space – have followed two very different paths to political development. Each path is influenced by its unique political history. In light of this, it would be rather unreasonable to expect that future Chinese political development will follow the same path that American political development once followed (I'm assuming that the United States is more developed, politically, than China). To be blunt, political development in China can occur even in the absence of a U.S.-style Bill of Rights; or a constitution that separates legislative, executive, and judiciary powers; or an electoral system that encourages competition between two independent political parties over positions that entail real political power. Just as important, the United States has the potential for greater political development, even after it secures basic individual rights and liberties (a possibility not always recognized in contemporary measures of democracy). Political development is *not* a dichotomous variable, where a country either has it or does not.

Europe in the late 18th century with those in Europe at the beginning of the 21st (or, for that matter, in South Asia).

In short, political development might entail progress, but that progress is difficult and contentious to capture in a linear fashion. Given the vast diversity in political experiences over time and across countries, we cannot expect very different countries to take the same steps or arrive at the same outcomes.

The third and fourth challenges are related and linked to the problem of aggregation. As both Nussbaum and Sen make abundantly clear, aggregate scales of development are problematic in that they gloss over individual differences in capabilities. Thus an individual can still suffer from a lack of capabilities while living in a community or state that scores high on an aggregate indicator of development.[19] The fourth difficulty is that political development can reveal itself in different forms at different levels of aggregation. Thus the institution used to capture political development at the national level can vary significantly from those that are found at the village or town level – even in the same country. Ideally, we need a measure of political development that can be employed at various levels (individual, village, state, nation, etc.) of analysis, because sometimes it is appropriate to measure at the nation-state level, but very often it is not.

WHAT THEN?

Given these conceptual challenges, how can we hope to capture political development across contexts that vary significantly over time and at different levels of aggregation? In the absence of a single indicator, I propose a practical solution that uses the more political aspects of the capabilities approaches, described earlier, as a broad umbrella concept. In this way, we can draw on existing databases and measures of political development (operationalized in various ways) when they are suitable, or we can use the capabilities approach to choose particular indicators in contexts that do not lend themselves to these cross-national databases. In other words,

---

[19] Similarly, Guillermo O'Donnell has criticized mainstream political science for its obsessive focus on the regime (see Reich 2002). Ringen (2007: 31ff) provides an innovative attempt to overcome this problem by using what he calls a "double bookkeeping" approach, which maps both regime-level and individual-level scores concomitantly. The 2009 UNDP *Human Development Report* does this also by including a measure of human development of people, as well as an indicator for the human development of countries. See UNDP (2009: 14).

we can allow the scope of political development to vary with the level of analysis, but each indicator will be informed by, and explicitly linked to, a capabilities approach to political development.

Thus when studying large-scale patterns that straddle several decades (even centuries), a very rough indicator such as Tatu Vanhanen's (2003, 2007) index of democratization or Polity's governance indicator (CSP 2009) can be employed. Although these indices provide only a very rough measure of political development, they stretch far enough back in time and over a sufficiently large number of polities to allow us to generalize about global political developments over almost two centuries. For more recent developments and higher levels of aggregation, we have access to better indicators, such as the HDI.

Given the roughness of the measure, the limitations of data that are collected at the national level, and the problems of relative insensitivity to path dependency and cultural variation, any approach that relies solely on this type of data will be severely hobbled. Still, when used carefully (and with an awareness of those caveats), available indicators of this type can be employed as rough surrogates for political development.

At the regional, state, or province level, it is possible to secure some patchy data for the level of human development (in recent years), and I use this data when possible. More often than not, however, I have chosen to employ more conveniently available indicators that capture the same sense of political development. Indeed, when statistical data are not attainable or existing measures of democracy are entirely insufficient for capturing any expected change, this study relies on case studies, anchored in particular contexts. In these situations, it is necessary to track perceptible changes in local (subnational) contexts: changes that allow each person more real freedom (Sen 1999: 3), changes that allow each person to be treated worthy of regard, and changes that allow each individual greater opportunities to live humanely (Nussbaum 2000: 74). What this means, in practice, varies significantly from one context to another.

The point is that the contextual setting itself determines the relevant aspects of development to be studied. In familiarizing ourselves with that context, we learn which aspects of development are seen to be most relevant and pressing. With this contextual understanding in place, we can then employ counterfactual and comparative-case approaches to isolate the role that emigration played in facilitating or deterring that development.

These varying levels of political development, even when captured by different measures over time and in different contexts, are not unrelated to one another. After all, the path to national (or, for that matter, global) political development is fundamentally shaped by class and social configurations and alignments, at any number of levels beneath the nation-state. Political development is exemplified by the far-reaching processes of internal restructuring, made possible by new balances of class power (and consequently new relations of production). These changing balances of power are evident at both national and local levels, even if they need to be captured by different indicators.

This is not a final solution to this difficult problem, as it complicates cross-national comparisons. Yet it is an honest attempt to do the right thing, under trying conceptual and empirical circumstances. I use hardened statistical indicators when they are available and contextually sensitive case studies and counterfactuals when necessary or useful. Yet whatever the measure, each is grounded in a capabilities approach to development.

It is the objective of this book to examine how emigration affects political development, measured in these sundry ways. The next chapter introduces a theoretical argument for linking the two phenomena.

3

Linking Emigration to Political Development

This chapter introduces an approach for studying how emigration affects political development. It does so in three cautious steps. Because emigration has the potential to affect political development at several levels of analysis, the first step is to justify a community-level approach to addressing the question. For the sake of convenience, community is operationalized as the state in the discussion that follows. Although it may be more common to begin by examining the motives of individual migrants, the state is both the most relevant agent of political development and the most convenient vehicle for measuring the effects of political development.

The second step constitutes the main body of the chapter; it outlines four approaches for studying state-level effects. It begins by considering the most obvious connection, in which political development follows on the heels of economic growth. Although such a straightforward approach draws from a large body of existing work and requires little theoretical elaboration, it fails to satisfy – if only because it links emigration only *indirectly* to political development. For this reason, I then describe three *direct* ways by which emigration can affect political development. The first considers the role of the individual migrant in facilitating political development at home. The second examines the relationship between individuals and the state to show how emigration affects the relative power of groups and individuals within the state. The third approach takes the state as its point of departure and explores how emigration can force states to compete with one another over potentially mobile residents. Although each approach leads us to expect that emigration can influence political development (either positively or negatively), each focuses on different causal mechanisms.

Because the remainder of the book tests these approaches in a wide-ranging empirical study, the third step concludes this chapter by elaborating on a case-selection strategy. Such a strategy is especially important in this type of investigatory study, in which little previous work has been done and the effects under scrutiny can be indirect and/or exerted in combination with other, more dominant effects. At the most general level, our objective must be to maximize both variation across cases and contextual sensitivity within cases. Yet the case-selection strategy is also designed to control for variation along a number of theoretically relevant dimensions. By the end of the chapter, I hope the reader will see how the subsequent design of the empirical studies can confirm the utility of each approach mentioned in step 2 and provide us with a fuller understanding of the effect that emigration can have on political development.

THE STATE AND POLITICAL DEVELOPMENT

The relationship between emigration and political development involves at least two types of actors (e.g., sending and receiving states), spanning a relatively wide array of contextual conditions. The nature of this relationship complicates any empirical study in ways that I elaborate on later in the chapter. The first order of business is to establish the appropriate level of analysis for the study.

Finding the appropriate level of analysis involves two related choices. The first concerns the relevant actors and motives. Emigration is an activity that involves many potential actors (the migrant, the migrant's friends and family, the migrant's home community, the migrant's new [host] community, any overarching political authority, etc.), any one of which is a legitimate agent of study. The second, related choice concerns what might be called the effect venue, or the level of aggregation that is appropriate for capturing the effect of emigration (e.g., individual, family, community, state or nation). The political development effects of emigration vary across different levels and agents.

Because we are interested in the *general* relationship between emigration and development, it is important not to bias the study by drawing too heavily on a particular context or the experience of any particular agent. Unfortunately, much of the migration literature has suffered from just this sort of analytical myopia. Many migration scholars build their analyses on assumptions about individual migrant (or family) motives, which tend to be economic in nature. In other words, these analyses tend to assume that the migrant (or his or her family) is *pushed* out of hopelessness and desperate local economic conditions or *pulled* toward foreign opportunities and rewards.

The desire to secure microfoundations blinds us to the fact that these individual/family motives depend critically on the degree of freedom that exists at higher levels of aggregation. Individual motives *might* matter in national contexts in which citizens can freely move about the country. Yet in many national contexts this sort of freedom does not exist.[1] More significantly, much contemporary migration occurs in an international context in which states monitor and control international border crossings. Under these conditions, the motives of individual migrants are relatively insignificant compared to the standing orders of the border guard that limit cross-border migrant flows.[2] In short, individual-migrant motives are important, but only within the broader parameters determined by larger (aggregate) political actors.

This is not to suggest that individuals do not matter: The political development effects related to individual migrants, in the form of social remittances or political brain drain, can be significant. I am suggesting instead that individual motives are less important than surrounding contextual factors for understanding patterns of emigration and their political effects.

This leads us to the second choice: the level of effects. This study chooses to examine those effects at the level of the sending community, and it has three reasons for doing so. The first is that the development effects of emigration on the individual migrant are so clear that they require little further elaboration: The span of individual opportunities is surely greater when that individual enjoys an opportunity to emigrate.

Making this argument in its full glory would draw us deep into normative and theoretical territory (a terrain that I hope to avoid at this juncture), but it can be sketched briefly as follows. Limiting the potential for migration restricts individual freedom. Because freedom and development are intricately linked to one another, and because this study employs a

---

[1] The UNDP (2009: 40) lists a handful of countries that impose strict restrictions on exit (e.g., Cuba, the Democratic People's Republic of Korea, China, Eritrea, Iran, Burma, and Uzbekistan), 20 countries that restrict the exit of women, and 8 additional countries that employ age-specific restrictions.

[2] Not to mention the sometimes exorbitant prices that states can demand when issuing external travel documents (McKenzie 2007) or the state's willingness to confiscate property, strip emigrants of their nationality, and even brand emigrants as traitors (Fitzgerald 2006: 262).

broad-based, capability approach to development, free migration, *ceteris paribus*, will open up more avenues for the individual's development. This argument reflects a key part of the liberal tradition of political thought, in which freedom is primarily conceived in terms of the absence of restrictions. The origins of this way of thinking are found in an argument about the effect of physical limitations placed on human mobility (think of slavery).[3]

Still, it is possible to argue that restricting a person's mobility is necessary for that person's individual political development. To make this argument, we need to accept that (1) an individual's development depends on the ability of the community to provide a context that is conducive to that development and (2) the community's capacity to provide such a context is jeopardized by allowing people free access to (or exit from) that community. This is a popular argument among those who reside in states that can provide such a nurturing context, but it rings rather shallow for the great portion of humankind that is less lucky.[4]

In the final analysis, this type of argument needs to be tested in a more normative and theoretical forum. Of course, it is possible to conduct a large empirical study of the individual effects of emigration. We can easily find examples of individuals who have benefited from and those who have been hurt by the opportunity to emigrate (indeed, Chapter 9 examines some of these examples). Yet it is nearly impossible to argue for the representativeness of such a sample across the wide spectrum of contexts in which we expect this relationship to hold. For these reasons I think it makes sense to put this individual argument aside and instead focus on the development effects of emigration on the sending community.

A second reason for focusing on the state level is that the state is clearly the most relevant and convenient means of operationalizing the "community." Although we know that many of emigration's effects occur closer to the ground (e.g., in the emigrant's village or neighborhood) – indeed, we can expect to find the strongest links at the lowest levels of aggregation – it is difficult to obtain good comparable data over time at this level of aggregation. As is shown in Chapter 8, fieldwork can trace these sorts of developments at the subnational level, but they are hard to compare across contexts. In addition, the modern state holds most of the

---

[3] See, e.g., Hobbes's definition of liberty in his *On the Citizen* (1998 [1651]: 111), or Locke's definition (and examples) of liberty in his *Essay Concerning Human Understanding* (1690 [BK II, chapter 21]: §10, §15, §22).

[4] I have argued against this position in other contexts; see Moses (2003, 2006: chapter 4).

other tools that we associate with broad-based development, and for this reason, it is the most common level of analysis in the broader development literature. Finally, and most important of all, the state remains the migrant's gatekeeper: In the world today, it is the state that decides who can (or cannot) enter and leave a given patch of territory (both within the state and across state boundaries).

Because of the state's central role in influencing developments on both fronts (emigration and political development), the international effects of emigration turn on the behavior of individual states. This is the third reason to focus on the state. After all, an individual's potential to emigrate is determined by the decisions of those who control the gates of two different communities (operationalized here in terms of states): the home community and the host community. When the world is divided up into a fixed number of states, and each state has the right and capacity to control the movement of people in and out of the territory it controls, then an individual's freedom to emigrate depends on decisions made by both the host and the home states. The right to emigrate freely – whether granted by an individual state or by the international community at large – is a hollow right if there are no states that are willing to open their gates to potential migrants. For this reason, the international regime effects of emigration also depend largely on the decisions made by individual states.

For these three reasons, it behooves us to focus on the role of the state when developing an analytical approach for studying the effects of emigration on political development. However, I hasten to emphasize that this focus on the state is merely a convenient means of operationalizing the political communities that exist at a variety of different levels. It is a sort of analytical shorthand for the theoretical discussion that follows. In the following empirical studies, the "state" is operationalized in terms of both nation-states and local and regional political authorities.

FOUR APPROACHES TO POLITICAL DEVELOPMENT

This section outlines four distinct approaches for studying the effects of emigration on political development. The first is an indirect approach that draws heavily on the existing economic literature and requires little further elaboration. The next three approaches trace out more direct influences. Each approach points to the possibility of either negative or positive effects, and each relies on different causal mechanisms.

An Indirect Approach

Perhaps the easiest way to think about the relationship between emigration and political development is to piggyback on the existing literatures. As described in Chapter 1, economists have already developed and tested numerous arguments for how migration facilitates economic development in the sending region or country. Underlying this literature is a growing realization among economists of the utility of emigration as an instrument for economic development.[5] Although the most dominant of these approaches tend to focus on remittance transfers, other factors may play an important role in linking emigration to economic development. Among these factors are a more efficient match of international supplies and demand for labor, a tightening of the sending country's labor markets, a (consequent) strengthening of the bargaining position of the labor force that remains, and the increased human capital of returning migrants (Moses 2006: 124–5).

A similar sort of link can be found in an older literature on the relationship between migration and development *within* countries: Here migration is often understood in terms of the uprooting of the peasantry in the process of industrialization. Most of these studies draw on the work of Arthur Lewis (1954, 1958) and Michael Torado (1969; Harris and Torado 1970), in which urban migration is seen to be a response to differences between urban and rural wages. This approach understands development as a process involving the movement of labor from low-productivity rural areas to high-productivity urban areas, in return for resources being sent from the city back to the countryside.

The lessons derived from these two literatures can be combined with that of a third, which links economic to political development. The ancestral roots of this argument run deep, but its modern reincarnation can be traced to Seymour Martin Lipset's (1959) influential article linking democracy to economic development. Lipset (1959: 75) compares European and Latin American countries in terms of their level of wealth, industrialization, education, and urbanization to show that the "more well-to-do a nation, the greater the chances that it will sustain democracy."

---

[5] If we take a step back, we see that economists' interpretations tend to ebb and flow along with the ideological tide. Before WWI, the benefits of emigration tended to be emphasized; in the interwar period and the 1970s–90s the negative effects tended to attract most attention. More recently, positive interpretations have again predominated.

Since the publication of Lipset's article more than a half-century ago, no other single subject has drawn more attention in the field of comparative politics. From all this attention, it is possible to catalogue a myriad of arguments about the relationship. Despite significant differences over its particular nature, the aggregate pattern is clear: There is a strong relationship between the level of economic development and the incidence of democratic regimes (see, e.g., Przeworski et al. 2000: 79, and their figure 2.1).[6]

Thus, it is possible to develop an argument about the potential political development effects of emigration by drawing on three well-established literatures. If political development is understood to mean the introduction of democratic regimes, we can simply extend the work of political economists to connect the dots that link (1) emigration to economic development and then (2) economic development to political development. Given the indirect nature of this link between emigration and political development, we can expect it to occur with a temporal delay (although the length of the lag is unclear).

This is not the only possible way to link the variables, and it is important to keep alternatives in mind when conducting the analysis. It could be that emigration generates economic atrophy and a corresponding decline in political development. Similarly, emigration could bring economic decline, yet still encourage political development. Both of these options are unlikely, if only because they challenge the growing consensus that links emigration to economic development. Still they are possible outcomes that need to be considered. A more interesting alternative is that emigration could bring economic development, but political decline. This might occur if the nature of economic development generated by emigration is skewed in such a way as to deter political development.

The indirect approach is tested in subsequent chapters, but there are at least three reasons to doubt its adequacy as a test of the underlying phenomenon. First, it is based on a very narrow understanding of development, one that suffers from the same sort of shortcomings found in the simple, economistic metrics of development described in the previous chapter. Indeed, most of the studies aim to explain the existence of democracy or its capacity to endure, not how it changes in strength over time. If we rely solely on narrow indicators of development (both

---

[6] See also Diamond (1992), Przeworski et al. (2001), and Landman (2003) for general overviews on the scholarship since Lipset.

political and economic), we fail to see the more important ways in which emigration can facilitate well-being. Second, an indirect approach tends to draw on simple causal models that may prove ineffective in the more complex terrain under study. Finally, the most important shortcoming of this approach is that it ignores the more direct effects that emigration might have on political development.

Direct Effects

At the most general level, it is possible to describe three direct paths along which emigration can affect political development. The first path considers the relationship from the perspective of the migrant, asking what the migrant has learned, experienced, or obtained, qua migrant, that might affect political development at home (in the sending country). The second approach considers how emigration can affect the relative influence of particular groups and interests. The resulting change in group influence can have significant effects on the state's level of political development. The third approach examines the relationship from the sending state's perspective. It considers how states might respond to increased levels of emigration and how these responses can affect a state's level of political development.

The Emigrant. The first of the direct approaches focuses on the role that individual migrants can play in the political development process by examining how they often act as agents of globalization by linking the distant with the local: In their exchanges and correspondence with those still at home or subsequently returning home, migrants introduce foreign ideas, skills, norms, and institutions in ways that are subtly adapted to local (home) conditions.

This approach draws from the work of those who study the economic effects of emigration in three related forms: remittances, skills transfers, and brain drain. Economists have long recognized the role that financial remittances can play as an important source of investment that is directly injected into the local economy (and hence avoids many of the more corrupt channels higher up in the political chain). This literature is careful to point out that more money is almost always better than less, yet the development and poverty-reducing effects of remittances depend critically on the way the money is spent. When remittances are sent home to friends and family to be spent in the local economy on essential items that are locally produced (e.g., food, clothing, housing), their effects can multiply out into the surrounding local economy, encouraging new investments, hiring, and a broad range of economic activity.

Just as important is the realization that a significant percentage of migrants return home (although the percentage varies across migration regimes). When they do come home, migrants bring with them capital, skills, and access to markets that prove useful in setting up new enterprises. For example, such entrepreneurial accounts can be read in frequent newspaper reports of returning Indian and Chinese migrants. It is also the reason that so many countries now encourage emigrants to return and start up businesses as part of their larger development strategies.[7]

Finally, economists are aware that there can be negative effects that follow in the wake of emigration, and these effects tend to fall under the rubric of brain drain: Freer emigration regimes allow skilled workers (e.g., teachers, doctors, and engineers) to leave economies that most desperately need them, thus undermining their development potential. After all, economically underdeveloped states commit scarce resources to train professionals to play an important role in their subsequent development. Obviously, training a doctor or engineer can take a great deal of time and resources. Because these skills are important for the development of the surrounding economy, states often help their citizens obtain them. Thus, when trained professionals leave their country to pursue lives and careers abroad (under much better conditions), their exit can have two dramatic and related effects on the sending country: It drains the economy of necessary skills, and it wastes the government's scarce resources by allowing an important skill, paid for by the state, to leave before its development effect can be harvested.[8]

Although these three types of economic effects are widely recognized, their political siblings are seldom considered. Yet each of the posited linkages (remittances, skills transfers, and brain drain) has a political parallel. Consider remittances first. By taking the concept of remittances and broadening it to include social and political resources, we can find

---

[7] The academic literature on this subject seems to be trailing behind developments on the ground. Until very recently, there were few studies that examined the entrepreneurial effects of return migration. Those that did tended to find that returning migrants had the potential to innovate in the nonfarm sector, but seldom did (e.g., Ballard 1987: 28–9; King 1985; King et al., 1984; Rhoades 1978). More recent studies are more enthusiastic about this potential. For a general overview, see Kapur and McHale (2005).

[8] The literature on brain drain is enormous. For a review and study of the effect of brain drain on economic growth, see Beine et al. (2001). It is also possible that the opportunity for emigration can facilitate conditions of *brain gain*. See Mountford (1997), Chau and Stark (1999), and Stark (2003) for details of this revisionist argument.

an important avenue of political influence. Such social remittances have the potential to encourage local political change in the same way that financial remittances can stimulate local economic activity. Returning migrants bring with them a myriad of new experiences, ideas, values, perceptions, and skills that have political and social meaning, as well as economic utility. Even if the migrant's original motivation to leave was economic, foreign experiences provide exposure to new laws, customs, traditions, ideas, and patterns of organization.

In an attempt to be more systematic, we can focus on two main channels through which social remittances can affect political development: emigrant exposure to (1) new ideas, values, and beliefs and to (2) new ways of doing things. By moving to a new place, migrants come to experience different behavioral norms as they apply to gender, ethnicity, class, and any other source of identity difference. Likewise, migrants are bound to experience different attitudes about any number of politically relevant norms, such as participation, social mobility, and respect for difference.[9]

Migrants also learn about alternative forms of organization and bring these experiences home to influence the activities and structures of local organizations. They can learn new ways to organize (e.g., in trade unions), as well as learn about how an organization should work (e.g., in the absence of corruption). In their host contexts, migrants can learn about the workings of different forms of governments (both good and bad), the behavior of different types of politicians (both good and bad), and the role of participation, recruitment, socialization, and leadership in a new and different light. In short, migrants are exposed to a broader organizational experience, and they can bring home this experience to influence and build local organizations.

All of this may sound vaguely familiar to those social scientists who are old enough to have cut their teeth on the modernization approach to development. This tradition understood development as a process that transformed traditional ways of life (culture, attitudes, and social and economic structures) in ways that were influenced by industrialization, urbanization, trade, and communications. The earliest modernization approaches tended to be unabashedly Western; Western capitalist

---

[9] Evidence of these effects can be found in a recent paper by Córdova and Hiskey (2009), which finds that individuals who were in contact with international migrant networks tended to participate more in local community affairs, were more supportive of democratic principles, and even were more critical of their own country's democratic performance. See also Smith and Bakker (2008). For a more pessimistic account of emigrant legacies, based on interviews with returning Italian emigrants, see Cerase (1974).

values and practices (i.e., secular, rational, materialist, individualist) were seen as both superior to traditional values and practices and as necessary foundations for the "modernization" of developing countries.[10]

Although the influence of social remittances parallels the sort of cultural and attitudinal forces that are found in early modernization theory, it is different in one important way. In the earlier literature we find a strong emphasis on the role of education, communication, and the media in spreading new attitudes and institutions that encouraged development. Consequently, modernization implied a strong role for the state, because the state tends to dominate and regulate these activities (education, communication, and media). The return of migrants, from across the country or around the globe, injects the same sort of impetus for attitudinal, institutional, and ideational change – but it does so at a lower level of aggregation (individual, family, local network) that is largely independent of the state.

This is not to suggest that distant or foreign ideas are naturally better – only that more ideas are better. Like financial remittances, more social remittances tend to be better than less. Yet the effectiveness of these social remittances also depends critically on the way in which they are "spent" in the local environment. Of course, it is entirely possible for repugnant ideas to be imported into a local political context, and such ideas might even overwhelm the local competition. In this way, emigration could lead to political atrophy or decline. It is also possible for emigrants to return with lessons that do not take root in local conditions. Here too, the effects of emigration on political development could be negative or indeterminate. Although we cannot know whether the influence of new ideas and practices will be good or bad, we can be confident that

---

[10] In the economic realm, modernization was associated with a transformation in both attitudes and institutions. Following Torado (1986), this transformation could be summarized in terms of the adoption of several ideational and institutional artifacts of industrialization and urbanization, viz. formal rationality and planning, social and economic equalization, improved institutions and attitudes, and the promotion of effective competition. In the political realm, analysts looked for the cultural conditions that supported democratic forms of government. Thus, Gabriel Almond and Sidney Verba (1963) found a "civic culture," and Daniel Lerner (1958) identified a "modern" personality as essential components in any participatory (i.e., democratic) society. Others, such as Karl Deutsch (1966) and Lucian Pye (1966), looked at the importance of an integrative system of mass communications for building social cohesion. At the summit of this research tradition sits the seminal piece by Seymour Martin Lipset (1959), as noted earlier, which pointed to a complex mix of interrelated social and economic conditions as prerequisites for political democracy.

the resulting ideational and institutional hybrids will lend themselves to more opportunity and choice.

Emigration and return provide important means for introducing new ideas, beliefs, and organizations into the body politic: Returning emigrants import new skills that can affect political development in the home context. The effectiveness of social remittances in bringing about development depends on several factors, such as the nature of the social remittances themselves (some skills/ideas/organizations travel better than others), the nature of the host culture (some host cultures are more fertile than others), the character and influence of the migrant who transmits these new skills/ideas, and the ideational/organizational distance that separates the foreign context from the local (see, e.g., Levitt 2005).

Finally, it is important to note that individual emigration can have a negative effect on a country's political development if it drains the pool of political (e.g., oppositional) talent. In short, countries might experience a sort of political brain drain. This is a reasonable expectation, if only because we know that many repressive states (e.g., the USSR, Castro's Cuba) actively used the deportation of political opponents and dissidents as a way of inhibiting political change. However, the costs and benefits of political brain drain are radically different from those of its economic counterpart in that (1) the costs of the dissident's political education are likely borne by the individual dissident (i.e., it is doubtful that repressive regimes support the education of political values that are subversive to that regime); and (2) it is unlikely that the political authorities want these political assets to remain in the country. Still, it is quite possible that emigration can entice away some of the people and skills necessary to lead a country's political development.

In closing this section, it is important to note that an approach focusing on the individual role of migrants can employ a very nuanced understanding of political development. At the most general level, we can expect the community to benefit from the expanded opportunities and skill sets that are introduced by returning emigrants or by the ideas sent home by emigrants abroad. The introduction of new political skills, new systems of practice, and new normative structures can enhance the possibilities for individual opportunity and understanding in the home country and bring about an increase in the sort of substantive freedoms that constitute development. Still, we must not be blind to the possibility that emigration can deter or undermine political development if it siphons off important skills and people in a political brain drain.

As a conduit of influence that emanates from abroad, emigrants (and their ideas) enjoy a relatively autonomous position vis-à-vis that of ruling political and economic elites, whatever the base of their power, be it in land, capital, the military, etc. This position of autonomy makes it easier for emigrants to challenge the grip that established groups often have on the ideas and organizations that can constrain political development. In short, emigrants can provide new ways to conceptualize, organize, and influence political developments at home.

Perhaps the best way to think about this potential influence is to imagine the nature of political development and the challenge to political authority in its absence. Without emigration, we can expect fewer new ideas to be circulated and fewer new organizations to be adopted, *ceteris paribus*. More to the point, we can expect existing institutions and ideas to reflect the interests of the status quo. Although change is of course possible in closed political contexts, it tends to happen endogenously and at a slower pace. (One might think of these changes in terms of a Marxist historical materialist account, in which change occurs when the relations of production are slowly overcome by changes in the means of production.) Emigration has the potential to break the status quo's hold on political power by offering new ways to think about and organize political development.

Constituent Groups. The second path of influence examines the way in which emigration changes the balance of power within states along two important dimensions. Along the first dimension, individual residents are able to exert more influence over political authority because the threat to exit provides them with an effective tool for voicing dissatisfaction. Along the second dimension, exit can generate changes in the underlying balance of class power that facilitate political development.

Albert Hirschman's (1970) influential book, titled *Exit, Voice, and Loyalty*, provides a useful approach for thinking about the effects of emigration in changing the balance of power. Although Hirschman developed his approach to consider the behavior of dissatisfied consumers and voters in America, his model can be extended in ways that allow us to generate expectations about state behavior in attracting and maintaining constituent[11] support (Moses 2005a, 2005b). At the core of Hirschman's

---

[11] I am avoiding the term "citizen," because it is linked to specific rights and obligations. The influence of exit extends beyond citizens, so it can be wielded by a much larger segment of the population residing within a given territory. For this reason, "residents"

argument is his recognition of two competing "forces of recovery" – exit and voice – by which firms and organizations learn of deterioration and correct it before becoming obsolete. Although Hirschman expects only one of these mechanisms to dominate in an organization (exit is more common in economic contexts, voice in political contexts), organizations need to rely on both mechanisms, at different times, to ensure that they can be aware of and respond to constituent dissatisfaction.

When applied to states, this model helps us see how the nature of the relationship between constituents and the state changes when the former have an opportunity to exit. In a context where states can inhibit exit, constituents are forced to develop elaborate alternatives for influencing the nature of political decisions. In such closed-polity contexts, the nature of political authority in each state varies according to the relative power of different interests within that state. The luckiest of us will end up in states that facilitate democratic expression through a number of different channels to voice dissatisfaction or support (voting, letter writing, protesting, etc.). Many others will be less lucky, finding themselves subject to a political authority over which they enjoy very limited influence. In the absence of exit, a constituent's potential to affect state policy depends largely on the size of the polity, as well as the nature and effectiveness of existing domestic institutions to channel voice (Moses 2005a: 60–3).

This balance of political power changes when residents have recourse to exit. In such a context, disgruntled constituents enjoy an additional (if costly) instrument of influence: Exit becomes an alternative to and amplifier of voice. When constituents employ voice and threaten exit, the political development of the community is enhanced in three significant ways. First, constituents are able to provide better information to policy makers about their preferences (and the intensity of those preferences). Second, constituents can expect the political authorities to be more responsive to those signaled preferences, because the constituent's voice is amplified by the threat of exit.[12] Finally, and most importantly, if these preferences are not attended to, constituents have recourse to

or "constituents," rather than citizens, is a more accurate way of depicting the individuals in this approach.

[12] Indeed, in a couple of subsequent pieces, Hirschman (1992, 1993) employs his approach to show how a combination of exit and voice forced the authorities in East Germany to concede power in a series of democratic reforms. This story has already been told in the introductory chapter, but see Moses (2006) for an extended application of Hirschman's approach to international migration.

exit: They can search for other states that better meet their needs and preferences.[13]

In short, the possibility of emigration strengthens the influence of individuals in their dealings with political authority. Consequently, political authority is forced to become more responsive to individual constituents' concerns. This change in relative influence, to the benefit of individual constituents, facilitates political development in the home community or state. This is the first dimension of influence.

The second dimension strengthens the political influence of those classes or interests that tend to be the traditional drivers of modern political development, especially workers and peasants. By strengthening the hands of individual constituents in a state, emigration strengthens the influence of the numerically dominant groups or classes in that state, thereby changing the underlying class balance. This class-balancing effect can be depicted with a simple illustration.

Imagine a preindustrial context in which there is a surplus of labor, living mostly off the land. Political authority lies in the hands of the landowners who exploit that authority to secure cheap labor for working their land. Without recourse to exit, farm workers would need to overcome a significant collective action dilemma: They need to unite and confront the landowners to secure better economic and political conditions. Although this sort of cooperation is possible, the odds for success are heavily stacked against the workers.

However, these odds change when workers are given an opportunity to exit, whether to the city or to another country. Before we consider this change, it is important to note that most workers would probably prefer not to leave, because they would want to stay near their friends, family, and homes. However, if conditions are bad enough, workers will be tempted to leave in search of opportunities that do not exist at home. When they do leave, they set into motion two related chains of events. First, landowners will need to be more responsive to the demands of their workers or risk losing them to "foreign" employers. The farm workers' demands will surely include higher wages, but may not be confined to economic benefits (because the landowner's power is not confined to the

---

[13] This framework implies that the individual's motivations to emigrate are purely political, and he or she migrates as part of an explicit and conscious political strategy. This may be a rather unrealistic assumption, because migration motives are surely more complex/manifold. In practice, as we shall see, the political effectiveness of this voice turns on how political elites interpret the motivation of mass emigrant exit.

economic realm). In exchange for not leaving, workers can make wide-ranging political and social demands – the sort of demands that both generate and reflect political development (e.g., the right to vote and/or organize in unions, land reform).

The second chain of events draws on the first. As a result of the threat to exit, the power and influence of the labor that remains actually increase, making it more likely that their demands will be met. The reason for this effect is simple and grounded in the law of supply and demand. As the pool of local labor evaporates, its relative price (and bargaining power) will grow: Landowners will be forced to respond with both economic and political enticements or end up with lots of land, but without the labor necessary to work it.[14]

Together these two chains of events show how emigration can encourage a new balance of class power and restructure local social relations in a way that can generate political and economic innovations. However, it is important to note that these effects depend on the relative size of the emigration pressure. For emigration to affect political development it has to be large enough (as a percentage of the total population) or focused enough (in terms of the share of a particular skill group, for example).

In short, emigration has the power to transform the class structure of the sending state. To the extent that emigration draws mostly from the working and middle classes, it strengthens those classes at the expense of propertied and capital (read upper) classes in a way that facilitates political development.

The State. We now turn to the third approach for studying how emigration can have direct political consequences. This approach changes the parallax from the individual migrant, or groups of migrants, to that of the surrounding community or state. In doing so, it asks two related questions: (1) How can we expect the state to respond to changes in the level of emigration? and (2) How do these responses affect political development?

To answer both these questions we need to consider how the state's perspective on political development might change as a consequence of emigration. One way to do this is to begin by recognizing that a sovereign

---

[14] In this way, emigration functions in a way not unlike the role played by war in Sandra Halperin's (2004) account of political development. By emptying the pool of workers in a country, emigration leaves a denser and more concentrated class, one better positioned to secure a more favorable class balance in the subsequent struggle.

government enjoys a spatial monopoly over the delivery of services and the capacity to tax residents to pay for those services. For some authors, this monopoly lends itself to Leviathan-like images of a monolithic government systematically exploiting its citizenry through the maximization of tax revenues (e.g., Brennan and Buchanan 1980; Buchanan 1975).

Yet even those of us who are less inclined to see monsters in government realize that the state faces a significant problem. This problem derives from the fact that one of government's main tasks is the production of public goods, the demand for which is especially difficult to identify correctly (Samuelson 1954, 1955). In short, states – even democratic states – lack an adequate mechanism for gauging the public-goods preferences of their residents/citizens. Even when we are generous and assume that the government *wants* to satisfy its citizens' preferences, we cannot avoid what amounts to a serious free-rider problem: Rational citizens will understate their preference in order to enjoy the goods being offered, while avoiding paying the bill (Musgrave 1939, 1959; Samuelson 1954, 1955).

Migration across political jurisdictions has the potential to signal these illusive resident preferences. This argument was made famous in an influential article by Charles Tiebout (1956), which suggests that local jurisdictions actually compete for mobile citizens by offering competing bundles of public goods.[15] In response, citizens sort themselves across jurisdictions according to their preferences, thereby efficiently allocating local public goods. In short, residents can (and do) vote with their feet: "There is no way in which the consumer can avoid revealing his preferences in a spatial economy. Spatial mobility provides the local-goods counterpart to the private market's shopping trip" (Tiebout 1956: 422).

If there are a large number of communities offering rival sets of collective goods (e.g., different combinations of taxation and spending packages), then migrants can choose the particular tax–service package that best suits their needs:

The act of moving or failing to move is critical. Moving or failing to move replaces the usual market test of willingness to buy a good and reveals the consumer-voter's demand for public goods. Thus each locality has a revenue and expenditure pattern that reflects the desires of its residents (Tiebout 1956: 420).

It is important to emphasize that Tiebout's focus was trained on the migrant (as a preference-signaling device), not on the community in

---

[15] For introductions to the vast Tiebout-inspired literature, see Zodrow (1983), Dowding et al. (1994), Oates (2005), and Fischel (2006).

question.[16] More to the point, and using Hirschman's (1970) terminology, Tiebout focused exclusively on the migrant's "exit" option, completely ignoring voice (Oates 2005: 14). It is also important to realize that Tiebout's focus, and that of most subsequent work in this tradition, is on local – not international – migration.[17] For this reason, a classical Tiebout approach is not directly applicable to the sort of question that motivates this study. Rather, Tiebout provides us with a vocabulary and a perspective for thinking about how emigration can affect a community's behavior with respect to political development.

In a context with greater opportunities for emigration, the state's position has been found to change in three important ways. First, the state is forced to face a constituency that now enjoys a much broader span of opportunities from which to choose. As a consequence, the state's relative position vis-à-vis its constituents changes in a way that benefits those constituents. Of course, this is the message of the previous (Hirschman-inspired) section, but it is interesting to find Tiebout bearing witness to the same sort of effect but in a more localized context: "The greater the number of communities and the greater the variance among them, the closer the consumer will come to fully realizing his preference position" (Tiebout 1956: 418).

The second point is related, in that the state in a context with greater opportunities for emigration finds itself in a position of de facto competition with other states. The possibility of migration generates competition among communities that can be seen as a powerful constraint on that feared Leviathan, because "the potential for fiscal exploitation varies inversely with the number of competing governmental units" (Brennan

---

[16] "In this model there is no attempt on the part of the local government to 'adapt to' the preferences of consumer-voters. Instead, those local governments that attract the optimum number of residents may be viewed as being 'adapted by' the economic system" (Tiebout 1956: 420).

[17] Tiebout (1956: 418, fn. 9) is clear on this point: "The discussion that follows applies to local governments. It will be apparent as the argument proceeds that it also applies, with less force, to state governments." Most subsequent scholars in this tradition are skeptical of trying to extend the approach to higher levels of aggregation. In this respect, Fischel's (2006: 20) account is typical: "The choice set for migrants is smaller, the instruments of taxation and regulation are less easily targeted, and mobility is more limited by cultural and family ties. Choosing between Budapest and Berlin is a lot different than choosing between Grosse Point Farms and Grosse Pointe Woods." Although it is difficult to disagree with this contention, it is important to point out that the rewards from long-distance migration correspond to the higher costs involved. For some, international migration can mean the difference between life and death, or life with or without significant political liberties. These opportunity differentials can surely provoke long-distance migration in the same way that, for example, property-tax differentials can provoke local migration.

and Buchanan 1980: 1985). "Citizen-voters weigh up the value of local services and the burden of local taxes and cross jurisdictional boundaries to get the best package of local taxes and services. This may act as an alternative form of local accountability to the electoral process" (Dowding et al. 1994: 767).

In a context characterized by competition, we can expect states to become more accountable and efficient. As with the previous (constituent group) path, the potential impact of emigration on state behavior will depend critically on the relative size of the emigrant stream. Indeed, if residents have an effective instrument to influence hesitant or unresponsive governments, it may become possible to jettison many of the institutional inefficiencies (read checks and balances) that we associate with today's democratic regimes (Moses 2006: 102). When states are forced, in effect, to compete over mobile citizens, they cannot afford to lean on their monopoly powers.

Finally, the greater the number of communities in competition with one another, the closer the analogy to a private market situation (Dilorenzo 1983; Epple and Zelenitz 1981). This insight was Tiebout's central contribution; he believed that migration allowed states to provide a more efficient allocation of public goods: "Politics that promote residential mobility and increase the knowledge of the consumer-voter will improve the allocation of government expenditures in the same sense that mobility among jobs and knowledge relevant to the location of industry and labor improve the allocation of private resources" (Tiebout 1956: 423).

This section has introduced several potential avenues through which emigration might affect political development. These effects are expected to be indirect and direct, positive and negative. We now know *what* to look for in the empirical study that follows and *why* it should matter. What remains is to find out *where* and *how* we should begin to look for these effects. The next section considers these challenges.

CASE SELECTION AND CONTROL

We know that the political effects of emigration are complex, that they are understudied, and that they can reside at different levels of analysis. These characteristics suggest that we should cast our analytical net as far and as wide as possible. In addition, we want to cast a net that can trap as wide an assortment of empirical bounty as possible and one that can help us presort the sundry catch. In short, we need the analytical equivalent of a trammel net.[18] Although this research strategy will inevitably trap a significant and somewhat wasteful by-catch (a nontargeted harvest), an excess of evidence can be a distinct advantage in any investigatory approach. This concluding section considers how we should test these four approaches in a way that will provide robust and dependable lessons about the political development effects of emigration.

This study should aim to establish the general relationships from as broad a sample of cases as possible, while recognizing the inherent short-comings of any database that could cover such a vast empirical terrain. At the same time, it should be able to examine the posited causal motors that link political development to emigration in individual, contextually sensitive cases.

At the heart of both these requirements is a case-selection strategy that can control for variation across the most theoretically relevant dimensions. From the discussion in this chapter, five particular types of variation are especially important to control.

Of these, the most daunting is the role that the surrounding regime[19] plays in influencing the tendency to emigrate. Consider the effects of international migration (although these regime effects also exist within nation states): Because the propensity to emigrate depends on the international regime that regulates that emigration, it is essential to control for this potential effect. To put it simply, emigration might generate positive effects under liberal international regimes and negative effects under protectionist international regimes. Controlling for the regime effect can be accomplished in three ways: (1) by first looking at the general (global) relationship over time, so that we consider both freer and more restricted international regimes; (2) by choosing cases that vary across those international regimes; and (3) by examining the political development effects of emigration within a given country. The sampling strategy that controls for regime type is used to ensure that the lessons we learn are not confined to a particular regime type.

Second, we can expect that outcomes depend on the size of the emigrant stream, because several of the causal mechanisms under study focus on the *relative* influence of important groups within the sending country. For example, if emigration is to affect the bargaining power of the

---

[18] Trammel nets contain three layers of netting. The inner layer consists of a slack, smaller meshed net. This net is sandwiched between two outer layers of netting, both of which are held taut and have a larger mesh.

[19] See Chapter 4 for further elaboration on what is meant by an emigration regime.

labor force that remains, the amount of emigration has to be significant relative to the overall size of the labor force in a given area or
state. In brief, the political effects of emigration are likely to be stronger
in smaller countries, because larger countries are swamped with deeper
pools of underemployed labor that are not easily drained by emigration. Realizing this, it may be necessary sometimes to disaggregate large
states and examine the effects of emigration at lower levels of political
organization.

Third, the case-selection strategy must be sensitive to temporal variation. Because underdeveloped (economic and political) contexts can provoke emigration, and because we are interested in how emigration can
affect the level of political development, it is important that we be able
to examine the effect of emigration over time. In the absence of this type
of temporal control, a simple correlational analysis might find that emigration is associated with political underdevelopment (because emigrants
may be fleeing nondemocratic regimes) and thereby overlook how the
effects of that emigration influence subsequent political development.

Fourth, because we are interested in the general relationship between
emigration and political development, we want to include a sample that
reflects the broad diversity of contexts in which political development can
occur. In short, it is important that our selection of cases is not confined
to a particular time, geographic area, type of economic activity, or level
of development.

Finally, the sampling strategy needs to be sensitive to variation in
outcomes. A good sample includes cases that show sufficient variation
in both dependent and independent variables. This is not a strategy for
sampling blindly on the dependent variable. Rather, I choose the cases
carefully so as to ensure sufficient variation on both sides of the causal
equation.

Before moving on, a sixth possible type of variation should be mentioned: the polity (or governance regime) of the receiving state. After
all, migration to more politically developed states will likely produce
different development effects than migration to less politically developed states. Unlike overarching regime type, size, temporal, context,
and outcome variation, however, polity variance does not need to be
controlled with a case-selection strategy. In part, this variance can be
dealt with by focusing on *voluntary* emigration and by assuming that
immigrants always choose states that are an improvement (in terms of
political development) over the conditions in their home (or sending)

state.[20] In this way, emigrant experiences always derive from more politically developed states. This is surely not an unreasonable assumption to make, if it will help us control for this potential variation.

In light of this control strategy, the empirical chapters that follow are organized mostly by level of aggregation. These chapters combine statistical and case-oriented studies in a way that is designed to address three related objectives: (1) to test whether the relationship exists (and at what lag, if any); (2) to test whether the mechanisms (posited earlier in the different approaches) exist; and (3) to test potential explanatory variables.[21]

---

[20] The reasonableness of this assumption is confirmed in the 2009 Human Development Report, which finds that the vast majority (about two-thirds) of emigrants leave to more developed states (UNDP 2009: 2).

[21] Because I do not want the details of the case-selection strategy to interfere with the story being told, an overview of this strategy is found in Appendix I for the more methodologically inclined reader.

4

Global Connections

International migration research has long been hampered by a lack of data. Although we have a general idea about the level of international migration and how it varies over time, migration scholars have tended to focus their study on those areas and in those times for which data have been most readily available. This is problematic for the study of emigration and political development, in at least two important ways. First, it is difficult to say anything useful about the effects of emigration on political development if we do not have systematic evidence of the level of and variation in international emigration over time. Indeed, I find it both insightful and embarrassing that policy makers have exerted so little energy to track international migration flows relative to global trade and financial flows, for example. The first place to begin any study of the effects of international emigration must be to document the extent of that emigration over time and across countries.

Second, the current limited focus of research is problematic because effects of emigration vary across migration regimes. Because we can expect the effects of emigration to vary with the extent of emigration (as described in the preceding chapter), and because the extent of emigration is likely to vary along with the opportunity to do so, then the political effects of emigration might be stronger at times when the global migration regime is more accommodating to migrants. In other words, the political effects of emigration should be strongest when the opportunity to emigrate is greatest.

For both these reasons, this chapter begins by introducing a new database that I created for international emigration: EMIG 1.2. This database collects 6,537 observations of annual emigration counts, covering 155 countries and 159 years (1850–2008). It allows us to document the changing level of global emigration and to develop a typology for different global migration regimes over time. Indeed, this typology is used in the following chapters to examine the effects of emigration under varying migration regimes: before WWI, after WWII, and the contemporary regime.

The second part of the chapter then maps variations in global emigration patterns against existing measures of political development as they change over time. At this level of aggregation, we are able to see that global political developments appear to be related to variations in global emigration trends. Indeed, in mapping these variations, we can establish a rough estimate of the sort of temporal lag by which political development follows emigration. Just as importantly, this global analysis allows us to single out particular cases that are then subjected to closer scrutiny in subsequent chapters.

EMIG 1.2

This section briefly introduces a new pooled, cross-national time-series database for global emigration, before using it to document the changing level of global emigration over time.[1] EMIG 1.2 aggregates emigration data from individual countries between 1850 and 2008 obtained by scouring national and international databases for official (i.e., government-reported) annual figures for the number of emigrant citizens moving to a foreign country.

This represents a very conservative approach on several counts. First, EMIG 1.2 does not try to capture total emigration flows – only those flows that governments are willing and able to count.[2] As a result, the number

[1] A more thorough introduction to the database is provided in Moses (2011a), whereas the dataset itself is available at: http://www.svt.ntnu.no/iss/Jonathon.Moses/EMIG/index.htm.
[2] This is generally the case. In a few unique, cases, I extended the inclusion criteria to capture important flows that were not included or to replace extreme observations that were having an undue influence on the trend. As an example of the former, I included foreign guest-worker figures from a number of South Asian countries (see elaboration later). As an example of the latter, I replaced patchy Mexican data (that were having a very strong influence on postwar emigration trends) with more consistent data on Mexican immigration into the United States. Whereas the Mexican figures are sparse and unreliable, the U.S. figures are very consistent over time (providing us with a longer trend), even though they must necessarily undercount total Mexican emigration (as we know that Mexicans emigrate to other places in addition to the United States). It is also

of emigrants in this data is smaller than in competing measures, and the differences generated can provide fodder for subsequent analysis. This conservative approach is helpful insofar as it diminishes the likelihood of double counting while providing a consistent source of emigration data, thereby ensuring a solid trend over time.

Second, this database embraces a narrow measure of emigration. For example, many states collect the number of annual departures, and this figure (larger than the number of emigrants) might be used as a surrogate for emigration. However, doing so grossly inflates the number of emigrants, and this inflation will grow over time, because the number of nonmigrant departures (e.g., tourists) is likely to rise as the cost of international travel falls. Similarly, by collecting citizen emigrant data I have intentionally left out alien (noncitizen) emigration figures, which many countries collected, especially before WWI.

Third, countries sometimes collect and publish emigrant stock data generated by national censuses. Including these data would have allowed me to expand the dataset in significant ways[3] – but at the cost of mixing flow and stock types of data.[4] For this reason, only flow data were included, unless the national statistical authority advised that the data were more reliable than the flow data, and only when the survey referred to the year of exit for the emigrant in question.

Finally, with data from more recent years, I had to decide what to do with foreign guest workers. Because the documentation of guest workers tends to be more accurate than for emigrants in general and because we know that a significant portion of international emigrants who migrated in the 19th century subsequently returned home, I decided to include these numbers when they were available. In short, for countries with large formal migrant worker export programs (Bangladesh, India, Indonesia, Philippines, Pakistan, Sri Lanka, and Thailand), I used the officially reported outflow of migrant worker figures, rather than the official emigration figures, if there was any discrepancy between the two.[5]

important to note that the U.S. immigration numbers of Mexicans were even larger than the total reported Mexican emigration numbers!

[3] France is a prime example, because it suffers from very poor emigration data. It is possible to obtain annual data for the number of French living abroad (for voting purposes), but these sorts of stock data were not included.

[4] Flow data count the annual number of emigrants crossing the border in a given year. Stock data count the accumulated number of emigrants abroad in a given year (even if they left the country in a previous year.)

[5] Bangladesh has only migrant worker data (1976–2008); India uses emigration data for 1850–1924, 1936–47, and 1953–75, but from 1976–2007 the data also include

TABLE 4.1. *Descriptive Characteristics of Component Datasets*

Dataset	Years (total)	Number of Countries	Number of Observations	Coverage Share
Ferenczi & Willcox (1929)	1850–1925 (76)	72	1,980	36.2
Mitchell (2003a, 2003b, 2007)	1850–1999 (150)	32	2,614	54.5
UN (1958)	1918–55 (38)	31	635	53.9
UN (1979)	1950–74 (24)	19	443	97.1
UN *Demographic Yearbooks*	1936–95 (60)	141	2,501	29.6
ILO (2009)	1986–2007 (22)	56	541	43.9
EMIG 1.2	1850–2008 (159)	155	6,537	25.4

To create this conservative measure, I drew mostly from six data sources: Ferenczi and Willcox (1929), Mitchell (2003a, 2003b, 2007), UN (1958), UN (1979), UN *Demographic Yearbooks* (various years), and ILO (2009). The basic components of each of these six datasets (and the resulting EMIG 1.2 dataset) are shown in Table 4.1. What is perhaps most striking about these datasets is their limited reach (either temporally or cross-sectionally) and the number of gaps in each. It is reasonable to assume that every country in the world, in a given year, can expect at least one person to emigrate. Given that assumption, then some of these datasets report a remarkably small coverage share[6] or amount of emigrant activity (e.g., the *Demographic Yearbooks* offer observations for

reported outflow of migrant workers; the Indonesia data (1996–2002) are based on official reported outflow of migrant workers; in Pakistan, the only numbers available are for outward-bound workers (1982–98); in the Philippines, the 1936–41, 1945–7, 1962–8, 1970, and 2006–8 figures are for registered emigrants, whereas the 1972 to 2005 figures are for registered overseas workers; in Sri Lanka, the numbers after 1975 represent reported outflow of foreign workers (whereas the data for 1878–1900, 1911–24, 1936–45, 1955–8, 1960–4, and 1966–71 are for registered emigrants). In Thailand, the numbers before 1973 and after 1999 are based on emigration, but the 1973–98 numbers capture Thai workers overseas.

[6] The total possible number of observations is equal to the number of years multiplied by the number of countries in the dataset. The coverage share is then set to be the number of actual observations divided by the total possible number of observations.

less than 30% of the total possible). Other datasets – for example, UN (1979) – do much better, capturing as much as 97% of the total possible (from an admittedly limited sample of just 19 countries).

After I collected these data from each of the six datasets, I then aggregated them into one large database. Doing this provided me with an opportunity to cross-check data and to look for entry errors and overlap in the different time series. At this point, I visited the Web site for the national statistical office/bureau for each country listed in the aggregate database (or the inheritors of now extinct states). If a country published a full emigration data series for the period under consideration, I stopped collecting data at this point. If any holes remained in the series, I then e-mailed the statistical bureau in question, described the data I had, and asked if the staff knew where I could find the missing data. I then followed any instructions I received from the responding agency. When there was a conflict between the data received from the statistics office and those found in the published reports, I relied on the former.

With this data in hand, now assembled in a large aggregate database, I waded through it – country by country – to piece together the most consistent and reliable time series possible. When there were discrepancies across databases, I examined the component parts to see which dataset best reflected my original approach. I then retained the longest stretch of uninterrupted data from the same source (to ensure comparability), or I chose the dataset that seemed to be in line with the longest run of, and most reasonable, numbers.

It is important to emphasize that EMIG 1.2 is a dataset under development, and I am currently soliciting help from migration scholars to help fill in its gaps. This project is necessarily bigger than can be done by any one researcher, because completing the dataset requires language skills and access to archives that only a collective effort can deliver. Still, EMIG 1.2 provides us with a good foundation (see Moses 2011a).[7]

Aggregate Results

EMIG 1.2's global aggregation is depicted as Figure 4.1, and its main components are listed in Table 4.1, so the reader can get an idea of how it compares to its component datasets. EMIG 1.2 covers the period 1850–2008; it includes 155 countries and 6,537 observations. Given its

---

[7] A more detailed table of countries, years covered, and sources used is found as Appendix II. Appendix III provides a list of the countries that were not included because of a lack of data.

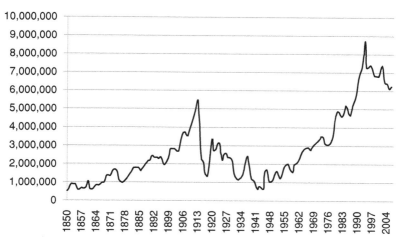

FIGURE 4.1. Global Emigration Trend, 1850–2005. *Source:* EMIG 1.2.

temporal and spatial spread, we should not be surprised to find that it has the smallest coverage share (about 25%) of all the datasets.

From Figure 4.1, it is possible to note five characteristics of the general trend in the level of global emigration, only the last of which is particularly surprising. First, the level of recorded emigration is consistent with general depictions of global emigration flows. This makes sense, because EMIG 1.2 primarily draws from the same databases used in other research efforts. In recent years, this level corresponds to roughly six million emigrants annually. Second, the cyclical nature of short-term global emigration trends is noteworthy – there is a steady flow and ebb in the aggregate data as if they were responding to global business cycles or some other patterned event. Third, most of the interwar period was characterized by relatively low levels of international emigration, mirroring the depression era of the 1870s and earlier. Fourth, it is possible to detect two peaks in the overall emigration trend: one in 1913 (when about 5.4 million people emigrated) and another higher peak in 1994 (when more than 8.7 million emigrated). Finally, it is surprising to find that the number of recorded global emigrants has been falling since 1994, even though the number of states reporting emigration figures has grown during this time.

Figure 4.1 can be used to divide the data into four distinct emigration regimes.[8] In the first period, stretching from 1850 to 1913, global

---

[8] I use a very weak definition of this term, without implying any sort of political or institutional links or agreements across states with regard to monitoring or regulating global

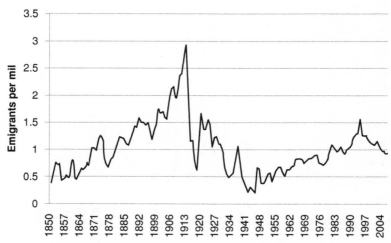

FIGURE 4.2. Global Emigration Trend, per Capita, 1850–2005. *Sources:* EMIG
1.2; Manning (2007). *Note:* Global emigration divided by the global population,
times 1,000.

emigration rates were rising rapidly. The second regime captures the interwar period, from 1913 to 1945, when the general trend was dramatically
downward. The third regime occurred throughout the postwar period
from 1946 to 1994, when global emigration gradually rose. In our own
contemporary period, we can see a new (fourth) global emigration regime
developing, in which global emigration rates are again falling.

From the discussion in the preceding chapter, we know that the effect
of emigration turns on its relative size. For this reason, a more relevant
indicator may be the size of global emigration flows relative to world
population. This indicator is presented in Figure 4.2, which takes the
emigration figures from Figure 4.1, divides them by estimates of the world
population for each year, and then multiplies them by 1,000.

By presenting emigration as a proportion of the world's population, the
emigration trend changes significantly. Most obviously, the relative size of

emigration patterns. In short, these regimes consist of evident trends whereby states
seem to agree about the proper scope of international migration. Thus, one can distinguish between an international migration regime that accepts high levels of international
migration and contrast it with a more restrictive regime, wherein there is an implicit agreement that international migration should be limited. In this way, international migration
regimes are not inconsistent with Stephen Krasner's (1983: 2) definition of a regime
as "implicit or explicit principles, norms, rules and decision-making procedures around
which actors' expectations converge in a given area of international relations." See also
Haggard and Simmons (1987).

global emigration flows today is small when contrasted against the prewar (WWI) flows; it corresponds roughly to the size of the flows associated with the last quarter of the 19th century and during the interwar period. Using this indicator, the postwar increase in global emigration levels is less sharp than in the raw data. This observation enables us to examine the expansive globalization literature in a more critical and nuanced light.

Whether we employ absolute or relative figures, it is possible to depict global emigration flows in terms of four distinct regimes, as described in Figure 4.1 – although the magnitude of each regime is reduced when weighted by the global population. Just as importantly, both absolute and relative measures indicate that global emigration levels have been falling since 1994.

POLITICAL DEVELOPMENT

We can now use the EMIG 1.2 dataset to examine the nature of the global relationship between emigration and political development. Given this level of aggregation and the need to cover such a large temporal and spatial area, we are forced to use relatively superficial indicators of political development. Nevertheless, we can use these indicators to attain two objectives: to establish (1) the direction of causal relationships at the global and international levels and (2) the length of the lag separating emigration and political development.

When considering the nature of the relationship between emigration and development at the global level, it is likely that the political effects of emigration will be found in two related channels. The first is through the individual migrant him- or herself. As global emigration levels increase, so too does the number of emigrants in circulation. These emigrants send home information about political conditions, institutions, and norms in their new homes. Other emigrants return home to collect friends, neighbors, and family or even to resettle. Political entrepreneurs in the home country can use these new sources of information to secure better political (and economic) conditions. In short, the emigrant community's capacity to spread information, social capital, and experience can motivate subsequent political development at the global level.

The second channel of influence is through state competition. In particular, during periods characterized by increased (global) opportunity for individual emigration, political authorities – of all types – will feel pressure from an increased threat of emigrant exit. One can imagine three possible responses of states under such pressure: They can (1) increase the number and scope of restrictions on emigration, (2) ignore the threat of exit and risk ruling over empty states, and/or (3) improve conditions at home to forestall further emigration (or encourage immigration and/or return). The first choice would lead to a decrease in global emigration numbers over time, until a new equilibrium is reached. The second choice would bring economic and political demise with time, in those places susceptible to emigration. The third choice would lead to the spread of political development, in response to the rise in emigration, until the level of development is sufficient to stop the outflow of emigrants (i.e., until another equilibrium is reached). In short, we can expect that global political development will follow on the heels of an increase in global emigration, after a period of time (e.g., $emigration_t \rightarrow political\ development_{t+x}$).

Just to be clear, these are not the only possibilities, and we should keep an eye open for other alternatives. It could be that economic development is driving both emigration and the subsequent political development (i.e., $economic\ development_t \rightarrow emigration_{t+x} \rightarrow political\ development_{t+x+y}$) or even that emigration follows in the wake of political development (i.e., $political\ development_t \rightarrow emigration_{t+x}$). In the study that follows, we can use the strength of the correlations at different temporal lags to establish which causal linkage is strongest and most likely.

Three Waves

The wavelike pattern of global emigration, as evident in both Figures 4.1 and 4.2, brings to mind Samuel Huntington's (1991) influential study of democracy, *The Third Wave: Democratization in the Late Twentieth Century*. In this book, Huntington points to the historical tendency for democracy to spread around the globe in a wavelike pattern in which surges of democratization (more specifically, the transition from nondemocratic to democratic regimes) are followed by a democratic backwash, when some of the new democracies revert to nondemocratic rule.

For Huntington, a regime is democratic "to the extent that its most powerful collective decision makers are selected through fair, honest, and periodic elections in which candidates freely compete for votes and in which virtually all the adult population is eligible to vote" (Huntington 1991: 7). This description also implies "the existence of those civil and political freedoms to speak, publish, assemble and organize that are necessary to political debate and the conduct of electoral campaigns" (ibid). In short, Huntington's measure of democratization is dichotomous: You are either democratic or not, and his operationalization is very rough (basically, a table on pp. 14–15 in his book). Otherwise, his general approach is rich and historical, with a focus on the third (most recent) wave.[9]

His very rough characterization of democracy makes it impossible to use Huntington's approach to establish degrees of political development and difficult to employ it in any sort of rigorous statistical study. Still, Huntington provides us with a narrative that has been largely embraced by political scientists: that the number of democracies in the global system has risen and fallen over the years and that this pattern of ebbs and flows can be characterized in terms of three waves of democratization. Despite the vague form of the argument, we may use it to start our investigation of the relationship between emigration and political development. In short, extending Huntington, we might expect that the larger the number of states in the global system that are democratic, the more politically developed is that system. We can then see whether the waves of emigration correspond to Huntington's three democratic waves.

Huntington points to the existence of a first "long" wave that washed across the globe for a full century, from 1826 to 1926. During this first period, democratization established a foothold in the 20th century, when a number of now developed states (Australia, Canada, Finland, Iceland, Ireland, New Zealand, Sweden, Switzerland, the United Kingdom, and the United States) established themselves as democratic and maintained themselves as such. Also included in this first wave were other states that eventually reverted back to authoritarianism; by Huntington's measure, these included a number of European and South American states.

After a short period during which the first wave of democracy ebbed (1922–42), Huntington describes a second wave that stretched from 1942 to 1962. This relatively short wave was propelled by the end of World War II and included several European states and Japan, as well as Chile, Colombia, and Argentina. This second wave was followed by an extensive backlash, in which a number of states – in Latin America, but also India, South Korea, Czechoslovakia, Greece, and Hungary – reverted to authoritarianism between 1958 and 1975. This period of retreat was significant. The third and final wave of democratization began in 1974 (with Portugal, Greece, and Spain) before spreading to Latin America and Asia. Because Huntington's book appeared in 1991, he could only hint at the possibility of a third reversion.

---

[9] See Doorenspleet (2000) for a discussion of the conceptual and empirical shortcomings to Huntington's approach, and Przeworski et al. (2000: 36ff) for a more general discussion.

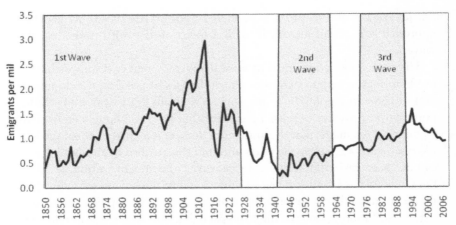

FIGURE 4.3. Three Waves of Democracy and per-Capita Emigration. *Sources:* EMIG 1.2; Manning (2007); Huntington (1991).

How, then, do these three waves correspond to the patterns of emigration evident in Figure 4.2? Figure 4.3 provides a simple visual test of the relationship by mapping Huntington's waves directly onto the emigration figures. Here the waves seem to correspond with emigration trends, but the measure is so rough that it cannot tell us anything about the nature (e.g., the causal direction) of that relationship. Curiously, the emigration data reveal a long postwar trend with little evidence of the second democratic backlash: The level of global emigration flattens out but does not decline over the length of that period.

Still, Figure 4.3 provides encouragement, showing what seems to be a rough relationship, and it behooves us to look closer at its nature. Each rise in democratization corresponded roughly with a period of increased emigration, and each drop occurred in periods with falling emigration (although the level of emigration seems to have dropped before the end of the first wave). As Huntington wrote in 1991, it is difficult to know where to end the third wave, but we can note that the emigration level began to fall in 1994.

Yet a healthy dose of caution is in order, because I can think of at least two equally reasonable and alternative explanations for the co-variation seen in Figure 4.3. First, both the emigration and democratization trends could be driven by changes in an endogenous (underlying) variable, such as economic growth. It is also possible that political developments (the democratic waves) are driving the global emigration trend. More careful analysis is needed to pinpoint the causal nature of this relationship.

Development Datasets

To gain a better understanding of the relationship between emigration and political development, we need access to data that can provide annual measures for the spread of democracy over time. To control for the possibility that the political effects are derived indirectly from economic effects, we also need an annual measure of global economic activity over time. Given the length of time under consideration (1850 to 2008), we are limited to rather superficial indicators on both (political and economic) fronts.

To measure political development over such a long span of time, we have recourse to two standard datasets: those generated by Polity (CSP 2009) and those generated by Tatu Vanhanen (2007). The Vanhanen dataset was briefly introduced in Chapter 2, but it is now time to elaborate on its make-up. Vanhanen created an index of democratization that depicts the degree of power sharing in every state's electoral system, as captured by two component parts: competition (measured in terms of the percentage of votes won by the largest party) and participation (the percentage of the total population who actually voted). The Polity dataset is often used as a surrogate for democracy, but is better understood as a measure of governance: It creates an index ranging from strongly autocratic (-10) to strongly democratic ($+10$) regimes, based on how a given state scores on three component measures: the competitiveness of political participation, the openness and competitiveness of political executive recruitment, and constraints on the chief political executive in that country. Thus, whereas Vanhanen captures the scope of voter influence, Polity measures the scope of constraints on political authority.

Because these two indicators have been highly correlated in the postwar period, much contemporary scholarship assumes that they are interchangeable. Yet this correlation tends to break down when the data are aggregated at the global level, over longer periods of time. Indeed, in the 1850–2001 data, the aggregate correlation is merely 0.46, and the measures diverge remarkably in the interwar period! Thus, rather than think of these two indicators as substitutes for one another, it is better to recognize that they capture different aspects of modern government: Polity is a measure of governance, which examines the nature of constraints on executive power; Vanhanen provides a more direct measure of democracy. *Ceteris paribus*, we expect emigration to affect the spread of the increase in both the quality of governance and democracy.

Finding a consistent measure of economic activity over such a long stretch of time is equally challenging, because current measures (such as GDP) do not extend very far back in time. For that reason, I turned to a surrogate indicator: energy consumption (thousands of coal-ton equivalents), as found in version 3.02 of the Correlates of War National Material Capabilities Data Set, covering 1816–2001 (COW 2002). Because the value of a ton of coal has changed significantly over time, I weighted the time series with a price deflator, based on U.S. GDP, with the index set at 100 in 2005 (Measuringworth.com 2010). This variable is called "Econ/Pop" in the tables to remind us that it is acting as a surrogate for relative economic activity.

Of course, changes in democracy and governance can be explained by a whole host of competing variables. Unfortunately, few data on such variables were collected at a global level before WWII, and the data one finds are remarkably patchy. For this reason, the models tested in this chapter are clearly underspecified, and their results reflect this shortcoming. Still, my objectives at this stage are quite modest: I only hope to establish a reasonable foundation for the relationship between emigration and political development.

To reach these objectives, I took three passes through the data: one that examined the time-series (no-lag) relationship among emigration, economic activity and political development in global aggregates; one that examined different lag structures to see if the effect of emigration only kicks in after a period of time (also in global aggregates); and one that looked at national patterns within the global dataset, employing time-series cross-sectional (TSCS) analyses.

In what follows I aim to keep the discussion as nontechnical as possible. For the statistically inclined, the regression output is available from me. For the rest, what matters are the relative strength, direction, and robustness of the relationships under consideration.

A STATISTICAL EXAMINATION

The first pass through the data was designed to gauge the importance of emigration as an explanatory factor and to get a rough feel for how it affects democracy and governance levels, when we control for economic activity.

First, I transformed the four variables so that emigration and democratic activity were weighted in terms of their national populations (in effect controlling for country size) and the Polity and Vanhanen scores reflected global averages.[10] The unexpected divergence in global averages across the Polity and Vanhanen scores over time meant that the effect of global emigration would vary across indicators, which complicated both the presentation and the interpretation of the findings. These complications only increased when different models were employed to study the nature of the time-series relationship. In an attempt to normalize the skewed distribution of the economic variable, I transformed it using natural logarithms (ln). The data were analyzed with two different models equipped to deal with the autocorrelation issues inherent in time-series data.

Global Time Series, No Lag

The unlagged relationship is complicated, fleeting, and varies with the choice of dependent variable. This is not very satisfying. Despite individual models that hint at a strong relationship, the overall picture lacks robustness as the direction and significance of the emigration coefficients vary rather significantly across models.

For example, when we study the relationship between emigration and the Vanhanen indicator (Models A and B in Table 4.2), we find that the direction of the effect from emigration varies across model types, so that emigration is negatively correlated with democratic development in Model A, but positively correlated in Model B (when controlling for the effect of economic development, logged). Our confidence drops further when we contrast these findings with those that are generated using the Polity indicator (Models C and D). Here we find positive relationships between emigration and political development, but these effects are only significant in Model C (not in D).

What do these findings this tell us? Not much. We know that a change in the global emigration level does seem to be related to changes in global democracy/governance levels, but the size of this effect and even our confidence in its direction vary significantly with the measure or model being used. Given that the models employed are underspecified because of the lack of relevant control variables, there is little point in devoting more analytical attention to this form of the relationship.

[10] In particular, I aggregated the national scores for a given year and then divided it by the number of observations (states). It is these global averages that are so remarkably different (0.46 correlation) over time. In addition, I transformed the Polity score to get rid of the negative values by adding 11: The new Polity score stretches from 1 to 21 (rather than from −10 to +10).

TABLE 4.2. *Global Time-Series Analysis, No Lags*

	Vanhanen		Polity	
	NW *Model A*	PW *Model B*	NW *Model C*	PW *Model D*
Constant	34.9***	8.71**	11.63***	11.94***
	(0.8628)	(3.9812)	(0.7088)	(1.1216)
Ln (Econ/Pop)	3.02***	−0.07	0.38***	0.23*
	(0.0946)	(0.3657)	(0.0815)	(0.1294)
Emig/Pop	−1.92***	0.60**	1.44***	0.09
	(0.4888)	(0.2955)	(0.2018)	(0.1267)
Prob > F	0.0000	1.000	0.0000	0.0001
Rho		.9854077		.9539118
Durbin-Watson		1.553072		1.369225

N = 152.

Note: ***$p < 0.01$, **$p < 0.05$, *$p < 0.1$. Standard errors are given in parentheses. NW is an autoregressive (AR1) model that employs Newey-West standard errors, max lag: 1; PW refers to a Prais-Winsten (AR1) regression with iterated estimates. The reported Durbin-Watson statistic is the "transformed" (not original) figure in the STATA readout. All regressions were run on STATA 11.0.

In light of these findings, we need to consider whether the effect of emigration is lagged. As discussed earlier, we have good theoretical reasons for thinking this might be the case, but little idea of how long the lag might actually be.

Global Time Series with Lags

As we learned in Chapter 3, there are good reasons to suspect that the effect of emigration on political development occurs after an unspecified period of time – because it takes time for the information, skills, human capital, and ideas to return home and make a difference. For this reason, it may not be possible for the static tests described in the previous section to capture the expected effect. My second pass at the data began with an investigatory search for the appropriate lag. Once the rough lag structures were established, I could conduct the subsequent analyses accordingly.

I began by conducting cross-correlation function (CCF) analyses to establish the nature of the lagged relationship for each of the relevant variables.[11] These tests allow us to see the strength of the correlation between two variables over time. Rather surprisingly (given the difference

---

[11] These analyses were done on the raw data, before log transformations were applied.

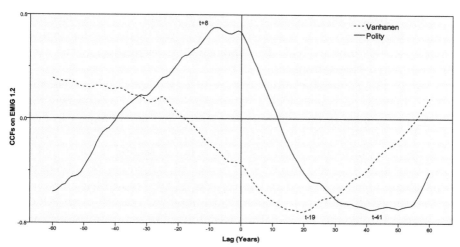

FIGURE 4.4. Cross-Correlogram on EMIG 1.2, Global Data. *Note:* The analysis was run on STATA 11.0, but the graph was made in SPSS 17.

in the Polity and Vanhanen indicators, as noted earlier), these relationships reveal somewhat similar lagging patterns: in other words, a wavelike relationship that peaks at different times.

Because Figure 4.4 includes both leads and lags, it is somewhat tricky to interpret, and some of the information it contains is not directly pertinent to our interests here. In particular, it contains information about two types of relationships: On the left side of the vertical line (at $t = 0$) we can see how political development (at time t) affects emigration (at time $t + x$); on the right side of the line we see how political development (at time t) is affected by emigration $(t - x)$. Although we might expect changing levels of political development to affect emigration (e.g., falling levels of political development will stimulate emigration), our focus is now on explaining the effect of emigration on political development, so our attention is directed to the right-hand side of the figure.

Figure 4.4 reveals how the correlation between emigration per capita and the Vanhanen (democracy) indicator increases in a negative direction over time, before reaching the bottom of its trough after 19 years $(t - 19)$. For the Polity indicator, the entire wave is evident in the temporal window under investigation, so we see both the (positive) peak at an 8-year lead-in time and an equally strong valley (negative) at a 41-year lag![12] This CCF

[12] At the individual level, a lag of 41 years hardly makes any sense, but it is not unreasonable to expect longer systemic effects in the aggregate data.

analysis suggests that as emigration increases at time *t*, political development *decreases* 19 or 41 years later (as measured by the Vanhanen and
Polity scores, respectively).[13] This finding is both surprising and contrary
to our initial expectations.[14]

Even though these relationships are not as originally expected, the
CCF analyses provide us with a point of departure for investigating the
nature of the lag in the multivariate settings: We should expect to find
the political effects of emigration some 19 or 41 years after the event
(depending on the indicator). As in the previous section, I conducted a
series of analyses, using two types of models to deal with autocorrelation
problems: One model used an autoregressive (AR1) model with Newey-
West standardized errors; the other model employed Prais-Winsten (AR1)
regression techniques. The analyses were limited to the strongest lags on
the right-hand side of the figure. Let me emphasize that these models are
not using paneled data but global (aggregate) time-series data, in which
global averages for democracy and governance are being regressed on
global emigration and global energy consumption levels.

Table 4.3 shows these results, and they are more disappointing than
those run without any lags. Only one of the models shows significant
coefficients for the emigration variable (Model A) – and this model used
Newey-West standard errors. Model A would have emigration generating
positive political effects with a lag of 19 years (Vanhanen indicator),
after controlling for the effects of economic development. The 41-year
lag models (C and D) had little of value to offer.

Because economic development may have been influencing the lag, the
next step in the investigation was to find the strongest and most significant
relationship, after controlling for the effect of economic development.
To do this, I regressed the global development data onto a constant, a
logged version of the economic development indicator, and the per-capita
emigration rate. I then tested the Emig/Pop variable with different lags

---

[13] In effect, this suggests that emigration is undermining political development, with a lag.
Because this interpretation is not evident from a first glance at the figure, it may be useful
to elaborate on it. The CCF shows that an increase (decrease) in political development
at time *t* is associated with a decrease (increase) in emigration levels at time *t* − 19
(Polity indicator). If we shift the time frame back 19 units, then a decrease (increase)
in emigration at time *t* leads to an increase (decrease) in political development at time
t + 19 (or 19 years later).

[14] Just as puzzling is the positive lead for the Polity score, which suggests that an increase in
global development levels at time *t* leads to an increase in global emigration levels eight
years later (*t* + 8). In other words, people are leaving, even though political conditions
seem to be improving.

TABLE 4.3. *Global Time-Series Analysis, Expected Lags*

	Vanhanen (t-19)		Polity (t-41)	
	NW *Model A*	PW *Model B*	NW *Model C*	PW *Model D*
Constant	31.50*** (0.9034)	12.17*** (3.7259)	10.86*** (1.0908)	11.32*** (1.2188)
Ln (Econ/Pop)	3.18*** (0.1039)	0.26 (0.4102)	0.01 (0.1211)	0.03 (0.1593)
Emig/Pop$_{t-19}$	2.73*** (0.4530)	0.17 (0.3276)		
Emig/Pop$_{t-41}$			−0.12 (0.2061)	−0.10 (0.1395)
Prob > F	0.0000	1.000	0.8192	0.0000
Rho		.9792426		0.9519285
Durbin-Watson		1.533299		1.332115
N	133	133	111	111

Note: ***$p < 0.01$, **$p < 0.05$, *$p < 0.1$. Standard errors are given in parentheses. NW is an autoregressive (AR1) model that employs Newey-West standard errors, max lag: 1; PW refers to a Prais-Winsten (AR1) regression with iterated estimates. The reported Durbin-Watson statistic is the "transformed" (not original) figure in the STATA readout. All regressions were run on STATA 11.0.

and leads, ranging from $+/-50$ years. The dependent variable was tested with both Vanhanen and Polity indicators. In short, the testing equation [1] was:

[1] Political Development$_t$ = α + β_1Economic Development$_t$ + β_2Emigration Rate$_{t-x}$ + ε

To illustrate the strength of the relationship at different lags, Figures 4.5 and 4.6 present the t-values for the Emig/Pop coefficients at different lead/lag times. A t-value above (roughly) $+/-2$ is considered statistically significant above the $p < 0.10$ level. Figure 4.5 shows the results when Prais-Winsten (AR1) regression techniques were employed; Figure 4.6 shows the results from analyses using an autoregressive (AR1) model with Newey-West standardized errors. The results are remarkably different.

Figure 4.5 shows that there is no stable lagging pattern that can be exploited in the analyses, regardless of which dataset is used. Indeed, remarkably few lags in the period under consideration were statistically significant. Although it is possible to choose a particular lag and secure significant results, the preceding/following year was likely to have an effect that was pointing in the opposite direction (and was probably

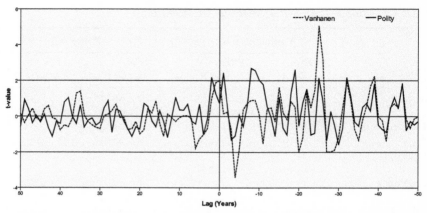

FIGURE 4.5. Lagging Pattern, Prais-Winsten Models, Global Data. *Note:* The figure shows the t-values for the Emig/Pop coefficients when the equation in the text [1] is run with a Prais-Winsten (AR1) regression model with iterated estimates, using Vanhanen and Polity as the dependent variables. The sign of the t-value indicates the sign of the coefficient, and its size reflects the statistical significance. The analysis was run on STATA 11.0, but the graph was made in SPSS 17.

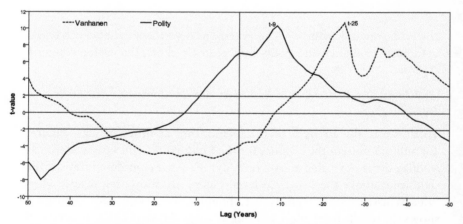

FIGURE 4.6. Lagging Pattern, Newey-West Models, Global Data. *Note:* The figure shows the t-values for the Emig/Pop coefficients when the equation in the text [1] is run with an autoregressive (AR1) model employing Newey-West standard errors, using Vanhanen and Polity as the dependent variables. The sign of the t-value indicates the sign of the coefficient, and its size reflects the statistical significance. The analysis was run on STATA 11.0, but the graph was made in SPSS 17.

TABLE 4.4. *Strongest Emigration Effects,
Newey-West Models, Global Data*

	Vanhanen$_{t-25}$	Polity$_{t-9}$
Constant	30.47***	11.11***
	(0.7595)	(0.7261)
Ln (Econ/Pop)$_t$	3.22***	0.32***
	(0.0859)	(0.0842)
Emig/Pop$_{t-25}$	4.12***	
	(0.3845)	
Emig/Pop$_{t-9}$		1.62***
		(0.1564)
Prob > F	0.0000	0.0000
N	127	143

Note: ***$p < 0.01$, **$p < 0.05$, *$p < 0.1$. Standard errors are given in parentheses. NW is an autoregressive (AR1) model that employs Newey-West standard errors, max lag: 1. All regressions were run on STATA 11.0.

insignificant). The hit-or-miss nature of these effects in the Prais-Winsten model makes them very unreliable.

Figure 4.6 presents a very different picture. Here the lagged emigration coefficients show a smooth pattern over time, so that we can locate the peak (and trough) of emigrant influence on political development. The reported t-values also extend beyond the level of statistical significance ($+/-2$), for both indicators. When using the Polity indicator of political development (and after controlling for the effects of economic development), the effect of per-capita emigration is positive and strongest after a lag of 9 years ($t-9$). Curiously, those effects become negative (and significant) after a very long lag (47+ years). For the Vanhanen indicator, the lag is longer, with the effect peaking after a 25-year lag ($t-25$) – and remains positive and significant throughout the period under consideration.

I do not know why these two models present such radically different results over time, but it is clear that the Prais-Winsten results are too unstable for subsequent analyses. By contrast, the Newey-West model generates effects that provide reasonable interpretations, whose characteristics are provided in Table 4.4. In short, all the variables are statistically significant (above the $p < 0.01$ threshold).

The interpretation of this table is straightforward. After controlling for the effect of economic development, we see that an increase in the global emigration rate results in a 4.12–point rise in the global Vanhanen score

25 years later. In contrast to the CCF results in Figure 4.4, this finding is consistent with our original expectations. Similarly, the global Polity score increases by 1.62 points (on the transformed scale, which now stretches from 1 to 21) nine years after an increase in the global emigration rate. Curiously, this relationship changes over time and becomes negative (and significant) over a much longer time horizon. Thus, 47 years after an increase (decrease) in emigration, political development falls (rises). In short, when we control for economic development, we find that global political development levels do respond (with a varying lag) to global emigration levels, in ways that are as expected. More importantly, we now have a good idea of the amount of time that it takes for emigration to affect the global level of political development.

TSCS

The final pass through this data allowed us to control for both temporal and cross-sectional variation by rearranging the data into a long-form format and running a pooled time-series, or time-series cross-sectional (TSCS), regression analysis. This analysis enabled an examination of national patterns, over time, within the EMIG 1.2 dataset.

I begin by transforming all the variables in an attempt to generate normal distributions (the two dependent variables were especially difficult in this regard, but natural logs provided a visible improvement). As in the global data (e.g., Figure 4.5), an attempt to employ Prais-Winsten regressions with correlated panel-corrected standard errors (PCSEs) resulted in very volatile signs and with mostly insignificant coefficients on the emigration variable. The Newey-West results, as depicted in Figure 4.7, were quite interesting in a number of respects, so they require some elaboration.

This figure (like Figures 4.4 and 4.6) displays two different sorts of trends, only the second of which is relevant for this study. On the left-hand side (left of the vertical line marking $t = 0$), the trends signal the effect that changes in political development have on subsequent emigration rates. More relevant for us are the trends depicted to the right side of this line: These reveal the effect that emigration has on political development, as captured by these two different (Polity and Vanhanen) indicators, when controlling for economic development.

It is important to stress that these t-values do not tell us anything about the size of the impact: They only tell us when they are statistically significant (t-values roughly over $+/- 2$, as marked by the horizontal

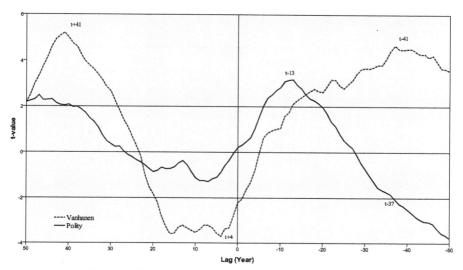

FIGURE 4.7. Lagging Pattern, Newey-West Models, TSCS. *Note:* See notes to Figure 4.6 for explanation. These t-values were generated by a pooled time-series regression model on long-form data, with Newey-West standard errors. The analysis was run on STATA 11.0, but the graph was made in SPSS 17.

lines in the figure) and the direction of the influence. Table 4.5 provides a closer look at the size of the impact, but the information in Figure 4.7 is enough to tell an interesting story.

For example, both indicators (Vanhanen and Polity) suggest that emigration has a curvilinear relationship to political development. In both indicators we see emigration rising some 40–50 years after a rise in political development (on the left-hand side of the figure).[15] As we shall see in subsequent chapters, this trend reflects the recent pattern of increased emigration from more developed democratic states. Yet the relationship flips inversely as we approach $t = 0$. Thus, on the Vanhanen indicator, states that experience falling (rising) levels of political development at time t experience falling (rising) levels of emigration 4–15 years later (around the point marked $t + 4$ in Figure 4.7).[16] Although our theoretical argument would expect emigration to be driven by political development, this

[15] Consider the effect at $t + 41$: As political development increases (decreases) at point t, emigration increases (decreases) 41 years later.
[16] The pattern is similar in the Polity indicator, but careful readers will note that the effect is only significant in the Vanhanen indicator, but not in the Polity indicator.

TABLE 4.5. *Strongest Emigration Effects, Newey-West Models, TSCS Data*

	Vanhanen	Polity	
	(t-41) *Model A*	(t-13) *Model B*	(t-37) *Model C*
Constant	1.25***	1.85***	2.38***
	(0.1651)	(0.0970)	(0.1097)
Ln (Econ/Pop)	0.20***)	0.12***	0.12***
	(0.0134)	(0.0067)	(0.0071)
Ln (Emig/Pop$_{t-13}$)		0.03***	
		(0.0097)	
Ln (Emig/Pop$_{t-37}$)			−0.023**
			(0.0110)
Ln (Emig/Pop$_{t-41}$)	0.07***		
	(0.0162)		
Prob > F	0.0000	0.0000	0.0000
N	2,541	3,946	3,180

Note: ***$p < 0.01$, **$p < 0.05$, *$p < 0.1$. Standard errors are given in parentheses. NW refers to a pooled time-series regression model with Newey-West standard errors, force lag (1). All regressions were run on STATA 11.

is not the focus of this study, and so these relationships are not examined in any more detail.

The trends to the right of the vertical line are what interest us now, and these trends are thought provoking. Consider how a rise in political development affects the Vanhanen indicator: It takes more than a decade before the influence becomes significant, but it continues strong before obtaining its highest t-value 41 years later. Thus, 41 years after an increase in a country's level of emigration we find an increase in its Vanhanen index, when controlling for that country's level of economic development. These results are entirely consistent with our original expectations – but the lag is perhaps longer than one would have guessed at the outset.

The effects of emigration on the Polity indicator are more interesting in that we see a brief ($t = -6$ to -19) positive relationship and then a slow decline into inverse territory, which becomes significant and negative after 37 years. As with the interpretation of Figure 4.6, this finding suggests that the relationship is quite complex: At first emigration has a positive effect on political development, but that effect becomes negative after a very long lag.[17] Table 4.5 lists the full regression results for the strongest (lag) models for each indicator.[18]

Interpreting the results from this table is complicated by the fact that all the variables have been transformed using natural logs, and the effects now need to be understood in terms of elasticities. In other words, a 1% increase in Emig/Pop is shown to result in a 0.07% increase in a nation's Vanhanen indicator, after a 41-year lag (Model A). Similarly, a 1% increase in per-capita emigration results in a 0.03% increase in a nation's Polity indicator after a 13-year lag (Model B). After 37 years, however, the effect of emigration on the Polity indicator flips, so that a 1% increase in a country's level of emigration results in a 0.023% decline in the country's level of political development (Model C).

CONCLUSION

This chapter is premised on a belief that more data are always better than less. It has endeavored to collect emigration data in a way that will facilitate subsequent empirical analyses over very long stretches of time. It is only with this type of data that we can begin to map the effects of international emigration in a systematic way.

Although EMIG 1.2 provides a useful picture of aggregate emigration trends over time, we need to be very cautious of the results that are generated by sophisticated statistical analyses, where we can easily lose our intuitive footing. There are two reasons for this caution. First, the

---

[17] When we stretch out the analysis even more in time, we find that these trends continue: The Vanhanen t-value stays positive and significant, and the Polity t-value remains negative and significant for at least another 25 years ($t + 75$). In effect, we are hitting the opposite side of the wave in the political development measures.

[18] The plot thickens when the reader realizes that this analysis is strongly driven by the experiences of three states: Norway, Ireland, and India. These three states experienced substantial levels of early emigration, but only became states (formally) after the largest waves of emigration had occurred. Because of this, the prestatehood statistics (Norway in 1905, Ireland in 1922, and India in 1947) are not usually included in traditional databases. However, the experiences of these states are very important for understanding the nature of the relationship under study, so I have collected independent (demographic) data for these states before statehood and included it in this analysis. When the prestatehood data are dropped for these three states, then the overall relationship between emigration and political development remains positive and significant throughout the entire 50-year period, when controlling for economic development. In other words, the drop we see in the Polity indicator does not occur in the truncated dataset. The lagging pattern for this analysis (the equivalent of Figure 4.7) can be found in Appendix VI.

nature and quality of the times-series data for this stretch of time – on both sides of the equation – are patchy and suspicious. We simply do not have adequate measures for political and economic development over long periods of time. Second, the nature of the empirical relationships uncovered are far from robust: They tend to vary by indicator, model, and the lagging structure used. In this light, great caution needs to be employed when interpreting the results.

With these caveats in mind, what can we say about the relationship between emigration and political development? At the most general level, it is reasonable to conclude that emigration is related to political development, as measured both in terms of governance (by the Polity indicator) or democracy (by the Vanhanen indicator). The political effect occurs even after controlling for the effects of economic development and tends to come after a variable lag. This finding suggests that the effects of emigration may be related to return migration or through indirect effects. Although statistical analyses of these sorts do not lend themselves to causal analyses, the existence of these lagged effects suggests that emigration is driving political development (i.e., emigration is not a result of either political or economic development).

This relationship is established in both the global average data and at the nation-state level (in the TSCS analyses). Yet the length of the lag varies across indictors and analyses. In short, we can be more confident that emigration affects political development, while controlling for economic activity, and we can expect the lag to be somewhat lengthy. At the global level, the political benefits from emigration are accrued after 9 years (Vanhanen indicator) or 25 years (Polity indicator); at the national level, the effects are similar, but the longest lags are now on the Vanhanen indicator (41 years), whereas the effect on the Polity indicator occurs much quicker (13 years). In both global and TSCS analyses, we find that the long-term effects on the Polity indicator change signs, suggesting that emigration can have a negative effect on the level of governance after a substantial lag (47 years in the global relationship, 37 years in the TSCS relationship).

Although further work could be done by assembling additional control variables and by tweaking the models, it would detract from the larger objective. The basic limitations of the existing data and the lack of suitable control variables covering the full period under consideration mean that additional regression analyses would need to be limited to recent periods in time, when the international regime for migration has been relatively restricted. Just as important, the complex nature of the posited relationships does not lend itself to such simple techniques and limited data.

For now, the EMIG 1.2 database has played the role for which it was designed: It has provided us both with an empirical baseline from which we can evaluate different emigration regimes and with a better understanding of the general relationship among political development, economic development, and emigration at the global level, over time. We can now turn to several case studies to examine in more detail the nature of that relationship in varying contexts over time.

5

The Free Migration Regime before World War I

As we learned in the previous chapter, the period before World War I exhibited the world's highest recorded level of global emigration as a percent of population, and that emigration corresponded with the world's first wave of democratization. Many states, especially in Europe, adopted democratic institutions and expanded their suffrage during this period of substantial emigration. This chapter asks whether these two trends can be related. In doing so, we need to consider three questions. Can increased opportunity for emigration help explain the timing and spread of the first wave of democratization? Are these two trends linked by some common underlying explanation? Or is the co-occurrence of these two trends just some odd coincidence of history?

To answer these questions, we begin by using the EMIG 1.2 database to examine the general relationship between emigration and democratization during this period. This examination finds little support for the argument that emigration alone was driving the democratization wave, because many young democracies came about without having experienced substantial emigration.

We then turn our attention to the experiences of a single state that was especially exposed to the pressures of international migration: Norway. By tracking the Norwegian experience during this relatively liberal period of international migration, we can see how political leaders often exploited the threat of emigration in their struggle to reform the state in a more democratic direction. Here we find that emigration was clearly an important element in a larger push for Norway's political development, but that emigration alone cannot explain Norway's early embrace of democracy. In short, emigration appears as a supportive, rather than a determining, factor in the Norwegian case.

EMIGRANT TRENDS

We first examine the general relationship between emigration and democratization during this period so we can get a sense of the representativeness of the Norwegian case, which we later consider in detail. During the period before World War I (1850–1913), overlapping emigration and demographic figures are only available for 18 states, and some of these states are fictitious (in that they represent areas or districts that would only later become states); therefore we restrict our analysis to these 18 countries. With these statistics, it is possible to calculate the per annum, decade-average, and gross emigration rates (per 1,000 of the population, or per mil) for each of these 18 states for the period 1850–1913. By averaging across decades, we can smooth over the sharp annual fluctuations evident in the national data.

Table 5.1 provides these emigration rates, in which states are divided into three groups according to their decade-average rates of emigration.[1] The first six states are high-emigrant states: These states experienced at least one decade with a very high rate of emigration (more than 10 per mil). These high decade averages are highlighted with bold print in the table. The next group of states experienced medium levels of emigration (i.e., at least one decade where 5 to 10 per mil of the country's population emigrated). These decade averages are also marked with bold print. The bottom group of countries includes those that experienced decade-average emigration rates that were always lower than five emigrants per mil.

The last column in the table provides a rough indicator of the level of political development for each state in 1913, using Vanhanen's democracy index. This provides us with a simple measure of a country's degree of political development at the end of the period under consideration. In studying the table carefully we find that there is no clear relationship

---

[1] Given the patchy nature of emigration data, I have taken some liberty in generating the decade averages. For example, if data only exist for a single year in a given decade, I have assumed that the given year was representative. Thus, the decade averages were constructed by dividing the sum of observations by the number of observations in that decade (e.g., $\sum (t_1, t_2, t_3, \ldots, t_{10})/n)$. I think this solution, although problematic, is better than discarding the data altogether or watering them down (by dividing the single observation by ten [e.g., $\sum (t_1, t_2, t_3, \ldots, t_{10})/10]$).

TABLE 5.1. *Gross Emigration Rates, 1850–1913 (per mil, per annum, decade averages)*

	1850–9	1860–9	1870–9	1880–9	1890–9	1900–13	Level of Democracy in 1913
High Emigration							(4.6)
Yugoslavia	–	–	–	29.61	40.53	30.59	–
Ireland	21.35	16.69	12.78	18.06	10.89	8.26	–
Uruguay	–	–	–	11.92	22.42	6.76	0
Italy	–	5.59	4.31	6.10	8.64	17.99	6.3
Argentina	–	–	8.01	6.18	9.02	12.46	0
Norway	2.60	5.03	4.50	10.11	4.63	7.19	12.1
Medium Emigration							(6.1)
UK	8.80	6.14	6.21	7.16	4.61	7.16	5.5
Spain	–	–	–	3.92	4.59	6.74	1.8
Portugal	–	1.71	2.94	3.60	5.34	7.20	0
Chile	–	–	–	–	–	5.15	0
Netherlands	0.50	1.65	2.69	4.06	4.64	5.39	8.9
US	–	1.77	2.51	3.10	3.85	5.15	24.9
Sweden	0.36	1.76	2.10	5.83	3.76	3.91	6.5
Greece	–	–	0.01	0.09	0.59	7.71	0.5
Low Emigration							(4.4)
Belgium	1.89	2.18	2.01	2.92	3.28	4.23	10.8
Brazil	–	–	–	–	–	2.72	0.9
Denmark	–	2.45	1.97	3.73	2.61	2.78	9
Russia	0.98	2.92	3.14	1.26	2.26	3.87	0
Germany	3.58	2.08	1.49	2.94	1.19	0.43	3
Switzerland	–	1.93	1.17	3.17	1.57	1.40	7.8
India	0.32	1.02	0.90	0.99	1.53	1.47	–
Austria	0.13	0.10	0.23	0.53	0.95	2.29	3.5
China	–	0.06	0.20	0.41	0.45	0.66	0
Japan	–	–	–	–	0.51	0.31	0.3
Turkey	–	–	–	0.01	0.17	1.09	0
Mexico	0.04	0.02	0.05	0.04	0.01	0.49	0
France	0.11	0.12	0.15	0.27	0.18	0.15	15

Notes: Per mil (o/oo) refers to the number of emigrants per 1,000 of the population in the sending (home) state. Bold figures refer to the decade averages that justify their inclusion in each grouping. See text for clarification. Because the demographic data come from the COW dataset and COW only collects data for independent states, I have had to collect extra demographic data for three states, which arrived relatively late on the international scene. Consequently, the Norwegian demographic data come from SSB (2009b), whereas the Irish and Indian data draw from Lahmeyer (2003a, 2003b).

Sources: EMIG 1.2; COW (2002); SSB (2009b); Lahmeyer (2003a, 2003b); and Vanhanen (2007).

between emigration and political development in the prewar period. High-emigration countries averaged just 4.6 on the democracy index, whereas medium-emigration countries tended to enjoy much higher levels of democratization (averaging 6.1 on the Vanhanen index). More to the point, Table 5.1 lists examples of strongly democratic states in each of the three emigration categories: Norway was both a high-emigrant and a strongly democratic state; the United States enjoyed the highest level of democracy, yet only experienced a middle level of emigration (mostly of European migrants returning home after a short stay); and the country that experienced the lowest level of emigration in this sample, France, had a very strong democracy score (15)! The inverse relationship is also evident, in that nondemocratic states can be found in each of the three emigration categories.

Right off the bat, then, we can write off any simple argument about emigration driving political development, at least as captured by these simple statistics during this turbulent time. However, it is possible to look beneath the statistics to uncover relationships that may be obscured by aggregation and complex causal patterns.

After all, students of French history know about the important role that emigration and passport controls played before, during, and after the French Revolution (see, e.g., Torpey 2000: chapter 2). The revolutionary government sought to employ passport controls as a means to regulate the suspicious movements of those who challenged the new regime. If this history is used to explain the subsequently low levels of emigration from France, it might also be used to explain why France is seen as the premier example of the strong-state tradition in Europe.

Similarly, emigration may be feeding political development at lower levels of aggregation, even if this effect is not evident in the national figures. For example, China experienced substantial (absolute) levels of emigration, but these are not evident in Table 5.1 because of the size of the overall Chinese population. If we consider that most emigration from China during this time came out from five coastal regions (Hong Kong, Shantou, Xiamen, Hainan, and Macao) in the southeast part of the country (Guandong, Hainan, and Fujian provinces), we might speculate about whether these regions were more susceptible to political development. These two examples can only illustrate the potential that might lie in the prewar context, even if a relationship is not clearly evident in the aggregate data. For now, they must remain as suggestive illustrations, as I direct our attention to a case that is representative of the high-emigration states.

When we turn to the category of high-emigration states at the top of Table 5.1, we find that the two South American states (Uruguay and Argentina) were not democratic in 1913 (although each state had enjoyed some prior level of democracy, according to the Vanhanen index). The four remaining states are all from Europe and are more difficult to characterize in terms of political development, because Ireland and Yugoslavia were not actually states in 1913. Indeed, the four European states in the high-emigration category share a common feature: Each gained statehood relatively late: Italy in 1861, Norway in 1905, Yugoslavia in 1918, and Ireland in 1922. Of course, late-blooming states are not confined to this group, as both Germany (1871) and India (1947) arrived late to the international stage and had lower levels of emigration.

Of the European cases, conflict-torn Yugoslavia is arguably unique and so is not examined in any detail.[2] Any of the three remaining European cases (Ireland, Italy, and Norway) could be used to study the phenomenon in question, because each experienced massive emigration before WWI. As space limitations prohibit me from addressing all three cases, I chose to dive into the details of one single case, rather than skim across the experiences of three relatively similar cases. In the end, I settled on the Norwegian case, because it is both nearer at hand (I live in Norway) and less familiar than the Italian and Irish exoduses.

Norwegian Emigration Characteristics

From Table 5.1 we learn that Norway represents one of a handful of states that experienced massive emigration before WWI. However, this fact tells us very little. Before we can begin to examine the nature of the relationship between Norwegian emigration and its political development, we need to have a better idea of the nature, size, and type of emigration that Norway experienced over these six and a half decades. This description can then function as a backdrop for the analysis of Norwegian political development that follows.

---

[2] The area, which in 1918 became the Kingdom of Serbs, Croats, and Slovenes (colloquially, the Kingdom of Yugoslavia), experienced significant levels of violence and at least four wars during the period in which we find these massive levels of emigration (the Montenegrin-Ottoman War of 1876–8, the 1885 war between Serbia and Bulgaria, and the two Balkan wars of 1912–13). The area was also especially hard hit by an agricultural crisis at the end of the 19th century. See Schierup (1995) for a brief introduction to the history of emigration from Yugoslavia.

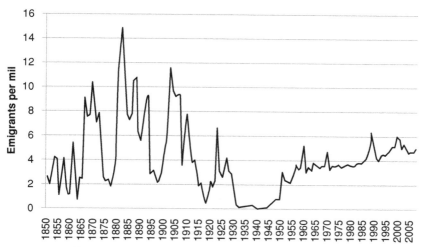

FIGURE 5.1: Norwegian Emigration, per Mil, 1850–2008. *Sources:* EMIG 1.2; SSB (2009b).

Norway's prewar emigration was spread out over several decades, beginning in the 1820s and culminating with very high levels in the decades immediately preceding World War I. The vast majority (98%!) of these emigrants were heading to the United States (Semmingsen 1960: 157). Like most countries, the Norwegian emigration trend is characterized by much short-term volatility. This trend is illustrated in Figure 5.1, where we find the pre-WWI period to have three peaks: from 1866 to 1873 (totaling some 111,000 people), from 1879 to 1893 (more than 250,000 people), and from 1900 to 1910 (when another 200,000-plus people emigrated).

At least three general features of the emigration trend should attract our attention. First, Norwegian emigration historians often distinguish between two different emigrant streams: one early and the other late. Although it is not easy to establish the exact date of the transition, we might suggest that the nature of emigration before the 1870s was different from that after that time in at least three ways: motives, occupation, and geographic point of departure.

The problem in documenting this change lies in the lack of systematic information covering the earlier emigrants. For the most part, the official mapping of the emigrant stream began in the mid-1860s, when the number of emigrants began to take off. With this caveat in mind, we might describe the earliest emigrant flows in terms of small rural family or community groups, at odds with the authorities (for mostly religious, but sometimes political and economic reasons), fleeing the country in search of a better life. It is customary to date Norway's modern emigration history from the 1825 departure from Stavanger of the *Restauration*, a small sloop filled with 52 mostly religious dissidents. In the 1830s and 1840s, the number of emigrants rose fairly steadily, until taking off in the middle of the 1860s, as evidenced in Figure 5.1.

Over time, most Norwegian emigrants continued to be pulled from the countryside, but it is possible to see a gradual change in their motives, occupation, and regional point of departure. After 1880, when emigration rates accelerated, the migration's character began to change, as fewer women and more young (single) men left the country. If we are to believe the survey evidence, the latest emigrants (those departing after 1905) tended to be motivated more by economic gain[3] and (presumably) less by social, political, or religious motives. For earlier emigrants, we have to rely on homebound letters to establish their motives.

Along with this change in motives and gender composition, there was a subtle change in geography. In the latter half of the 19th century, much of the emigration came from mountainous, poor, and inland districts in the southern part of the country (e.g., Oppland, Hedemark, Telemark, and Buskerud counties). Over time, the source of emigration began to spread out along the southern coast (Rogaland, West and East Agder) and farther up the western coastline (Hordaland, Bergen, Møre, and Trøndelag). The northernmost part of the country was least exposed to massive emigration (except for an early bout in Finnmark).[4]

Finally, the occupational make-up of most emigrants was fairly constant. Before 1880, most Norwegian emigrants were tenant farmers or crofters (*husmenn*)[5]; after the turn of the century, a growing number of emigrants were engaged in traditional Norwegian trades associated with the natural resource extraction and shipping sectors (SSB 1965: 174).

---

[3] Only in 1905 did the authorities begin to ask the emigrants directly about their motivation for emigration. In the period between 1905 and 1914, 86% of the men and 68% of the women cited "lack of opportunity for profitable work" (SSB 1965: 178).

[4] See SSB (1965: 165, table 91).

[5] See, e.g., Semmingsen (1950: 215) and Mørkhagen (2009: 346–8). *Husmenn* tends to be translated into English as either cottars or crofters. As both terms refer to English peasant conditions/relations, which are not exact equivalents to the conditions in Norway, it is difficult to know which term is most appropriate. For the sake of clarity, I have translated *bønder* as "freeholder" and *husmann* as "crofter."

THE NORWEGIAN CASE

We can now take a closer look at the Norwegian case. In addition to being both easily accessible and relevant, the Norwegian case is interesting in that the country was, in many respects, a democratic forerunner: In 1814 it already enjoyed one of the most liberal and democratic constitutions in Europe! This history poses an interesting challenge, because we might expect relatively less emigration from a more (politically) developed state, such as Norway. Our interest in the Norwegian case might be further piqued when we recognize that the country's subsequent political development has skyrocketed Norway to one of the world's richest, egalitarian, and most developed states today – a state that consistently scores atop the UNDP's Human Development Indicators index.

Norway's Political Development

During most of the 19th century, Norway was a rural and relatively backward country.[6] Although its level of economic development (measured in GDP/capita terms) was above the European average by the middle of the century (Bairoch 1997: 252–3), its wealth was drawn mostly from natural resource extraction (fishing, lumber, sailing/transport). Industrialization and the class cleavages we associate with it came quite late to Norway. It was only in the 1890s that a majority of Norwegians were employed outside the primary sector, and as late as 1920 most Norwegians still lived in the countryside (Hodne 1975: 370).

It was only in the political sphere that Norway stood out as a leading or advanced state. In the upheaval that followed the Napoleonic wars, Norwegians managed to convene a constitutional assembly in Eidsvoll and to declare their independence in 1814. Although the independence was ephemeral (Norway ended up in a rather unbalanced union with Sweden, which lasted until 1905), the constitution that resulted was arguably the most democratic in Europe at the time.

The source of the democratic nature of this constitution is often traced to Norway's unusually equal distribution of land and wealth. In the words of a foreign (British) contemporary, Samuel Laing (1851: 304–5),

---

[6] There are surprisingly few books written in English on Norwegian political development or emigration. For the former, general readers could consult Derry (1973) and Danielsen et al. (1995), whereas political scientists may find more utility in Rokkan (1967). For English accounts of Norwegian emigration during this period, see Blegen (1931) and Semmingsen (1978).

There is not probably in the history of mankind another instance of a free constitution, not erected amidst ruins and revolutions, not cemented with blood, but taken from the closet of the philosopher, and quietly reared and set to work, and found to be suitable without alteration to all ends of good government. The reason of this apparent singularity is, that all the essential parts of liberty were already in the country. The property was in the hands of the people. The ancient laws and institutions affecting property were in full operation and were conceived and administered in the very spirit of liberty.... There was nothing in the condition of the people, the state of property, the civil or religious establishments, which did not fit in with a free constitution, in which legislative power was vested in the people. These had all emanated from the people in ancient times; and, there being no hereditary privilege, or power, or property vested in any class of the community, had been handed down unbroken through ages. The new constitution was but the superstructure of a building of which the foundations had been laid, and the lower walls constructed, eight centuries before, by the ancestor of the present generation. Esto perpetua! must be the earnest prayer of every man who sees this contented and amiable people enjoying the blessings of rational liberty under laws, institutions, and a constitution the most liberal of which any modern nation can boast.

This interpretation of Norway's egalitarian and law-abiding history is common and accurate: Norway's constitution was indeed a radically progressive document for the time. Yet if Norway was such a beacon of liberal freedom, with a democratic constitution that was the envy of many, why would so many of its residents risk everything and flee to an uncertain fate in a foreign and distant land?

To answer this question, we need to jettison simplistic measures and conceptions of democracy and political development. By the standards of the time, Norway was clearly a democratic forerunner. In the Vanhanen dataset, only four states (Norway, Sweden, the United Kingdom, and the United States) were characterized as democratic in 1814. Of these, only the United States scored higher than Norway in terms of participation and in the overall index of democracy.[7] Yet in the eyes of many contemporary Norwegians, and from our own perspective in the 21st century, the country's democratic constitution was anything but satisfactory. Despite Norway's egalitarian traditions and democratic constitution, there was

---

[7] Their requisite scores for competition, participation, and the overall *index* were Norway (27, 1, 0.3); Sweden (37.5, 0.5, 0.2); the United Kingdom (15, 0.3, 0); and the United States (41, 2, 0.8). Interestingly, Norway scores less well on the Polity2 index in 1814. This indicator has only two countries being democratic in 1814: the United States (scoring a 9) and Korea (scoring a 1). On the Polity2 index, Norway scored a -7, behind nine other countries (United States, Korea, United Kingdom, France, Afghanistan, China, Morocco, Nepal, and Oman)!

a significant and growing level of dissatisfaction among a sizable share of the Norwegian population. In other words, there was much room for political development.

Although the Norwegian constitution of 1814 ensured that legislative power lay in the hands of the Norwegian people, it operationalized the "people" in a very narrow way. Paragraph 50 granted suffrage to only three types of residents – public officials (*embetsmenn*), town citizens, and freeholders (*bønder*) – and the latter two categories came with explicit property requirements. In 1814, these three groups represented about 45% of Norwegian men over the age of 25 and just more than 10% of the total population (Kuhnle 1972; Rokkan 1967: 378, 380). Over time, as Norway's population grew and Norwegians moved away from the primary sector, these percentages shrank. Even within the primary sector, early population growth forced many sons of freeholders to become crofters (Lorenz 1972: 22). By the 1870s, only 7 to 8% of the entire Norwegian population had a right to vote in parliamentary [*Storting*] elections, whereas just 34% of the men over the age of 25 were qualified to vote (Rokkan 1967: 378, 380). Only in 1898 was suffrage extended to all men, regardless of property and circumstance, whereas women had to wait until 1913 to gain that right.[8]

In effect, 19th-century Norway was run by a class of public officials. They were relatively well educated and conscientious and because they were not part of the titled nobility, they were justly proud of a constitution that provided them with the right to vote. The problem is that there was still a world of difference separating this cadre of public officials from the general population over which they governed – and this difference was growing throughout much of the early 19th century.

Despite these inequalities, the nation's political system – for most of the period before 1884 – seemed to have been put on hold. As T. K. Derry (1973: 17) writes in his history of Norway, in a chapter titled "Government by an Élite, 1815–1884," "In domestic politics this was an age of small things. In seventy years the only substantial changes were the setting up of local self-government (1837) and the introduction of annual sessions in the Storting (1869)."

Then, in 1884, things began to get interesting. In that year, parliamentarianism was introduced: In a legal battle of epic proportions, the sitting

---

[8] In 1901, all women who paid a certain level of taxes (400 kroner in the city, 300 kroner in the countryside) were allowed to vote in local elections. In 1907 women won the right to vote in general elections, but with a number of restrictions.

government was forced to answer to the Norwegian Storting, not to the king (in Sweden). This change was driven by a new political movement, propelled by growing freeholder support, which was flexing its growing political muscle. In 1905, Norway broke away from its union with Sweden and established full independence.

As in the political sphere, Norway's economy was developing rapidly, and with substantial volatility, in the three decades preceding World War I. During this time there were bursts of economic growth and bouts of economic depression, although over the period as a whole the Norwegian economy did remarkably well. Between 1870 and 1910, Norway's economy grew by more than 50% (as measured in both per-capita and per-worker terms), and the real wages of its workers rose by nearly 150% (Moses 2005c: 112).

In the remainder of the chapter I describe these political developments as they relate to the emigration of a growing number of Norwegians. Before I do so, however, I encourage the reader to reflect on the sequence of events described here. From this brief outline it is difficult to depict Norwegian political development as a spin-off of its economic development. If anything, the relationship was the other way around. In the Norwegian case, a skeleton of political development was secured *before* the country experienced industrialization and the growth and wealth associated with it. The country's economic development and its further political development occurred only late in the 19th century – after decades in which thousands of Norwegians had already fled the country. At the close of almost a century of flight (1825–1913), during the three decades immediately preceding WWI, economic development, political development, and the embrace of free international mobility became complementary ingredients in a Norwegian stew of liberal government policies. On the one hand, economic and political underdevelopment drove early emigration in Norway. On the other hand, that very emigration helped generate the economic and political developments that we find in the late 19th and early 20th centuries. It is to these complex linkages that we now turn.

The Idea of Freedom

Because the indirect effects of emigration are not all that visible in the broad outline of Norwegian political development, it might be helpful to search for more direct linkages between political development and emigration at the level of the emigrant him- or herself. As the reader will recall from Chapter 3, these effects can be wide ranging and potentially contradictory. On the one hand, emigrants send home money, ideas, and experiences that can facilitate political development. On the other hand, the country's political development can be hindered, even retarded, by the emigration of political entrepreneurs and activists.

As Jon Gjerde (2007: 56) notes, the least quantifiable, yet perhaps the most important, influence that Norwegian emigration had on developments in Norway was the diffusion of foreign ideas. With so many Norwegians emigrating to the United States and then writing letters home, the United States became in effect the measuring stick of Norwegian political progress. As early as 1844, a Norwegian newspaper asserted that emigration and conditions in America had become the theme of the day.[9] The emigrants' letters home and the public debates that resulted from them prompted an

extensive expansion of the common man's horizons. They increased his sense of self-esteem and self-confidence and provided him with arguments and slogans when he needed to develop them, as demands. In this way, the influence of America, the influence that emigration created, in its widest sense, has had a significant influence on the growth of Norway's democracy (Semmingsen 1950: 486).[10]

Thousands of letters home reached into the deepest corners of Norwegian society, spreading word of a world that seemed very different from their own. Peasants and craftsmen learned of a place where the fruits of their labors could be sold freely, where the influence of priests and public officials was circumscribed, and where social differences and privileges were not institutionalized by legislation:

Under his daily strife, it is reasonable that the freeholder's mind journeys to where many of his relatives are, most often under favorable conditions. In comparing the conditions there, with those in which he finds himself, the freeholder realizes that things could be much different and better here too. No longer is his spirit confined between the mountains and fjords that surround his village; his vision has been extended, and an impression is made that challenges old, accustomed opinions and awakens in him a sense of one's position in society (*Dagbladet*, May 12, 1869).

The emigrants' letters were read over and over again and shared widely with friends, families, and neighbors. Many made their way into newspaper print. The most famous one may be the Muskego-Manifesto, which

---

[9] *Bratsberg-Amts Correspondent* (Skien), January 1, 1844.
[10] I made all translations from the Norwegian, unless otherwise noted.

is an open letter to the people of Norway signed by eighty men from Muskego, Wisconsin, and eventually published in the *Morgenbladet*, April 1, 1845. Here is an excerpt:[11]

We have no expectation of gaining riches; but we live under a liberal government in a fruitful land, where freedom and equality are the rule in religious and civil matters, and where each one of us is at liberty to earn his living practically as he chooses; such opportunities are more to be desired than riches; through these opportunities we have a prospect of preparing for ourselves, by diligence and industry, a carefree old age. We have therefore no reason to regret the decision that brought us to this country.

In these many letters home came ideas that influenced some of the country's most influential writers at the time. Henrik Wergeland (1808–45) – perhaps Norway's greatest lyric poet – was a frequent commentator on the conditions that fueled the country's growing stream of emigrants. He believed that Norwegians were leaving because of a shortage of economic and religious freedoms. We have to accept, he wrote, "that North America's freedom and the lack of such freedoms in our own legislation, is the real motive. If we enjoyed freedom of religious and business practice, then our emigration would stop on its own. Our lives could then be transformed and the desire for freedom would not have to travel across the Atlantic to become satisfied" (Wergeland 1837). For Wergeland, the freedom enjoyed by Norway's priests and public officials – although novel in the broader European context – meant little to the peasant or craftsman. These Norwegians found themselves ensnared in a dense thicket of taxes, laws, and regulations that protected trading privileges, limited real competition, and kept them from bringing their goods to market.

Similarly, Johan Reinert Reiersen (1810–64) used his position as the editor of *Christiansandsposten* to link the need for liberal reforms in Norway with the growing wave of emigration: It was the authorities' regressive policies toward ordinary farmers, craftsmen, and crofters that were driving emigration. For Reiersen, America stood out as a beacon of liberty and republican government where the masses could no longer be

reduced – through the power of individuals or of capital – to the same slavish dependence that supports the thrones of Europe. Personal freedom is something the people suck in with their mother's milk. It seems to have become as essential to every citizen of the United States as the air he breathes. It is part of his being, and will continue to be until his whole nature is cowed and transformed in the bondage of need and oppression (Reiersen 1981 [1844] 182–3).

[11] A reprint of the letter can be found in Blegen (1958: 178–80).

Whereas Wergeland found emigration to be a national shame or embarrassment that needed addressing, Reiersen found it only natural and proper that people should use their freedom to secure a better life abroad. Indeed, Reiersen himself left Norway in the spring of 1845, but he continued to agitate from abroad. In this decision to leave, he was not alone: Many political activists gave up on the Norwegian struggle, in frustration over the lack of progress. Agnes Mathilde Wergeland (her father was Henrik's cousin), the first Norwegian woman to earn a doctoral degree (in Zurich), left for America because she could not find satisfying employment in Norway, where all the doors to a bright future seemed closed (Andersen 1990: 95). She landed on her feet, securing a position in 1902 as a professor of history at the University of Wyoming. When she reflected on her decision twenty years later, she wrote, "Can one wonder why people with initiative, drive and the capacity to break new ground do not wish to stay in a country where one risks beings treated like a lout as soon as one shows some gumption?" (Wergeland 1906: 174).

A similar story can be told in the lives of two very influential members of the Norwegian labor movement in the 1870s. The founding member of Norway's first explicitly social democratic labor union (*Den Norske Arbeiderforening*), Marius Jantzen, eventually immigrated to the United States in 1880. He was accompanied by the union's very last leader, Christian Hagen, who emigrated after the union folded. Both men had tired of fighting for workers' rights in Norway (Bull 1947: 112). Each of them, in turn, was following in the illustrious footprints of Marcus Thrane, Norway's first socialist agitator, who left in the late 1840s.

From 1825 to the turn of the century, Norwegian society was forced to reflect on its shortcomings, because they were constantly juxtaposed against the promise of American society. It matters little that the American promise was often exaggerated; what matters was that many young and talented Norwegians were drawn away – tempted by the promise of a better life abroad. Those who remained used the American example to motivate reforms at home.

When Norwegian emigrants returned – and they did so increasingly toward the end of the 19th century, and especially after independence in 1905 – they brought back skills, attitudes, and money that contributed to economic development. These social and economic remittances facilitated a rationalization and mechanization of Norwegian agricultural techniques and the cultivation of new fields – allowing farm workers to become more productive, freeing others to move to the city in search of better-paying jobs.[12]

Indeed, the government's Emigrations Committee of 1912–13 explicitly recognized this effect:

> The returned Americans put their stamp upon it all; the rural districts are hardly recognizable. The farmers are not so burdened with debt as before; people live better, eat better, clothe themselves better – thus the population itself improves. All those who come from America begin to till the soil better than it was tilled before. They work the land more intensively and dispense with less productive processes and traditions. Crop rotation is introduced, machinery is acquired, the buildings of the farm, dwellings as well as others, are improved, more rational dairy methods are practiced, and gardens are laid out. In all these respects, there have been great advances in Sörlandet [the Southern region] during the past 10–15 years; the returned Americans have had their very considerable part in it, in some places even the largest part. They bring home with them much practical experience and understanding, which benefits the whole region. Furthermore, they have a will to take hold, and have in America learned a rate of work, which is different from what people are accustomed to here at home (*Utvandringskomiteen 1912–13*, 1915b: 3).

Thus, emigration provided an important source of ideas and inspiration for subsequent political development; Norwegians were able to envision a better world for themselves in the transatlantic communities described in the emigrants' letters home. By focusing on the power of these ideas, we do not ignore the costs of brain drain to the burgeoning movement for political change. Emigration skimmed off much of the cream of Norway's opposition, whether they were freeholders (e.g., Hans Barlien, an early farmer activist), newspaper editors (e.g., Reiersen), or labor organizers (e.g., Thrane, Jantzen, and Hagen). In the final balance, however, the benefits of emigration seemed to have outweighed these real costs. Emigration offered a realistic alternative to an aspiring opposition; it provided an alternative model for political development. Just as importantly, emigration altered the balance of power among disparate social groups and classes.

---

[12] It is difficult to measure how much money was remitted home, because much of it came in the form of bills, tucked inside envelopes, alongside letters home. Semmingsen (1950: 456) suggests that more than 12 million kroner were remitted annually in the years between 1905 and 1917. Like the experience of returning emigrants, this money helped fuel transformations (both political and economic) that characterized the decades preceding WWI.

Strength in Numbers

Shifting demographic and class cleavages occurred throughout the 19th century, and these changes help explain important economic and political developments in Norway. At the same time, these differences in opportunity and advantage surely motivated much of the early emigration. The growing stream of emigrants shifted the balance of Norwegian power across three important political cleavages: (1) between crofters and freeholders, (2) between workers and employers, and (3) between supporters of political reform (and independence) and defenders of the status quo.

The first of these shifting balances of power is the easiest to document. At the end of the period under investigation, Norwegian crofters more or less disappeared as a class. In 1855, the country had about 67,000 crofters; in 1900 their numbers had dwindled to 27,000; and by 1920 only 8,000 – mostly old and infirm – crofters remained (Hodne 1975: 363; Semmingsen 1978: 109). This demise cannot be explained by the adoption of mechanized techniques, because mechanization arrived late in Norway and only after the heaviest period of mass emigration (Haarstad 1978: 44; Tveite 1980). Rather, this class was decimated by emigration, their flight being a "protest with their feet" against the life of a crofter (Svalestuen 1980: 21).

The unfortunate plight of the crofter was not unknown among those who had already emigrated to the United States. There – in the mid-1880s – we find a group called "The Sons of Norwegian Crofters Association" (*De norske Husmandssønners Forening*), whose objective was to provide financial assistance to the sons of crofters and other workers so that they could emigrate to America (Semmingsen 1950: 218–19). Norwegian public opinion was also aware of the crofter's dilemma, as evident in an 1883 (August 15) letter to the *Husmanden* newspaper: "[I]f something is not done soon to begin loosening the strings on the crofter's straitjacket, then we cannot expect our young and strong workers to settle in this country, or adopt a crofter's role in life. Rather, we can expect them to set flight over the ocean to the free West, where forced labor is forever abolished."[13]

As the exodus of crofters continued, even the Storting came to recognize the need to act. In 1848, members of the judicial committee proposed a new law for regulating crofter affairs; their consideration had

[13] Cited in Semmingsen (1950: 216).

two noteworthy outcomes: (1) a new law (1851) that aimed to reduce the exploitation of crofters in Norway and (2) a stipend awarded to Sjur Fedje, politician and founder of the *Husmanden* newspaper, for travel around the country so that he could document the crofters' conditions. Fedje's report to the Storting included a proposal for the establishment of a fund to assist crofters in buying the land on which they toiled. It took nearly a half-century before this idea was implemented, but in 1894 the Storting created a Land Purchase Fund (*Jordinnkjøpsfondet*).

I do not mean to suggest that emigration was the only motivation for agrarian reform. The final quarter of the 19th century was a time of serious agricultural crisis across Europe when farmers were forced to respond to a radical fall in the price of corn caused by cheap imports from the New World. Charles Kindleberger (1951: 37) describes a plethora of policy choices implemented by states in response to the crisis:

In Britain agriculture was permitted to be liquidated. In Germany large-scale agriculture sought and obtained protection for itself. In France . . . agriculture as a whole successfully defended its position with tariffs. In Italy the response was to emigrate. In Denmark, grain production was converted to animal husbandry.

The Norwegian response relied on a combination of these strategies, the details of which would lead us too far astray (see Moses 2005c: 101f). However, a central, if implicit, part of the Norwegian strategy in response to this crisis was to export it on the backs of its emigrant crofters.

A second shift in the political balance of power grew out of the struggle between freeholders and the bureaucratic elite. As we have seen, the small class of public officials exerted an inordinate amount of influence. Although the 1814 constitution provided Norwegian freeholders with a unique opportunity to influence political power, they proved remarkably ineffective in exerting it. As early as the 1830s, two freeholders (Jon Neergaard and Ole Gabriel Ueland) had been elected to parliament – and this early influence was used to open the way for the local self-government act in 1837. Yet in general the freeholder movement proved to be either ineffective or uninterested in introducing the sort of reforms that could stave off the growing stream of emigrants. For this, they needed the help of Marcus Thrane.

Marcus Thrane (1817–90) had a turbulent and short career as a labor activist. His is the story of the explosive rise and fall of Norway's first organized opposition movement. In December 1848, Thrane started from scratch by organizing workers in the city of Drammen, at the time Norway's largest industrial center. By the summer of 1851 he had attracted more than 20,000 workers to that movement, across most of southern Norway (Bull 1947: 62). In the intervening two and a half years, Thane managed to do what the freeholders had not: He pulled together Norway's first organized form of political opposition.

Although Thrane's movement began in the cities, its political platform voiced the demands of a much larger segment of the population. Indeed, the Thranite movement was made up predominantly of crofters and rural workers from the eastern part of the country. In a petition to the king, which collected almost 13,000 signatures, the Thranites demanded suffrage for all men, a universal draft, cheaper goods and the dismantling of protective duties, an improved school system, and improvements in the crofters' condition (Lorenz 1972: 28–9). Indeed, one of their central demands was that the state should assist crofters in purchasing land (Bull 1947: 74). It was in this context that Sjur Fedje was proposing the same to the Storting.

What is perhaps most remarkable about Thrane and his movement was the emphasis placed on emigration as a tool for improving worker conditions. Thrane himself was a strong advocate of emigration for the lower classes – the very classes he was trying to organize! This lesson was not lost on other leaders in the movement, and subsequent research shows that about 25% of the Thranite leadership ended up emigrating before 1865 (Oen 1980: 62). This is not as paradoxical as might first appear, because Thrane recognized that emigration would reduce the number of those who remained, thereby strengthening their bargaining position (see, e.g., Oen 1980: 34–5). Indeed, Thrane himself left for the United States after the authorities clamped down on his movement and sentenced him to a lengthy stint in jail.

The Thranites embraced emigration as one tool in their struggle, because they were aware of the effect it could have on the political and economic demands of Norway's working classes. As emigration continued to grow throughout the latter half of the 19th century, this effect became increasingly evident in the rise of workers' real wages and in the growing influence of an organized labor movement.

The effect on wages followed from the law of supply and demand. Assuming that demand remains steady, the wages of workers will rise as the supply of their labor falls: This is elementary economics. The departure of 10,000 to 15,000 able-bodied workers from Norway each year on average, for most of the latter part of the period under investigation, was bound to affect the wages of those workers who remained at home. Indeed, as we have already seen, Norwegian real wages increased by an impressive 150% between 1870 and 1910. This increase is all the more remarkable when one realizes that much of this period was characterized by poor economic conditions and falling prices. Although many factors contribute to explain the rise in wages (e.g., expansion of Norwegian industry, large construction/infrastructure projects, improved production techniques, labor union pressures), massive emigration was clearly a major cause.

Norwegian public officials were aware of this effect. For example, in his 1885 report to the central authorities, the Lesja sheriff noted that emigration to America was making it easier for a shrinking labor force to make stronger demands – demands the sheriff felt were justified, given the poor wages that freeholders traditionally paid these people. Twenty years later, the district medical officer in Lom noted that emigration had forced many smallholdings to fold, as freeholders could no longer afford the improved agricultural wages and working conditions demanded by farmworkers (Semmingsen 1950: 453).

Yet the impact of emigration exceeded the focused effect on wages – it strengthened the labor movement as a whole. This statement requires some elaboration, given that emigration of its early leaders weakened the movement and later leaders of the labor movement opposed emigration for fear of the same sort of brain-drain effects. Emigration clearly operated as a safety valve for social discontent, and this effect may have delayed some of Norway's political development. As we have already seen, some of the labor movement's brightest stars – and many of its most radical foot soldiers – were enticed to leave the struggle for the promise of a better life abroad. One can only imagine the pressure that would have been generated by thousands of angry and mobilized crofters, had they not had an opportunity to emigrate.

Yet emigration also helped create the very conditions necessary for a vigorous labor movement.[14] In Norway, organized labor made rapid and impressive gains, on both political and economic fronts, at the outset of the 20th century. The movement was late in developing, but it exploded with activity once ignited. Norway's first trade union, for typesetters, emerged in 1882 through the efforts of Holtermann Knudsen

---

[14] Indeed, many of the founding actors in the Norwegian labor movement were foreigners or had spent significant time abroad as part of their apprenticeship. Among these were the Norwegian painter Martin Tranmæl (see Chapter 9), the Danish carpenter Sophus Pihl, the Danish cigar maker and broom maker Carl Jeppesen, the Danish saddle maker Marius Jantzen, and the Swedish carpenter J. O. Ljungdahl (Pryser 1980: 212).

(who later became chairman of the Labor Party and a member of parliament). Seven years later, Oslo was rocked by two long and bitter (if ultimately unsuccessful) strikes – one by the printers, another by female matchmakers – whose actions blazed a path for more substantial unions, such as the Iron and Metal Workers' and the General Workers' unions. On the eve of a new century (1899) a Workers' National Trade Organization (*Arbeidernes Faglige Landsorganisasjon* [AFL/N], subsequently *Landsorganisasjonen* [LO]) called together 16,000 trade unionists to create a new umbrella organization for Norwegian unions, proposing strong links to the nascent Labor Party (following the Swedish example). Its industrial partner, the Norwegian Employers' Organization (*Norsk Arbeidsgiverforening* [NAF], subsequently NHO) was established in response in the following year (1900).

However, only two unions, representing just 1,578 workers, joined the trade union federation at the organizing conference in 1899, because its membership fees and organizational requirements were seen to be exorbitant. Indeed, in 1904 there were as many unions outside the AFL/N as were in it. However, in 1905, several large unions joined, and the AFL/N's membership rose to 15,600; since then, the AFL/N (and the LO) has held a dominant position in representing Norwegian workers. After its slow start, the AFL/N proved to be a remarkably centralized and effective organization. By 1907 it had established a strike fund, controlled by a central leadership with considerable power. Indeed, this centralization became a point of contention within the Norwegian labor movement, as we see in Chapter 9. The same year, Norway experienced its first national strike and its first national wage agreement (signed by the Iron and Metal Workers' Union). By the eve of World War I, the AFL/N's membership had quadrupled in number.

The history of the political wing of the Norwegian labor movement was more turbulent than that of its economic wing. In 1873, a Danish saddle-maker's apprentice, Marius Jantzen, began the political movement with an advertisement in a local newspaper, appealing to like-minded socialists. The resulting *Norske Arbeiderforening* attracted just 37 members before collapsing – its leadership having died or been chased off to America, as we have already seen. Fourteen years later, in 1887, the Norwegian Labor Party (*Det norske Arbeiderparti* [DNA]) was founded, but it too experienced a difficult start, as it came to political maturity under the wings of the Left Party (*Venstre*), which stole much of its political thunder. Yet the Labor Party's luck seemed to change with the turn of the century: The DNA won its first parliamentary seat in 1903, and by

1912 (the last election before the war), it had become Norway's second largest party, mustering 140,000 votes, more than a quarter of all those who voted! Given Norway's rapid and intense industrialization at the turn of the century, the Labor Party drew its support from a radicalized class of workers. The result was a Labor Party that found itself far to the left of its Scandinavian brethren, made evident by its joining the Comintern in 1919.

By the start of World War I, the Norwegian labor movement was poised to take political control. In the interwar years it built a powerful working alliance with representatives of Norwegian farmers – a red–green alliance that allowed the DNA to dominate Norwegian politics in the postwar period. Indeed, the Norwegian historian Jens Arup Seip (1963) referred to the postwar period in Norway (1945–65) as an era of the one-party state, in which the party in question was the DNA.

How much of labor's success can be explained by emigration? It is impossible to tell, and perhaps it is too convenient to exaggerate the emigrants' potential effects. Still, the positive influences of emigration must have outweighed the negative: The Norwegian labor movement did not appear to be lacking in capable leaders, despite significant emigration from among its ranks. Quite the contrary, the Norwegian labor movement in both its political and economic forms proved to be remarkably astute and effective during its formative years before WWII.

More to the point, decades of emigration had laid the economic and social foundation on which the success of this leadership rested. At the close of the 19th century Norwegian industrialization entered a more intensive phase, and there was an increased demand for workers. At the same time, a global economic crisis began to affect Norwegian industry and trade, creating additional incentives for workers to emigrate.

Thus a possible oversupply of labor threatened to be drained away, wages of those who remained tended to rise, and labor was placed in a strong bargaining position. It became possible to build up very effective organizations, capable of enforcing respect for higher demands in the matters of wages, hours, conditions of work and living. Emigration may, therefore, confidently be viewed as one of the reasons for the growing radicalism of the Scandinavian labor movements, especially that of Norway; it operated to create the prerequisites of its success and encouraged it to increase its demands (Hovde 1934: 272–3).

This shift in class power is important for explaining Norway's subsequent political development. Although its precise effect is difficult to gauge, emigration clearly played a significant role in facilitating this shift and encouraging the red–green alliance that came to dominate Norway's politics in the postwar era. Yet there is still one more way in which emigration helped facilitate Norway's political development. This third shift in political power happened in the more explicitly political arena. Emigrants abroad were active in supporting the *Venstre* and its democratic reforms, and emigration can be seen as a surrogate measure of political discontent or dissatisfaction.

Similar to contemporary examples from Latin America (cf. Córdova and Hiskey 2009), Norwegian emigrants remained engaged in Norwegian politics even after they settled in the United States. Norwegian settlers in the United States established their own leftist (*Venstre*) associations to provide moral and financial support for *Venstre*'s fight for parliamentarianism in Norway (Gjerde 2007: 56; Semmingsen 1950: 482–3). When a fight for independence with Sweden appeared as a distinct possibility, similar groups collected money to support Norway's rearmament. One Chicago group even sent a telegram to the Storting, expressing "warm participation in the fatherlands' fight for might." When independence was gained ten years later, the Storting expressed its gratitude to Norway's "emigrated sons and daughters for their work for the National Cause" (Gjerde 2007: 57–8).[15]

Other researchers have found emigration to function as an important signal of political discontent. Thus, Lowell (1987: 191) found a correlation in Norwegian regional data between liberal political attitudes (in 1891) and emigration: The Right Party (*Høyre*) vote was strongest in those districts around Oslo, where industry was most firmly established, but which experienced relatively little emigration, whereas the Left found its greatest support in those districts that experienced higher levels of emigration. These findings allow Lowell to conclude that "[i]t is probable that emigration did, therefore, represent both the result of political disenchantment and a feedback effect on the political system" (Lowell 1987: 192).

Similarly, Aarebrot and Kuhnle (1976) found emigration to be strongest in those regions where voter turnout was low, suggesting that exit and voice were acting as functional alternatives in Norway before WWI. If we interpret voter turnout as an indicator of allegiance or satisfaction, we can expect high levels of political disenchantment in those areas with less voter turnout. Aarebrot and Kuhnle's finding that county-level emigration rates were inversely related to voter turnout rates suggests

---

[15] See also Andersen (1990: chapter 8).

that many Norwegians were signaling disenchantment with the political system (or Norway, in general) when they chose to emigrate.

Across each of these three fronts (rural/urban, labor/capital, and political) it is possible to trace the effects of emigration on Norway's political development. The exodus of crofters played the role that industrialization played in other contexts: It emptied the countryside of its exploited labor and forced landowners to rationalize their production. Most importantly, by emptying the Norwegian workforce of its excess labor, emigration strengthened the bargaining position of the labor force that remained – providing the leverage necessary to obtain better wages and working conditions, on the one hand, and a more responsive state, on the other. Finally, Norwegian immigrants to the United States played an important supporting role in political developments at home, and their very act of emigration signaled to the political authorities that they needed to do something to deter further emigration.

The Home Front

The third level of emigration effects concerns the way in which the Norwegian state responded to the threat of emigration. This response might be characterized in terms of increased engagement, over time, as the level of emigration rose. In the early years, the Norwegian government understood emigration as a natural response by free individuals; it did not think it necessary to influence these decisions, even when public opinion was increasingly adamant about the need to counteract the trend. Over time, political elites became more aware of the need to change course. This change in course was first visible in parliamentary discussion about the need to extend suffrage, but it became more evident after 1880, when the state introduced a number of measures directly aimed at placating those groups of Norwegians who were most likely to emigrate.

Before the 1880s, the Norwegian government's response to mass emigration was laissez-faire: The early Norwegian state can be seen as a caricature of the liberal night-watchman state, unwilling to interfere in the decisions of its citizens. In the realm of emigration, the state's role was confined to collecting information about emigrants and considering regulatory legislation to ensure that emigrants were not being exploited.

This early attitude is most clearly evident in the government's response to a report by the Norwegian-Swedish consul in Havre on the poor condition of Norwegian emigrants abroad. In 1843, the government's Finance, Trade, and Tariff Department had turned to F. C. Borchsenius (the

Bratsberg county governor [*amtmann*]) to chair a committee to study the emigration problem.

Borchsenius's position was that emigration from a country such as Norway, with its thinly spread population, was in itself an oddity that needed explanation. It was his impression that the root of the problem was "not to be found simply in the character of its people, but also in defects in the economic and social conditions" of the country.[16] In particular, Borchsenius pointed to the problem of access to land, referring to particular laws that affected the parceling out and inheritance of property. Most emigration, he argued, was occurring in the poorest districts, where land parceling had been extensive and where small farmers were being forced to leave in droves.

The Finance Department seemed to agree with Borchsenius about the nature and motivation for emigration, but it believed it to be a temporary problem, one that would correct itself in due time. The full committee's final report seemed to concur more with the Finance Department's position than that of Borchsenius. It failed to recognize that emigration was being driven by "any absolute lack in the conditions in our native land, either in institutions or in the physical character of the land." It diagnosed the problem as one of overpopulation, not political underdevelopment: After all, Norway's political context was one of the most liberal in Europe! "[I]t is not the political institutions of our country which occasion the desire to leave the country, for they must be considered among the freest in Europe, and the country people – especially in the recent period[17] – seem to know very well how to exercise their political rights."[18]

Having said this, the committee did recognize that emigration could be deterred if the government assisted poor farmers in securing access to land, but it felt that a recommendation of this type lay outside its mandate. The bill it proposed was an attempt to protect both the home country and its emigrants from the dangers of unregulated emigration. In spite of its limited objectives, the bill failed to generate enough support in the Storting to pass.

Although Borchsenius's argument did not sway the committee, the parliament, or the government, his opinion was echoed in the broader public debate. In 1852, the newspaper *Stavangeren* wrote that the government's

---

[16] *Stortings Forhandlinger* (1845), I (6): 1.
[17] This is a reference to the fact that the 1842 Storting election brought almost as many freeholders (42) as public officials (50) to parliament.
[18] *Stortings Forhandlinger* (1845), I (6): 25.

policies were responsible for emigration. The freedoms promised in 1814 had not been delivered in practice, and it was for this reason that peasants fled. In 1857, the newspaper *Aftenbladet* concurred, writing that "emigration could be seen as the direct result of a conscious and universal political dissatisfaction with the state of our country" (Semmingsen 1941: 449–50).

The attitudes of leading political elites seemed to change over time, and emigration was increasingly employed as a rhetorical lever in Storting debates. This is clearly the case when parliament discussed extending the suffrage – first in 1868, in debates over expanding the suffrage in county elections, and, again before 1884, in debates over expanding the suffrage in national elections. The influential freeholder representative, Søren Jaabæk, seemed to invoke emigration more than anyone else. For him, emigration was the best evidence of political dissatisfaction: High interest rates, a heavy tax burden, the draft, and exorbitant pay to public officials were all driving emigrants from the country.[19]

Yet others also played the emigration card.[20] For example, in an 1873 discussion about extending the suffrage, P.C. Bjørnsgaard asked the Storting rhetorically, Why do people emigrate? The answer, he argued, was not simply a search for the means to make a better living:

They leave because they feel like they are not appreciated and they want their humanity, their personality, and their individuality respected. This is the main reason driving them to America. These many capable men could contribute much to this country, but they now settle in the far West, because a small minority in this country has introduced a class-system that is all too pervasive in our social conditions (Storthingstidende 1873a: 432).

Even conservatives wishing to limit the suffrage drew support for their position from the threat of emigration. Thus, a conservative parson, Albert Henrik Krohn Balchen, responded to Bjørnsgaard's argument by doubting that anybody emigrated because he lacked the vote in Norway. Even if emigrants left for that reason, he argued that this was of less concern than the capital and brains that would leave Norway if the suffrage was to be extended! Balchen feared that increasing the influence of the masses would drive out the sort of people that Norway needed most

[19] See, e.g., Scott (1952).
[20] Semmingsen (1950: 418–19) tells us that Jaabæk did so in 1875, Jørgen Olafsen did in 1879, and Sivert Nielsen followed in 1881. With the help of Stian Saur, I have found additional mention by Jakob Velde (May 1, 1873); Jørgen Olafsen (already on December 1, 1868, but also on April 23, 1879); as well as Ludvig Daae and Johan Sverdrup (November 30, 1868).

of all: those with necessary skills and capital (Storthingstidende 1873b: 519).

I am not suggesting that emigration alone can explain the expansion of Norwegian suffrage; the reform is much too complicated to be explained by a single variable. Indeed, an earlier attempt to correlate the timing of suffrage expansion with emigration levels has shown that those countries with negligible levels of emigration were more likely to take dramatic steps to democratize: "[T]he right to use *voice* was generally more widespread at an *earlier* stage in countries which came to experience the most excessive waves of out-migration, and only minor extensions were granted after the exit-waves started to roll" (Kuhnle 1981: 513, emphasis in original). Kuhnle found that suffrage was extended gradually in those countries with higher levels of emigration, but more abruptly in the low-emigration countries. The Norwegian experience corresponds with this general pattern, as we see supporters of expanding the suffrage willing and able to use the threat of emigration, on several occasions over time, as a sort of political crowbar.

Indeed, as we saw in Table 5.1 there are states that enjoyed political development and democratization without experiencing emigration, and many commentators in Norway were skeptical of the effect that increased political development would have on further emigration. For example, in 1903, members of the Political Economy Association (*Statsøkonomiske Forening*) met to discuss how to deal with the emigration problem. Their discussion pointed to many potential explanations for the massive emigration; there were simply too many hindrances on the ability of individuals to go out and create a better life for themselves. Yet their focus was limited to economic regulations; they did not think that Norway's political context could explain the emigration. Indeed, they noted with some apparent surprise that recent constitutional changes and the expansion of political rights did not seem to have any effect on the rate of emigration! At that time Norway enjoyed a democratically responsive government, a Norwegian flag was flying from its ships at sea, and it had introduced universal suffrage (for men) – but none of these reforms seemed to have dampened the desire to emigrate among Norwegians.[21]

---

[21] Reported in *Aftenposten*, April 28, 1903. See also Mørkhagen (2009: 456–7). Although emigration did not seem to decrease noticeably after independence, the number of returning emigrants did increase. Between 1891 and 1896, about 2,000 people returned, but in the five-year period after independence (1906–10), more than 9,000 returned home (NOS 1921: 75).

As the 19th century came to a close, the government's attitude seemed to change. The continued outflow of emigrants was beginning to take its toll, and officials began to consider explicit measures to stave off the exodus. The need for a response was most evident in the countryside, where farmers were finding it difficult to find workers at a suitable (low) wage. Yet as WWI approached, there was also an increased effort to improve the general conditions facing industrial workers.

The situation was exacerbated by a recognition that the pace of emigration was beginning to slow down in other countries. Both Sweden and Denmark were experiencing falling rates of emigration. In Sweden in the years before WWI, emigration was 60% of what it had been in the 1880s, and return emigration seemed to be higher as well. In Germany and Switzerland emigration levels were at a standstill. Only Ireland was experiencing the same pace of emigration over time.

By the closing decade of the 19th century at last, the cries of Thrane and Fedje were heard. In 1891 the Department of the Interior finally began to consider the effect that peasant access to land was having on emigration. It noted that emigration was draining labor from Norwegian agriculture, which suggested that the working conditions of agricultural workers were worse than in other occupational groups. It also recognized that agricultural workers were increasingly unwilling to accept crofter status. Something needed to be done to help agricultural workers secure land (Semmingsen 1950: 429).

As we have already seen, a new fund (*Jordinnkjøpsfondet*) was established in the 1890s to provide finances for those workers who wanted to build their own house and to buy small patches of agricultural land. In 1900, another proposal was presented to the Storting to encourage the clearing of new land and to help peasants secure land and homes of their own. The resulting Land Cultivation Fund (*Jorddyrkingsfondet*) came into effect in 1900 and lasted until 1908, providing 3.3 million kroner to 4,014 newly cleared farms, most of which presumably went to crofters (Mørkhagen 2009: 458).

In 1903 another proposal made its way through parliament for a state-financed bank that could provide loans for agricultural workers to buy their own homes and cultivate new lands. In the parliamentary debates there now seemed to be consensus about the needs for these loans; there was only disagreement about how much funding should be provided and how long support should be given to these frontiersmen. The bill passed on June 10, 1903, creating the Norwegian Agricultural Workers and House Bank (*Den norske Arbeiderbruk- og Boligbank*). By 1915, this bank had lent out 40 million kroner to 27,690 workers and peasants (Semmingsen 1950: 430).

In 1908, representatives from several important producer groups in the Norwegian economy met to establish the Society for the Limitation of Emigration (*Selskabet til Emigrationens Indskrænkning*). In the original mission statement, they voiced their intent to investigate the reasons for and to consider appropriate countermeasures to extensive emigration. The organizing committee realized that some level of emigration might even be useful as a regulatory device during periods with high unemployment, but it was concerned that emigration "saps the strength of our agriculture, depopulates our mountain districts, transports our skilled seamen on foreign ships, and deprives us of our most skilled tradesmen and industrial workers" (Selskapet til Emigrationens Indskrænkning 1910: 4).

Toward that end, the group produced an impressive amount of pamphlets, newspaper editorials, local speeches, and political agitation with the goal of discouraging emigration. Over time, the Society became increasingly convinced that the best way to deter emigration was to secure new, virgin lands for cultivation. Indeed, in 1916, it reorganized to focus its attention on this effort, changing its name to New Land: Society for the Nation's Home Colonization and the Limitation of Emigration (*Ny Jord, selskap for landets indre kolonisation og emigrationens indskrænkning*).

At the same time, the government introduced a number of measures aimed at helping the growing class of industrial workers. For example, an important Labor Commission was appointed by a unanimous Storting in 1885, and its report led to an 1892 law on factory inspection and an 1895 law on accident insurance. A 1906 law established local unemployment offices, which at least one observer believed would help deter emigration and assimilate returning emigrants (Mellbye 1909: 11). In 1909, the government introduced the world's first compulsory sickness insurance scheme that automatically covered the spouse of the insured (Kuhnle 1981: 519).

Finally, a new parliamentary committee – the Norwegian Emigration Committee of 1912–13 (*Utvandringskomite*) – was established to coordinate legislation related to emigration issues. As in the earlier, mid-century attempt, most of the attention of this committee was aimed at regulating the conditions of emigration. However, the committee also considered the effect of emigration, especially returning emigration, on Norwegian political and economic development: "[E]migration has contributed to a continued rise in the workforce's demands with respect to both wages and working conditions. It has forced employers and capitalists to organize and to develop more rational methods" (*Utvandringskomiteen 1912–13* 1915a: 216).

If we band these reforms together and think of them as components in a developing welfare policy, it is not unthinkable that emigration was an important motivation for the government's move to improve political developments in Norway. These reforms were consistent with Stein Kuhnle's (1981: 519) observation that "governments in countries ridden by persistently high levels of exit, responded more actively to the challenge of satisfying vital population needs in order to make their societies more attractive in comparative terms."

CONCLUSION

Gustav Sundbärg, the eminent Swedish statistician and chair of Sweden's official emigration committee (1907–13), noted, "To discuss 'Swedish emigration' is the same as to discuss 'Sweden;' there is hardly a single political, social or economic problem in our country, which has not been conditioned, directly or indirectly, by the phenomenon of emigration" (Sundbärg 1913: 660).

The same thing could be easily said of Norway. Emigration clearly matters, but its effect is found in complex relations, buried beneath the aggregate figures introduced at the beginning of this chapter. By examining Norwegian political development before World War I, we get a better sense of the sundry ways in which emigration influences political development, at each of the posited levels (individual, group, and community). In the particulars of the Norwegian case we uncover the mechanisms that lie beneath the lagged effect found in the statistical analyses from the preceding chapter.

This was a remarkable time in the modern era, when migration was a real opportunity for many of the world's residents. This relative freedom of mobility provided a context in which it was possible to talk about politically motivated emigration and for governments to consider the need to respond to the threat of emigration by improving local shortcomings. Although this motivation surely exists today – every country can benefit from greater political development – this way of thinking about emigration is almost foreign to modern policy makers, except in countries that are suffering from a brain drain. We tend to think about migrants in terms of economic incentives or as asylum seekers.

Yet the degree of restriction on modern migration surely limits the effect that emigration can have on the sending political authorities. When emigration is easier, its effect on political change can be significant, which is quite evident in the Norwegian case. In the agricultural sector, emigration led to a reduction in the number of available workers, which forced farmers to adopt machines and introduce more modern and efficient means of production. This development also led to a change in the system of agricultural labor: When the number of crofters and servants fell drastically, family-based agriculture became the new form of agriculture. This transition, in turn, influenced the nature of Norwegian industrialization and its nascent labor movement. By draining the country of potential labor, emigration strengthened the hand of those workers who remained. It was the strength of Norwegian labor – in the countryside, at sea, and in the growing industrial sector – that explains the country's subsequent political development. In this light, emigration can be seen to have propelled both waves of Norway's political mobilization: that of the freeholders in the 19th century and that of the workers in the century that followed.

To consider the importance of its effect, we can try to gauge what Norway's labor markets would have looked like in the absence of massive emigration. This can be done by comparing Norwegian demographic developments with those of Denmark. In 1845, both countries were roughly the same size (ca. 1.3 million people). Because Denmark experienced less emigration than Norway, its population grew relatively more: In 1910 there were 2.75 million Danes, compared to just 2.4 million Norwegians.[22] Consequently, real wages in Norway grew faster than they did in Denmark. In Hatton and Williamson's extensive analysis of *The Age of Mass Migration* (1998: 208), they find that the Norwegian labor force effectively shrank by 24% between 1870 and 1910 because of emigration. (In Denmark, the corresponding decline was 14%.) On the basis of these figures (p. 224), they estimated that Norwegian wages would have been 15% lower (and Danish wages 11% lower) in the absence of emigration.

Alternatively, we might consider a broader counterfactual scenario in which we try to imagine what the Norwegian polity would have looked like in the absence of emigration (but otherwise being exactly the same). Norway's underlying balance of class power – in particular, its lack of an indigenous bourgeoisie or landowning class – makes it likely that Norway would have experienced significant political development during

---

[22] When projected into the future, the numbers are even more dramatic. In 1950, Denmark's population was 4.6 million, whereas Norway's was only 3.6 million. See Mørkhagen (2009: 410).

this period, even if the country had not experienced massive emigration. Yet this development would have probably taken longer to achieve, and it would have been less accommodating to small farmers. In short, in the absence of emigration we might have seen later and more radicalized political development in Norway.

When we consider subsequent political development in Norway and Europe, emigration's effect on timing and moderation is not unimportant. On the domestic front, Norway's subsequent political development rested heavily on the ability to secure a red–green alliance in the interwar period. It is difficult to imagine modern social democracy in Norway without strong links to small farmers. On the international front, if Norway's political development had been delayed, it would have occurred in a much more tumultuous international environment – in the crisis-prone interwar period that followed the Bolshevik Revolution.

In the end, we must recognize that it is difficult to measure the impact of emigration on political development. We can see its effects by studying the Norwegian example, but only if we dig for them. This evidence seems to confirm Albert Hirschman's general hunch:

Throughout the 19th century and up to World War I, the right of suffrage and other civil rights were extended in many of the very European states from which large contingents of people were departing. In other words, exit and a certain kind of voice increased hand-in-hand, even though at the same time, exit lowered the volume of another more militant kind of voice. These two developments may be causally connected: because a number of disaffected people had departed, it became comparatively safe to open up the system to a larger number of those who stayed on. In this manner, exit-migration may have made it possible for democratization and liberalization to proceed in several European countries prior to World War I without political stability being seriously imperiled (Hirschman 1978: 102).

When we contrast the Norwegian experience with other cases from the same period, it is also evident that emigration alone is not enough to explain its political development. The effects of emigration seem to be bundled together with the effects of other variables. In this way, emigration probably cushioned the discontent that accompanied Norway's industrial transformation. In doing so, it lessened the likelihood of alternatives (revolution or political oppression) and facilitated Norway's peaceful and piecemeal political transformation.

6

Guest-Worker Programs after World War II

As the reader will recall from Chapter 4, international emigration suffered a dramatic decrease in the interwar period – both in absolute and real terms. Only after the end of World War II did global emigration figures begin to rise slowly and steadily until the mid-1990s.

This chapter takes a closer look at the unique character of the postwar emigration regime from 1947–76. In doing so, it adopts the structure of the preceding chapter in first briefly reviewing the general pattern of the period as reflected in the EMIG 1.2 data. It then turns to a comparative study of guest-worker programs in North America and Europe.

PERIOD PATTERNS

Table 6.1 uses the same criteria as in the last chapter to distinguish between high-, medium-, and low-emigration countries for the period 1947–76. By ranking countries in this way, I hoped to be able to distinguish general period patterns and choose case studies accordingly.

Table 6.1 confirms that the relationship between emigration and political development does not lend itself to simple indicators and analyses. By comparing the average level of democracy in 1979 across the different groupings (high, medium, low) of emigration states, we find that there is no clear relationship between the level of postwar emigration and the strength of democracy. Among the high-emigration countries are examples of both strong and established democracies (e.g., New Zealand) and authoritarian regimes (e.g., El Salvador). Indeed, on average, high-emigration states had lower levels of democracy (14.3) than did

Emigration and Political Development

TABLE 6.1. *Gross Emigration Rates, 1947–76 (per mil, per annum, decade averages)*

	1947–56	1957–66	1967–76	Average 1947–76	Level of Democracy 1979
High Emigration					(14.3)
El Salvador	31.17			31.17	0.0
Guatemala	22.61			22.61	5.9
Seychelles			21.18	21.18	0.0
Algeria		17.96	23.00	20.48	0.3
Jamaica		19.68	15.45	17.56	15.4
New Guinea			16.86	16.86	21.0
Botswana			16.86	16.86	4.1
Malta		22.30	8.74	15.52	30.2
Cyprus		10.81	4.96	7.89	15.0
New Zealand	3.81	6.05	10.15	6.67	32.9
Israel	13.17	2.34	2.68	6.06	32.2
Medium Emigration					(25.6)
Costa Rica	9.29			9.29	20.7
Guyana		8.17	8.20	8.19	13.8
Liberia			7.25	7.25	0.0
Fiji			7.15	7.15	16.0
Zimbabwe		8.93	3.91	6.42	
Denmark	6.28	5.68	6.28	6.08	38.2
Australia	3.14	5.62	7.31	5.36	34.0
Iceland		4.42	6.20	5.31	35.1
Italy	5.74	6.19	2.89	4.94	40.0
Portugal	3.40	5.70	5.69	4.93	25.3
Ghana		4.51	5.26	4.89	6.1
Germany	2.45	4.90	7.18	4.84	31.6
Greece	1.71	7.93	3.57	4.40	32.2
France	0.82	2.81	8.27	3.97	35.8
Ireland	6.04	0.9		3.47	29.1
Low Emigration					(9.9)
Canada	3.51	4.35	3.78	3.88	29.3
Yemen			4.64	4.64	0.0
Finland	2.95	3.76	4.90	3.87	26.4
Zambia		3.07		3.07	4.5
Norway	1.83	3.62	3.65	3.03	32.8
Trinidad and Tobago		0.61	5.35	2.98	13.0
Sweden	2.00	2.34	3.65	2.66	37.3
Haiti			2.49	2.49	0.0
Mauritius			2.29	2.29	23.5

	1947–56	1957–66	1967–76	Average 1947–76	Level of Democracy 1979
Japan	1.37	1.79	3.14	2.10	25.8
Morocco	2.00	2.17		2.09	0.9
Taiwan	2.61	2.76	0.74	2.04	0.0
Spain	1.79	1.67	2.02	1.83	31.8
Switzerland	1.59	1.62	1.63	1.61	41.2
Rwanda		1.59		1.59	0.5
Yugoslavia	3.17	1.12	0.38	1.56	0.0
Venezuela	3.60	0.51	0.45	1.52	21.7
Kenya		1.15	1.53	1.34	0.0
Colombia	2.47	1.03	0.37	1.29	9.9
Czechoslovakia	1.59	1.22	1.00	1.27	0.0
Poland	0.96	1.67	0.43	1.02	0.4
Turkey	0.34	0.86	1.76	0.99	20.6
Mexico	0.54	0.80	1.29	0.88	1.7
Thailand	0.37	1.64	0.44	0.82	3.7
Austria	0.55	0.34	1.42	0.77	31.2
Bangladesh			0.75	0.75	5.4
Ethiopia		0.95	0.41	0.68	0.0
South Africa	0.82	0.59	0.48	0.63	1.3
Sri Lanka	0.25	0.44	1.00	0.56	5.3
Nigeria		0.52	0.48	0.50	15.0
Korea, Rep. of		0.49		0.49	0.0
United States	0.16	0.80		0.48	24.9
Dominican Rep.		0.42	0.50	0.46	15.2
Tanzania		0.35	0.54	0.44	2.0
Uganda		0.38	0.47	0.43	0.0
India	0.26	0.48	0.49	0.41	17.7
Russia		0.41		0.41	0.0
Philippines	0.18	0.36	0.70	0.41	0.0
Pakistan			0.40	0.40	0.0
Bulgaria	0.39	0.18	0.63	0.40	0.0
Somalia			0.37	0.37	0.0
Burma			0.35	0.35	0.0
Nicaragua	0.26			0.26	0.0
Hungary	0.23		0.21	0.22	0.3
Indonesia			0.14	0.14	4.3

Notes: Per mil (o/oo) refers to the number of emigrants per 1,000 of the population in the sending (home) state. Bold figures refer to the decade averages that justify their inclusion in each grouping. See text in Chapter 5 for clarification. The guest-worker cases studied later in the chapter are highlighted with italics.

Sources: EMIG 1.2; COW (2002); Vanhanen (2007).

medium-emigration states (25.6), whereas both groups scored higher than did low-emigration states (9.9).

In examining the data closer, we find that the group of high-emigration countries is remarkably disparate. Scattered across the globe, these countries seem to share few, if any, obvious characteristics. Worse, the data that generate this ranking are patchy in nature – the highest emigration states earn their ranking with observations from only a single decade or two. Consequently, there is a real possibility that the ranking is being driven by outlier observations of very particular (and nation-specific) circumstances.

I suspect that the period under consideration (1947–76) is too diverse in character to be easily captured by such simple indicators. The nature of international exchange changed significantly during this period, which began with efforts to rebuild national economies in the immediate aftermath of WWII and ended with an expansion of global markets. Therefore I chose to focus analytical attention on examples from the beginning of the period, when political constraints on emigration were more evident.

In the wake of World War II, global emigration patterns were driven by two pressing needs: (1) to repatriate millions of people displaced by the war and (2) to rebuild national economies affected by that war. The latter need was fulfilled in part by extensive guest-worker programs in both Europe and North America. These programs were structured according to a number of bilateral and multilateral agreements that channeled the flow of a specified type of migrant. As a consequence, the nature of international migration at the time was more limited in scope and regulated in nature than before the war and in the preceding century.

To study the political effects of emigration under such a highly regulated regime, this chapter selects examples from all three emigration categories. These examples are indicated by italics in Table 6.1 and include high-emigration countries (Algeria); medium-emigration countries (Italy, Portugal, and Greece), and low-emigration countries (Morocco, Spain, Yugoslavia, Turkey, and Mexico). Each of these states agreed to participate in bilateral programs to supply guest workers. The rest of the chapter considers how these regulated agreements affected political development in those countries that supplied workers to the burgeoning economies of the United States and Europe.

In the process we find that the nature of the restricted international regime allowed some states (e.g., Mexico and Algeria) to channel emigration streams in ways that strengthened the control of the political authorities. However, in other countries (e.g., Spain, Portugal, and Italy), access to foreign labor markets, combined with stagnant demographic conditions, helped secure a more favorable balance of class power that facilitated political development. A restrictive international context seems to make political development more difficult because workers who remain are not able to fully flex their political muscle. However, under certain conditions (e.g., in the growing European Community), workers were able to secure political gains, even in this restricted international climate.

NORTH AMERICA

The North American guest-worker program begins during the war, and looks like a shotgun wedding: It was a convenient arrangement sealed by an external threat. The U.S. government – recently attacked at Pearl Harbor – needed to secure a stable supply of farmworkers to maintain domestic production, because its own men were being sent to fight in the war. Under these circumstances, in which the labor needs of the United States outweighed those of Mexico, the Mexican government was able to secure a remarkably favorable agreement (at least at first): It had a strong say in the number of men being sent, where they came from, what they would be paid, and how they would otherwise be treated.

Officially, this marriage of convenience is known as the "Mexican-United States Program of the Loan of Laborers." More commonly, it is called the Bracero Program, referring to the manual labor that was being exchanged (*brazo*, in Spanish, means arm). Like most shotgun arrangements, no one expected this marriage to last: Both sides understood it to be temporary. Yet the partners involved – the U.S. growers, both governments, and the workers themselves – found the arrangement useful enough to let it last for more than 20 years, from 1942 to 1964.[1] In fact, the number of braceros grew over time, with more workers arriving each year in the 1950s than during all the war years combined.

This is not to suggest that the program did not have its detractors or that it was without faults. For the United States, in the memorable title of Truman Moore's 1965 book, the Bracero Program provided *The Slaves We Rent*. Mexico, in turn, in needing to find outlets for its idle hands, had to face the political humiliation that accompanied that need. Yet the Bracero Program was a novel agreement: a formal and bilateral

---

[1] There were two legislatively enacted Bracero Programs: from 1942–7 and from 1951–64. In the interim years, employers recruited braceros directly, but the system was administered by the U.S. Immigration and Nationality Service.

attempt to manage migration across a common border, at a time when international migration was increasingly being restricted.

Migration from Mexico to the United States began long before 1942, nor did it stop after 1964. Neither were the levels of emigration especially high during the intervening 22 years. What the Bracero Program offers this analysis is a managed regime of international migration. This section considers whether such a unique institutional context affected the way in which emigration influenced Mexican political development.

Mexican Political Development

Mexico's relationship to the United States is a long and complicated one: Not only do the two countries share an extensive common border but they also have at times managed to share the same territory and people. With the 1848 Treaty of Guadalupe-Hidalgo and the 1853 Treaty of La Mesilla (colloquially known in the United States as the Gadsden Purchase), Mexico lost almost half of its territory and about 1% of its population to the United States.

In many ways, the political development of modern Mexico is intricately linked to its northern border. In the bloody aftermath of the 1910 revolution, perhaps as many as a million Mexicans fled to the United States, and revolutionary groups often took refuge on the other side of the border. Consequently, emigration, exodus, and revolution were all parts of a potent political cocktail, in which every side expressed concern about the size of the exodus and the exploitative conditions meeting Mexicans when they arrived in the United States. This concern was reflected in the 1917 Mexican constitutional convention, which drafted Article 123 to include safeguards for Mexico's emigrant workers (García y Griego 1988: 56).

Throughout this entire period, from the 1910 revolution until the first Bracero agreement, emigration haunted the postrevolutionary government. Before the revolution, critics of the old regime could point to emigration as evidence of the human costs of Porfirio Diaz's government: His policies were said to be depopulating Mexico. Emigration was used as evidence of the need for land reform and state-subsidized repatriation policies, which were designed to encourage emigrants to return home and work on their farms in Mexico. By the late 1920s, emigration had become an integral part of the Mexican development mantra.[2]

---

[2] I have in mind the influential work of Manuel Gamio (1930). Based on a survey of Mexican immigrants to the United States in the mid-1920s, Gamio concluded that

Although emigration played an important role in the rhetoric of Mexican development, it was not a leading role. That role was played by a party that became the *Partido Revolucionario Institutional* (Institutional Revolutionary Party [PRI]). Indeed, Mexico's political development in the postwar period under study can be characterized by two striking and related features: the complete dominance of the governing party and a long period of economic and political stability.

At a time when coup d'états and military dictatorships were the norm across Latin America, Mexico enjoyed a remarkably stable period of constitutional rule, with regular elections and peaceful government transitions (albeit with little participation by the opposition). In examining the country's social indicators (fully aware of their contentious and probably fictitious nature), one sees a country at rest: Election statistics were churned out year after year with remarkable regularity, the level of unemployment was consistently below that found in the United States, and the level of industrial action was, well, tranquil (Wilkie 1971).

This stability was secured by the political dominance of the PRI. Founded in 1929 as the National Revolutionary Party (*Partido Nacional Revolucionario* [PNR]), it governed Mexico without interruption for nearly 70 years (having changed its name to the PRI in 1946). During this time, it enjoyed remarkable electoral success: From its inception until the late 1980s, the PRI won every gubernatorial election and more than 95% of local elections (Hiskey and Canache 2005: 264)! Although this power was consolidated over a long stretch of time, it blossomed during the time of the Bracero Program. To paraphrase the Peruvian author Mario Vargas Llosa, the party enjoyed a perfect dictatorship (Hiskey and Canache 2005: 258) – an arrangement secured by buying the support of two important interests: workers and farmers.

Agrarian support was secured by way of land reform. The revolution halted the trend of land concentration that had been encouraged by the prerevolutionary (Porfirian) government, which relied heavily on the power and legitimacy of the landlord class (*hacendados*). Land reform was designed to undermine support for the old regime and contribute to a new type of political identity, borne of the *ejido* (communal farms):

emigration was by and large favorable for both Mexico and the migrants, despite the hardships and abuses they suffered. Significantly, Gamio's work set the intellectual context into which the Bracero Program entered: He described the emigrant experience as part of a modernization effort, in which migrants learned to improve their diets, hygiene, and expectations. They developed "discipline and steady habits of work," they "learned to handle machinery," and they experienced (and came to expect) a certain degree of social mobility (Gamio 1930: 184; see also 128, 156–7, 178–84).

"But if the *ejido* system is not economically warranted, it is surely justifiable on political grounds. For the granting of land to the *campesino* was the one act which could secure his loyalty to the Revolution and assure that in future revolts, he would support the government, and not, as had almost invariably been the case in pre-Revolutionary Mexico, the insurgents" (Needler 1961: 310).

The support of labor was secured by similar means. Conventional wisdom points to Mexico's record of strike activity as evidence of an ineffective labor movement. There is little doubt that the movement was subservient to the interests of the PRI: Its leadership moderated rank-and-file demands in exchange for numerous benefits. This tradition of *charrismo* (government-appointed labor bosses) is evidence of the difficulty that Mexicans have had in creating a strong and independent civil society – one that is strong enough to oppose the state and the interests embedded there (Collier and Collier 1991).

This combination of political dominance and political stability produced a striking example of what the literature came to call "dependent development" (e.g., Evans 1979; O'Donnell 1973). By co-opting important worker and peasant interests and securing power across different levels of government, the party was able to use its influence to create a broad-based development platform that included major land reform, the nationalization of several industries (railroad, steel, mining, transportation, and communications), and a broad package of import-substitution industrialization (ISI) policies. While the Bracero Program was in effect, Mexico experienced its longest stretch of political and economic stability, which became known as the "Mexican Miracle." Between 1940 and 1970, Mexico's GNP grew by 6.5% a year, and its per-capita growth rate was 3% a year; from the mid-1950s to the mid-1960s its real wages increased steadily (Villarreal 1977). The miracle extended to the agricultural sector as well: Mexican agriculture grew by 6.3% per year between 1940 and 1960: equaling the world's highest rates of growth at the time (Sandos and Cross 1983: 53)!

Although Mexico's economic performance during this period is impressive, it is more difficult to characterize changes in the national level of political development. The Vanhanen and Polity indicators show no clear sign of political development, despite Mexico's impressive economic growth and political consolidation. As shown in Figure 6.1, the Polity indicator shows absolutely no change during the Bracero period (and beyond): Mexico scored a constant -6 from 1930 to 1977. The Vanhanen indicator shows more volatility, with a general increase over time:

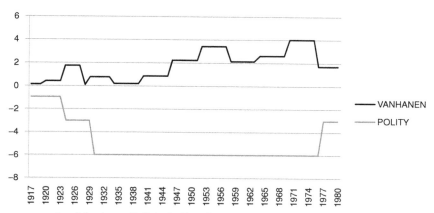

FIGURE 6.1. Mexican Political Development, 1917–80. *Sources*: Vanhanen (2007) and CSP (2009).

At the beginning of the Bracero Program (in 1942) Mexico scored 0.8; by the end of the program (in 1964), this score had risen to 2.6, but by 1980 it had declined to 1.7.

In short, the Mexican picture of political development is a complex one: We know that there was significant economic growth during this time, and we know that a process of political consolidation was under-way. However, it is not clear whether political consolidation (that pro-duces economic growth) should be understood as an indicator of political development, political decline, or just plain political stability.

The Bracero Program

The Bracero Program was established to secure a stable flow of labor for American employers, mostly in the agricultural sector; with time it was seen as a useful vehicle for limiting undocumented or irregular immigration. From an international and historical perspective, the num-bers involved were modest, especially when seen as a percentage of the Mexican population: averaging about 0.88 per mil over the entire (1947–76) period. Obviously, if we add the number of irregular immigrants to the mix, the numbers increase, but they do so in inverse proportion to the comparative value of the exercise.

It is not necessary to go into all the legal twists and turns of the Bracero Program, even though it is a fascinating exercise in (good?) neigh-borly negotiations (see García y Griego 1988 for the play-by-play). It is sufficient to note the degree of control exhibited by the countries on both sides of the border. Although the balance of power between the countries changed over time, the desire to regulate these flows (with the hopes of deterring irregular migrants) remained constant.

The original arrangement tended to favor the Mexican government. The U.S. government was the formal employer of the workers, and negotiations were aimed to ensure that they received adequate wages and protection from mistreatment in the United States. The program was so tightly managed that braceros signed a contract requiring them to stay on a given farm, which prevented them from moving freely or seeking work on the open labor market. The Mexican government was able to ensure that braceros would not drain the domestic labor supply by securing guarantees that they would return in time to service the Mexican fields.

The Mexican government's concern with controlling the stream of workers is most evident in the almost continual bickering between the two countries over the placement of bracero recruitment centers in Mexico. The U.S. growers, who were paying for the transportation between those centers and their fields, wanted to locate these centers as close as possible to the border to minimize costs. In contrast, the Mexican authorities argued for the need to recruit braceros from the interior of the country, because unemployment rates were higher there, and northern Mexico needed its farmhands.

The Bracero Program resulted in the export of 4.6 million temporary workers from Mexico. Most braceros ended up in three U.S. states (California, Arizona, and Texas), but a total of 30 states participated in the program. Figure 6.2 provides a glimpse at the relative size of different migrants flows between the 1910 revolution and 1976: The number of braceros towered over the number of registered emigrants and the number of Mexicans formally removed from the United States. The latter measure can be used as a surrogate indicator for the size of the undocumented or irregular migration flow from Mexico into the United States. That statistic indicates that the Bracero Program was relatively effective in constraining the number of irregular emigrants from Mexico; we also know that the number of irregulars increased substantially after the Bracero Program ended. Indeed, despite successive amendments to the U.S. Immigration and Nationality Act (in 1965, 1976, 1978, and 1980) – each of which was intended to restrict Mexican immigration – the number of legal immigrants rose from 38,000 in 1964 to 67,000 in 1986; over the same period gross undocumented migration is estimated to have grown from 87,000 to 3.8 million entries per year (Durand et al. 1999: 519).

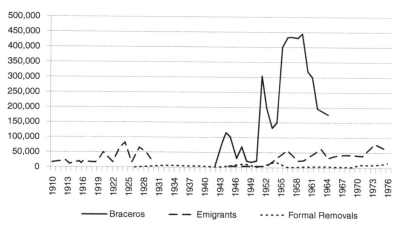

FIGURE 6.2. Mexican Emigration to the United States, 1910–76. *Sources:* Garcia y Griego (1988: 87, 205); and DHS (2009, 2010). *Note:* Braceros are the number of registered braceros (Mexican count); Formal Removals refers to the combined number of Mexicans excluded and deported from the United States; and Emigrants refers to the official Mexican immigration figures from the U.S. Department of Homeland Security.

At the national level in Mexico, the numbers of emigrants alone between 1947–76 were insufficient to create the sort of pressure that we associate with political development. The share of the Mexican population that emigrated freely was relatively small (0.88 per mil), as shown in Table 6.1. If we add the regulated flows associated with the Bracero Program, the level of Mexican emigration jumps into the next category, and Mexico becomes a medium-emigration state.[3] Given the highly regulated nature of the program, it is possible to identify the source of bracero workers and then look for signs of political repercussions in those regions. In short, although the Bracero Program did not seem to have a positive effect on political developments measured at the national level of aggregation, these effects may be more evident at lower levels of aggregation.

Table 6.2 describes the share of Mexican emigrants to the United States, by Mexican state of origin, for a sampling of years preceding, during, and after the Bracero Program was in place. Here we see that most emigration occurred from a handful of states, with four states in the north central part of the country being particularly involved: Guanajuato,

---

[3] By combining the bracero and emigration numbers, the decade averages corresponding to Table 6.1 are as follows: 1947–56 = 7.11; 1957–66 = 7.55; 1967–76 = 1.28; and average 1947–76 = 5.31.

TABLE 6.2. *Share of Mexican Emigrants to the United States, by Region and State of Origin (%)*

	1926–32	1944	1964
Historic Region	44.0	54.0	56.1
Aguascalientes	1.5	2.3	3.0
Colima	0.2	0.0	0.0
Durango	2.2	3.1	4.1
Guanajuato	10.3	13.8	11.1
Jalisco	14.2	6.5	6.7
Michoacán	9.4	18.7	16.3
Nayarit	0.3	0.4	2.2
San Luis Potosí	1.6	2.9	3.9
Zacatecas	4.3	6.3	8.8
Other regions	66.0	46.0	43.9
Total	100	100	100

Source: Durand et al. (2001: 110).

Jalisco, Michoacán, and Zacatecas (these regions are italicized in Table 6.2). Although each of these regions sent a sizable proportion of emigrants to the United States before the Bracero Program went into effect, the share of emigrants dropped off in the state of Jalisco, whereas it rose in the other three states, after the program was introduced (see the 1944 statistics).

As I have only patchy data on the actual number of braceros being sent from each region in a given year (e.g., Sandos and Cross 1983: 45),[4] and I do not have regional population figures at these points of time, we cannot see how important this emigration was, relative to the state population. However, it is possible to find sporadic references to problems of emigrants undermining the local labor supply. For example, we know that the governors of Jalisco, Guanajuato, and Michoacán prohibited bracero contracting between 1943 and 1944 out of fear that it would erode the local labor supply. Officials in other regions (e.g., Coahuila, México, and Baja California) adopted similar measures (Fitzgerald 2006: 275).

Because the allocation of bracero permits was the responsibility of the Mexican government (first through the Bureau of Migratory Farm Labor Affairs and after 1953 through a new federal Labor Exchange

[4] To give the reader an idea of the numbers involved, we can take a sampling from the end of the Bracero Program in 1960–4. We know that Michoacán received 143,527 bracero permits, whereas Guanajuato received 132,263, Jalisco 110,054, and Zacatecas got 91,831 (Sandos and Cross 1983: 45).

Office), the government was able to transform them into political capital. In principle, these permits were to be allocated on the basis of need (i.e., unemployment rates) to state governors, who would then distribute them to local authorities.

From the government's perspective, the Bracero Program was part and parcel of a larger modernization drive, the explicit contents of which dovetail nicely with our expectations, as described in Chapter 3. Experienced agricultural hands, currently unemployed, would be sent to the United States with the expectation that they would return home transformed. The government expected these braceros, having left as simple peasants, to return as small, independent, skilled, and capitalized farmers (see, e.g., D. Cohen 2001, 2006, 2011):

> The government suggested that migrants working in the technologically superior United States would learn modern agricultural skills and be exposed to 'modern' values and habits. It also touted the Program's forced saving plan as promoting modernization. Returning migrants would buy modern machinery with money they had saved, ultimately enabling returning braceros to not only modernize production on their own land but to promote this process gradually throughout Mexican agriculture (D. Cohen 2001: 113–14).

Even *El Popular*, the official newspaper of the Confederation of Mexican Workers, was riding the modernist bandwagon: It proclaimed that, having served in el Norte as "citizens on a mission," these agents of change were coming home "to serve a fighting brigade in the struggle for Mexico's economic awakening."[5]

Such, at least, was the rhetoric. In practice, the Bracero Program offered just another means for the governing party to spread its political reach. The work of Cross and Sandos (1981; Sandos and Cross 1983) documents the selective allocation of bracero permits and shows how they were used to placate regions that were unable to participate in the larger agricultural reforms, tied to the Green Revolution. The rewards of modern agricultural reform went to those with large landholdings, water, rural infrastructure, new seed strains, and credit – features that were distinctly lacking in the most prominent sending states: Durango, Guanajuato, Jalisco, Michoacán, San Luis Potosí, and Zacatecas (Sandos and Cross 1983: 50–1).

Instead what these sending states had to offer was a history of political uprising (in the form of the Cristero Movement) and a growing level of dissatisfaction, now solidified in a new radical movement. The

---

[5] *El Popular* (Mexico City), October 21, 1944. Cited in Snodgrass (nd: 17).

Sinarquismo movement was propelled by the realization that the 1910 revolution had impoverished central Mexico: This area had been especially hard hit by the land reform, the violence of the revolution, and the government's subsequent inability to provide water, credit, and technical assistance for agricultural development. Central Mexico represented the biggest threat to internal stability as the PNS (*Partido Nacional Sinarquista*) grew rapidly, claiming 50,000 *Sinarquistas* in 1941 and more than 900,000 by 1944 (Sandos and Cross 1983: 51)!

In effect, the government used the allocation of bracero permits as a means to secure political support in these unstable regions. As these permits made their way down the chain of government (from the central government, to state governments, to local magistrates), they could be used to reward political allegiance and strengthen party ties. Because workers often obtained a permit in exchange for a bribe, bracero permits became a fountain of political and financial capital for whoever controlled their allocation.[6]

Thus the Mexican government allocated bracero permits to meet two related objectives: to pacify a region prone to political revolt and to secure political support in that region. Emigration was offered as a palliative for 30 years of previous political turmoil: More than 50% of the permits went to a region of the country with only 23% of Mexico's rural population. "The Mexican government gave the people of Durango, Guanajuato, Jalisco, Michoacán, San Luis Potosí, and Zacatecas twice as many opportunities to work in the US as it gave to any other area" (Sandos and Cross 1983: 44). By directing the flow of braceros through local and regional administrative offices (and allowing these local officials to collect bribes on these activities, the national government was able to purchase the loyalty of local officials.[7] This reading is consistent with that of other researchers: The PRI system "is at once tragic and brilliant: Tragic in that

---

[6] Having a permit was not enough, in itself, to secure a job in the United States. A worker with a permit still needed to show up at one of the designated migration centers, where a further selection process occurred (and a new round of bribing began). Local officials sold places in line, and workers with permits had to compete with those who did not (so-called *libres*). Those who ran out of money might work on large local farms (for a short period at very low wages to pay the bribe) in order to secure a job in the United States (Sandos and Cross 1983: 54).

[7] See also Snodgrass (nd: 21–3), who is skeptical of the argument that quotas were allocated to placate political radicalism, because states such as Guerrero and Morelos were subjected to military repression (rather than bracero quotas) to deal with their own problem with growing agrarian radicalism. However, Snodgrass does buy the political machine argument and adds evidence of its effect.

it forces citizens to accept massive corruption, low levels of government service, and highly inefficient policies; brilliant in that it forces citizens not only to accept these features, but to play their role in maintaining the system" (Diaz-Cayeros et al., 2000: 2–3).

In the Mexican case it seems that the highly regulated nature of the exchange allowed the government to turn the tables on our expected political effects. Under these conditions, emigrants were unable to exploit their enhanced bargaining position, because the government could direct the exit option to its advantage – strengthening its relative position vis-à-vis Mexican peasants and workers.

Although we cannot be certain that this result is an artifact of the international system and the highly regulated manner of this labor exchange regime, most other aspects of the pressure we saw in the Norwegian case (in Chapter 5) are evident in Mexico. In particular, it is not difficult to find evidence among Mexico's political elites that emigration was understood to be a sign of political failure:

[T]he failure of the Revolution to provide social justice, the failure of agrarian reform to provide everyone with an adequate parcel of land, the failure of the growing economy to absorb the labor force, the failure of Mexico, as a nation, to provide an attractive place for her children to stay. Mexican workers were only incidentally a labor drain; they were, first and foremost, prodigal sons. These are not reasons to oppose emigration *per se*, but they were employed to argue that the Mexican government had no business in promoting emigration by recruiting workers to be sent abroad (García y Griego 1988: 103).

Indeed, in his dissertation, García y Griego references a number of editorials in Mexico's leading newspapers to conclude that there was almost unanimity among Mexican elite opinion at the end of Bracero Program: The problem of emigration was social and economic, and the appropriate response was to improve the welfare of the rural poor, not to employ punitive or police measures to keep emigration at bay (García y Griego 1988: 751).

However, this widespread recognition that emigration was being driven by political, economic, and social inadequacies did not seem to influence the government's attitude or policy. The outcry we see in the Mexican headlines in the mid-1950s was fueled by a concern that the Mexican government was employing force to restrict the flow of undocumented workers. In mid-February 1954, the Mexican president's office launched a number of vague plans for economic development (earmarked mostly for the northern part of the country), but there appeared to be little concerted effort to improve the political and social conditions that were fueling the exodus.

The reason for this lack of effort may have been that the voices of any potential opposition had already been co-opted: Local politicians, labor organizers, and peasant representatives were participating in a system whose very substance drew from the exploitation of emigrants.

Conclusion

The Mexican experience under the Bracero Program contrasts strongly with what we saw in the Norwegian case in an earlier and more liberal international regime. In Mexico, the Bracero Program coincided with a period of significant economic growth (a Mexican Miracle!). Yet it was also a period of political stability, even stagnation, under which a single political party was able to secure its hegemonic grip on the Mexican body politic. In Norway, political entrepreneurs could exploit the precarious position of emigrant crofters: Their misery could be exchanged for political capital as parties competed for their votes and vied for political authority.

Three factors explain why the Norwegian case differs so much from the Mexican. The first is simple numbers: The percentage of Norwegians emigrating was much larger than in Mexico, even under the Bracero Program. The second factor is the nature of the international regime in place. Before WWI there was no discussion about how to forcefully restrict emigration (and thus bleed off pressure for political change). The third factor concerns the nature of the national political landscape. The Norwegian context was one of political competition: Because of their growing influence that resulted from the threat of exit, workers and crofters found a voice in new political parties that were willing (and able) to challenge the status quo. As a consequence of these three important factors, Norwegian workers and peasants could wield a real threat of exit and an opportunity to channel voice in an effective manner.

In Mexico, by contrast, the government was able (and at times even willing) to employ its authority to physically deter any threat of exit. The emigration that was permitted was channeled in ways that allowed the authorities to strengthen their position vis-à-vis those groups that we expect to be helped by emigration. In addition, the stream of Mexicans did not reach a level that could threaten political authority. Whenever labor shortages popped up, the government jumped in to relieve the pressure by either restricting emigration forcefully or rerouting it from other sources. In short, the Mexican authorities took cover in an international system that allowed them to control the pressure exerted by emigrants. As a consequence, emigration was used as a release valve on the Mexican pressure cooker.

EUROPE

My interest in the European case can be traced to an important book from the late 1960s: Charles Kindleberger's *Europe's Postwar Growth: The Role of Labor Supply*. Kindleberger (1967) employs a Lewis-based growth model (as introduced in Chapter 3) to explain Europe's remarkable economic growth after 1950. He argues that Europe's growth was fueled by its access to additional sources of labor. In some countries, this labor was delivered by a high rate of natural increase (e.g., in the Netherlands); in other countries this labor came from rural emigration into Europe's growing cities (e.g., in Germany, France, and Italy); and in other countries the additional labor was supplied by international immigration (e.g., France, Germany, and Switzerland). Those European countries without access to additional labor reserves (Britain, Belgium, and Scandinavia) suffered lower growth rates in the immediate postwar period.

Kindleberger was not interested in migration alone, nor was he especially interested in the effects that emigration had on the sending regions/countries that supplied Europe with the labor it craved. However, he does note, with an appropriate degree of caution, that the main labor exporters (Greece, Spain, Portugal, Turkey, and southern Italy) had experienced some economic gain from the relationship (save Turkey): "Bloodletting need not be stimulating. Exodus can lead to collapse and ghost communities. . . . Providing it does not go too far, however, the loss of excess supplies of labor can speed up the growth process" (1967: 106).[8]

Kindleberger's analysis raises two important issues. First, as in North America, a formal, heavily regulated arrangement facilitated international

---

[8] This is not the place to engage Kindleberger's (tempered) claims about the economic benefits from exporting Europe's guest workers. Yet I hasten to note that political economists were starting to cast a more critical eye on these efforts in the years that followed. See, e.g., Böhning (1975: 251), OECD (1975), and Lucas (1981).

labor mobility in postwar Europe. The second issue is more significant, but escaped Kindleberger's otherwise watchful eye (to be fair, it came about after Kindleberger published *Europe's Postwar Growth*). Although Kindleberger noted the apparent economic gains derived by the sending countries of Greece, Portugal, and Spain (and the absence of those gains in Turkey), our attention should be drawn to the fact that these three countries are the very ones that propelled Huntington's third wave of democratization (as described in Chapter 4).

Is this just another coincidence of history? Or is there an underlying connection between the role that these countries played as labor exporters to a growing European economy and their subsequent democratization? How do these experiences mesh with the account in Mexico?

The Guest-Worker Program in Europe

It is estimated that between 20 and 30 million people participated in this large-scale experiment in labor migration (Rogers 1985b: 3). In the first three decades after the war, the vast majority of emigrants left expecting to return home after a relatively short stay abroad (Rogers 1985b: 12). European employers and their sponsoring states expected the same: This labor was meant to be secured on a temporary basis. With time, of course, Europeans came to realize that, although they had asked for a temporary workforce, they got men instead (to paraphrase the Swiss author, Max Frisch).

An intricate weave of international agreements supported this network of supposedly temporary and mobile workers. In Europe, two international organizations were particularly important for setting the legal context that paved a path for subsequent guest-worker emigration. In 1953, the Organization for European Economic Cooperation (OEEC, subsequently the OECD) adopted a rule that facilitated movement across member states: When a job opened up, native workers were given priority for a specified period of time (usually four weeks), after which foreign workers were allowed to compete on an equal footing with native workers. Four years later, in 1957, the European Community's Treaty of Rome also embraced the free movement of labor (alongside the free movement of goods, capital, and services). Just as importantly, in securing these rights, the Rome Treaty did not distinguish between the treatment accorded to member state workers and to nonmember state workers. This made it easier for foreign workers to secure jobs (and rights) in Europe.

TABLE 6.3. *Bilateral Guest-Worker Agreements in Europe, by Year Signed*

	Austria	Belgium	France	Netherlands	Sweden	W. Germany
Algeria		1970	1962			
Greece		1957				1960
Italy		1946	1946			1955
Morocco		1964	1963	1969		1963
Portugal			1963			1964
Spain		1956	1961			1960
Tunisia		1969				1965
Turkey	1964	1964	1965	1964	1967	1961
Yugoslavia		1970	1965			1968

Note: This table is meant to be illustrative, not exhaustive.
Sources: Heisler (1985: 474); Abadan-Unat (1995: 279); and de Haas (2005: 7).

The Treaty of Rome established the European Community (EC), which at first was limited to just six states.[9] Of the labor-exporting countries, only Italy was an original signatory state, and most of its labor came from the southern and most impoverished part of the peninsula. Greece and Turkey were associate members of the EC and thus entitled to membership privileges (without reciprocal obligations). Spain and Portugal had not yet negotiated associate status, but had made separate treaties with individual member states to secure access.

Yet even states without formalized relationship to the EC were able to secure access for their emigrant workers. Indeed, a network of bilateral guest-worker agreements crisscrossed Europe, as shown in Table 6.3. In this table we can also see that Europe's labor needs were being supplied by a much larger number of sending states than those named in Kindleberger's study: Algeria, Morocco, Tunisia, and Yugoslavia also secured access to the European labor market.

These bilateral agreements solidified a regulatory framework that was clearly controlled by the *receiving* country. Of all the sending countries, only Algeria seemed to have managed to maintain any influence over the number and type of workers allowed to emigrate (Heisler 1985: 476). The other sending countries simply supplied the type and number of workers requested by the receiving states. In this way too, the European arrangement was quite different from what we saw in North America.

[9] In 1975, the EC had nine member states, three of which had joined in 1973 (Britain, Denmark, and Ireland). The original treaty states were Belgium, France, Italy, Luxembourg, the Netherlands, and West Germany. Greece joined in 1981, Portugal and Spain in 1986, and Turkey applied in 1987.

Employers in Switzerland (before the 1970s) were the least regulated: They were allowed to contract directly with foreign workers, who
were then granted a work and residency permit. As Swiss xenophobia
increased, however, so too did the number of regulations and stipulations.
British immigration was also characterized by a more liberal regime at
the time, as Britain's Commonwealth workers enjoyed legal access to the
British labor market. However, in most of Europe, the immigrant flow
was controlled and managed by government offices that decided which
types of workers and how many were needed.[10] Even so, compared to the
Bracero Program, European guest workers enjoyed much greater freedom
of movement.

Sending-Country Characteristics

To gauge the potential political effects of guest-worker emigration, we
need to begin by defining the universe of cases. It would be too convenient
and potentially misleading to look only at the cases that Kindleberger has
(cherry) picked for us.

Table 6.4, drawing from Papademetriou (1978: 379), provides us with
a standardized point of departure. Papademetriou lists the size of the foreign population in different European countries in 1975, the conventional
end point of the European guest-worker programs. From these figures, we
can get an idea of how important the accumulation of annual emigration
(i.e., the stock of emigrants) was for any given country.

From Table 6.4 we can see that only two sending states (Austria and
Finland) were not located around the Mediterranean basin, and these
states supplied relatively few workers to a limited market (in mostly
Germany and Sweden, respectively). We can also see that the United
Kingdom was bringing in many foreigners from across the Commonwealth (mostly from the Caribbean, Pakistan, and India) – witness the
large "other" category in the U.K. column – but these flows were related
less to labor market demand and more to Britain's postcolonial policy
(see, e.g., Anwar 1995; Spencer 1997).

What remains are nine states hugging the Mediterranean coastline:
Algeria, Greece, Italy, Morocco, Portugal, Spain, Tunisia, Turkey, and

---

[10] For example, in Germany, this role was played by the Federal Labor Institute, whereas in
France it was played by the National Immigration Office. Employers in these countries
turned to these organizations to supply them with the foreign workers needed. See
Martin and Miller (1980: 317).

TABLE 6.4. *Migrants in Europe by Countries of Origin/Destination, December 1975*

	Austria	Belgium	France	Germany	Luxembourg	Netherlands	Sweden	Switzerland	UK	Total
Algeria		3,000	420,000	2,000			200		500	425,700
Austria				78,000				21,000		99,000
Finland							103,000			103,000
Greece		8,000	5,000	212,000		2,000	8,000		56,500	237,500
Italy	2,000	85,000	210,000	318,000	10,700	10,000	2,500	281,000	1,000	975,700
Morocco		60,000	165,000	18,000		28,000	500		4,000	272,500
Portugal		3,000	430,000	70,000	12,500	5,000	1,000	4,000	15,500	529,500
Spain		30,000	250,000	132,000	1,900	18,000	2,000	72,000		521,400
Tunisia			90,000	15,000		1,000	200			106,200
Turkey	26,200	10,000	35,000	582,000		38,000	4,000	16,000	1,500	712,700
Yugoslavia	136,000	3,000	60,000	436,000	600	10,000	23,000	24,000	3,500	696,100
Other		76,000	235,000	328,000	21,100	104,000	60,000	135,000	690,000	1,670,100

Source: Papademetriou (1978: 379). Reprinted with permission.

Yugoslavia. Of these, Italy is a somewhat special case in at least two regards: (1) It was the only EC member state at the time, and 2) its economy was divided between a relatively prosperous northern region and a relatively poor southern region. The Italian emigration stream came mainly from the southern region, but the statistics are collected at the national level, which problematizes the analysis.

How, then, can we see whether emigration facilitated political development in these very different countries? Some of these countries had long traditions of emigration (Spain, Italy, Portugal), whereas others did not (Turkey). Some emerged out of collapsing empires (Turkey and Yugoslavia), whereas others just recently broke free from their colonial ties (Algeria, Morocco, Tunisia). Some of the countries were already democratic (Italy); others were state socialist (Yugoslavia), one-party states (Turkey), or outright authoritarian (Spain, Greece, and Portugal). We also know that this handful of counties was scattered across the emigration rankings in Table 6.1: Algeria was a high-emigration country; Italy, Portugal, and Greece were medium-emigration countries; and Morocco, Spain, Yugoslavia, and Turkey were low-emigration countries.

The best way to sort through these sundry variables is to list the relevant country attributes in a table to facilitate comparisons. Table 6.5 allows us to sketch out the more visible patterns.

On the left part of Table 6.5 we find three political variables: Column 1 reports the nature of the regime in 1950, column 2 lists the regime type in 1979, and column 3 reports the change in Polity score from 1950 to 1979.[11] The countries are then ranked mostly by their change in Polity score.[12] Of course, not every country experienced linear political development over this time – some countries experienced some improvements and then setbacks over time – but this score gives us a rough indicator of political developments during the era of guest-worker

[11] In 1980 there were radical changes in both Turkey and Yugoslavia, which were not especially representative of the period under consideration. For this reason, the change index was limited to 1950–79. If we included 1980, then Turkey's Polity Change score would drop from +2 to −13, and Yugoslavia's would change from 0 to +2.

[12] The Vanhanen index was not used, because many of these states were not democratic in 1950. For those colonies that enter the dataset only after their independence, I used the first score in the dataset for measuring Polity change (e.g., in Morocco, Polity change is from 1956 to 1979). Italy is moved up in the ranking, because its Polity score was pegged out at the maximum (+10) in 1950 and remained there throughout the period. Thus, if Italy had experienced political development, it could not have been traced by the Polity indicator. However, Italy's political development is traceable in the Vanhanen indicator, as described later in the text.

TABLE 6.5. *Characteristics of Europe's Guest-Worker Sending States*

	(1) Regime Type 1950	(2) Regime Type 1979	(3) Polity Change	(4) Emigrant Stock	(5) Population Growth	(6) Economic Growth	(7) GNI/ Capita	(8) Export Share	Signal Dates
Portugal	Autocracy	Democracy	18	0.060	0.5	4.6	3,111	0.002	Democracy 1974
Spain	Autocracy	Democracy	16	0.015	0.9	4.1	5,958	0.001	Democracy 1975
Greece	Autocracy	Democracy	4	0.026	0.7	4.8	5,831	0.001	Democracy 1974
Italy	Democracy	Democracy	0	0.017	0.5	3.2	8,182	0.003	Hot Autumn 1969
Turkey	Autocracy	One-party state	2	0.018	2.4	3.6	2,031	0.001	Military coups 1960, 1971, 1980
Morocco	Colony	Autocracy	1	0.016	2.6	2.7	1,036	0.003	Independence 1956
Tunisia	Colony	Autocracy	0	0.018	2.2	4.7	1,363	0.004	Independence 1956
Yugoslavia	State socialist	State socialist	0	0.033	0.9	5.2	3,435	0.003	Tito dies 1980
Algeria	Colony	Autocracy	−1	0.025	2.9	4.2	2,186	0.004	Independence 1962

Notes: Polity Change (column 3) is the change in Polity indicator from 1950 to 1979; Emigrant Stock (4) is the total foreign population of the country living in Europe in 1975 (the last column in Table 6.4) divided by the country's population in 1975; Population Growth (5) is the annual population growth rate 1960–88; Economic Growth (6) is measured as the average annual growth in GNP per capita, 1965–80; GNI/Capita (7) is the 1980 gross national income, per capita, at current prices in U.S. dollars; and Export Share (8) is the annual average export to the core 6 EC countries from 1956–80, divided by the country's 1980 GDP (current U.S. dollars).

Sources: Polity Change: CSP (2009); Emigrant Stock: Papademetriou (1978: 379) and *UN Demographic Yearbook 1975* (1975: 142–8); Population Growth: UNDP (1990: 166–7); Economic Growth: UNDP (1990: 166–7); GNI/Capita: UNDATA (2010); and Export Share: IMF (2003) and UNDATA (2010).

migration.[13] Here we see that the top three countries (Portugal, Spain, and Greece) had become democratic by 1979. Italy's democratic status remained unchanged in the Polity score, but it enjoyed a significant increase in the Vanhanen indicator during this time (from 29.6 in 1950 to 40 in 1979). At the bottom of the table we see that Turkey, Morocco, Tunisia, Yugoslavia and Algeria had mixed experiences (some improvements, some setbacks), but none of these labor-exporting countries were able to secure substantial political development, as measured by the Polity indicator.

The right-hand side of the table lists a number of variables that might be used to explain this change in political development. These variables include the relative size of the emigrant population, the rate of population growth, the pace of economic growth, and the share of exports going to the core six EC countries (as a percentage of GDP).

What can we glean from this table? To begin with, we can see that emigration alone is not a determining factor for explaining political development. Although the size of the emigrant stock is roughly correlated with political development, there are cases of political development with relatively small emigrant influence (e.g., Greece) alongside cases with no significant political development, despite significant emigration (e.g., Yugoslavia). This finding is not surprising, of course, because we did not expect emigration to be the sole determinant of political development.

The second column is more interesting. Population growth alone is not a good predictor of political change, but it seems to work well in league with emigration. In particular, states that experienced democratization tended to have low rates of population growth, combined with high rates of emigration (note, again, the Yugoslavian exception). This is the opposite of what we saw in the Mexican case, which had relatively low rates of emigration with high rates of population growth: Indeed, Mexico's population growth for the same period (1960–88) was the same as Algeria's (2.9%; UNDP 1990: 167). Alternatively, those states in the bottom half of the table experienced high rates of population growth and low levels of emigration (except, as noted, Yugoslavia). In short, from these two

---

[13] For example, the table obscures Turkey's turbulent political development during this time, when it experienced three military coups; it vacillates on the Polity score: from +7 (1950–3), to +4 (1954–9), to +7 (1960), to +9 (1961–4), to +8 (1965–70), to −2 (1971–2), to +9 (1973–9). In the following year (1980), Turkey's score fell to −5. The 1950 reference in the table (one-party state) is to the regime before the election victory of the Democratic Party in May 1950. See Karpat (1972) for a description of events during the early period.

columns, it would seem that political development occurs in those countries that experience high levels of emigration, combined with relatively low rates of population growth. This general trend provides support for our initial hunch that it is the relative size of the emigration stream that matters – and it may be an indication that the remaining labor force in these sending countries (Portugal, Spain, Greece, and Italy) was better positioned to exploit its position because its relative strength as a class (vis-à-vis capital) was on the rise in these states.

On its own, economic growth (column 6) is surprisingly poor at explaining political development. Yugoslavia scores the highest growth rate for the period, and Tunisia's growth rate was nothing to sneeze at. Yet Italy's growth rate is among the lowest on the table (but above Morocco's). In short, in this small sample, democratization is not explained by higher economic growth rates. Less surprising is what is revealed in column 7: Here we see that democratization is related to wealth, because the four most democratizing countries enjoy higher per-capita income than the nondemocratizing countries (except Yugoslavia, again).

The most surprising finding in the table is in column 8, which shows the relative importance of exports to the core EC countries. We might expect the young democracies (Portugal, Spain, Greece) to have increasingly strong economic ties with the core EC states (ties that included not only emigration but also investment and trade flows), that the political development of these sending states was derived from a stronger economic (and political) engagement with the EC, and that it would be difficult to distinguish the emigration effect from the other economic integration effects. Yet the export share column in Table 6.5 suggests otherwise: Here we see that those states with the strongest export relationship to the EC (Algeria, Tunisia, Yugoslavia, Morocco, and Italy) are those states that experienced the least political development (and, except for Italy, did not manage to democratize).

Of course, there is a great deal of history underlying Table 6.5, and I would very much like to dive into each of these cases to trace out the causal mechanisms involved. Additional study might reveal why Yugoslavia appears as a frequent outlier. Similarly, it would be interesting to examine the Italian case in more detail. We know, for example, that the emigration of workers from southern to northern Italy and abroad resulted in labor shortages and changes in investment sites during the "Hot Autumn" of 1969 (Ascoli 1985: 191–3). It would also be interesting to look at the way in which the newly independent states in Africa chose different emigration strategies vis-à-vis their old colonial masters. For example, in postcolonial Algeria, the state first tried to manage the emigrant flow and then cut it off altogether in 1975 (Heisler 1985: 476–7). In postcolonial Morocco, by contrast, the state consistently encouraged emigration as an explicit tool to manage domestic unemployment levels (Fargues 2004: 1359). Most of all, it would be interesting to contrast the Algerian and Mexican cases more directly, because Algeria was the only sending state in this sample that managed to control the size and the nature of its emigrant outflows – and Algeria, like Mexico, did not experience political development.

Yet the scope of this research project is meant to be exploratory, and we are forced to shove aside these temptations. With the notable exception of Yugoslavia, Europe's guest-worker states reveal a relationship among emigration, population growth, wealth, and political development. This relationship seems to suggest that emigration improved the relative strength of labor (as a class) in Portugal, Spain, and Greece and that this influence was exerted to bring about political development. The Italian case is more difficult to analyze, because although we would expect to find the effects in southern Italy, we have no means of netting out that effect. The remaining emigrant states (minus Yugoslavia) experienced relatively high levels of population growth, so that the rise in emigration was not able to change the underlying class balance in these countries. Perhaps this is the reason that these states were unable to realize political development.

CONCLUSION

World War II and the immediate postwar period introduced two very different guest-worker programs in North America and Europe. Although the international context was one in which migration was severely restricted (compared to before WWI), these arrangements provided these two growing economies with a managed and limited supply of temporary workers. In North America, the Bracero Program produced little notable effect on Mexican political development. By contrast, a handful of states in southern Europe did manage to secure significant political development while participating in a managed emigration regime.

By comparing results of these two experiments with guest-worker programs, we again find that the relationship between emigration and political development is neither simple nor direct. Instead, the political effects of emigration appear to be contingent on other, more contextual variables. In particular, three contextual factors seem to matter during the period.

The first concerns the international regime and the degree of control that the regime provided individual states. In Mexico, the Bracero Program allowed the authorities to manipulate the emigration stream in a way that benefited established political elites and interests, at the expense of workers and peasants. Because the international context did not allow for other emigrant opportunities, the Mexican threat of exit was severely constrained. As a result, progressive political forces were unable to exploit the political leverage that might have resulted from greater, or freer, emigration streams. Although I have not been able to explore the link in any detail, a similar correlation – between heavy state control of the emigrant flow and negative or stagnant political development – is evident in Algeria. Clearly, however, more research is necessary to examine whether such a connection is merely coincidental or spurious.

The second evident factor concerns the role played by demographic pressure. Like the first factor, this is not surprising in that we expect the effects of emigration to work, in part, through the relative influence of the labor force that remains. That strength is determined only partly by emigration; natural demographic growth plays an even more important role in this regard. In these cases from the immediate postwar period, we find that the effects of emigration can be leveraged when they exist in a context of relatively modest population growth. In countries with that level of population growth, emigration of a significant number of workers does seem to influence their ability to secure political gains.

Finally, it would seem that the effects of emigration are more potent at a certain level of economic development. With the exception of Portugal, economic development was a factor shared by all the Mediterranean states that experienced political development. Of course, it is possible that political development could have occurred in the absence of emigration in these countries. After all, there is an extensive literature (reviewed in Chapter 3) that has documented this sort of effect, without considering the role of emigration. Yet the Mexican case should prevent a hasty conclusion, because that country's relative wealth and its impressive Mexican Miracle were insufficient in themselves to deliver the expected political gains. The lesson from this chapter must be that Mexico could have enjoyed political development if it had allowed a much higher level of emigration, liberalized that emigration, and secured a lower rate of population growth.

In conclusion, it would seem that the nature of the political effects from emigration turn on a number of contextual variables. Among these, the nature of the international regime (and the consequent opportunities available to emigrants) is an important one. In the next chapter we consider how today's international regime seems to be affecting the nature of this complicated relationship between emigration and political development.

7

Limited Mobility in the World Today

This chapter considers the political effects of international emigration from 1994 to the present. As we have already seen, the contemporary period is characterized by falling global levels of emigration, which implies increased regulation and control of international migration flows. Yet beyond this general impression, because our attention is drawn so easily by any number of captivating examples of individual emigrants' stories in the media, it is difficult to know where to begin a study of recent developments.

To overcome this difficulty and in an attempt to be systematic, this chapter lets the existing data shape our understanding of the general relationship between emigration and political development and then points us to the most interesting cases. These data reveal a fairly strong relationship between emigration and political development in recent years. Perhaps a more surprising result is the discovery that this relationship is most striking in a number of very small (often island) states. Although these states are more exposed to the pressures of international emigration, they seem be able to leverage this exposure to generate better than expected political returns (given their relative wealth).

To arrive at this conclusion, the chapter is divided into four short sections. The first section considers some of the methodological challenges associated with the study of contemporary emigration. The second section turns to the EMIG 1.2 database used in previous chapters to examine how emigration is related to political development. The third section does the same with a recent UN dataset of emigration stocks. This dataset proves to be especially useful, because it covers a much larger sample of countries in a more systematic fashion than does the EMIG 1.2. On the basis of analyses conducted with these two datasets, the fourth section looks more closely at the experiences of those very small states that experienced the highest levels of emigration in recent years.

METHODOLOGICAL REFLECTIONS

In approaching the study of recent emigration trends, I have had to deal with the threat of potential sampling bias related to perceptions of the scope of international migration and the most relevant or important sources of that emigration. Obviously, these types of bias also existed in analyzing earlier periods of emigration, but the passage of time allows much analytical dust to settle, so that the more prominent contours of the relationship become visible. This sort of conceptual settling has yet to occur in the contemporary data, so our attention is easily drawn to particular and often spectacular (but not necessarily representative) events.

From the evidence presented in Chapter 4, we know that the level of international emigration has been falling in recent years. However, politicians, public officials, and media editors do not seem to be aware of this fact, and our newspapers are filled with stories of the developed world's borders under threat and international migration run rampant. Of course, the EMIG 1.2 database does not include measures of undocumented or irregular migration, so we can expect some disconnect between its findings and public outcries about levels of international migration. Yet in a highly politicized context like ours, researchers need to be especially cautious about generalizing on the basis of what appear to be common truths in the eyes of politicians and their countries' media.

It is not just perceptions of the level of emigration that can be swayed by public discourse. Our attention is easily drawn to those cases that generate the most hype, even if they are neither unique nor analytically relevant. I must admit to being guilty in this regard, as my initial research design for this chapter was driven by two very visible examples of contemporary emigration: migration within the European Union (EU) and from South Asia to the Gulf region.

At the turn of the millennium, politicians began pushing for a radical liberalization of European markets, encouraging millions of migrants to move from one end of the EU to the other. This movement has generated much political heat as established member states erected a number of temporary barriers to keep emigrant workers from new (eastern and southern) member states at bay.[1] In this political context, the Polish immigrant worker has secured almost legendary status. Reading contemporary European newspapers, which contain many accounts of labor markets across northern Europe being inundated by cheap but highly skilled Polish workers, one could easily get the impression that the Polish exodus was particularly onerous.

In South Asia, another migration phenomenon has also received much attention. Here we have learned about several states that encourage the export of their domestic labor force as part of larger development strategies. Governments from across the region (e.g., Bangladesh, India, Indonesia, the Philippines, Sri Lanka, Thailand, and Vietnam) have encouraged their citizens to seek temporary jobs in the Gulf states (and beyond) in hopes of reducing pressure on the domestic labor market, accessing foreign exchange, and encouraging development. These worker-export programs are supported by government bureaucracies set up to encourage, monitor, and channel workers to foreign jobs. Indeed, the ebb and flow of emigrant workers constitute the only reported emigration figures for many of these states, as we saw in Chapter 4.

Such examples inform public opinion about the nature and scope of international migration. They also mold our expectations as researchers about where to look for relevant examples. My initial intent was to examine the political effects of Polish and South Asian emigration flows, because these cases have drawn so much public attention. Yet the relative size of the emigrant flow in these familiar examples is not particularly large or unusual: The level of Polish emigration is not especially high relative to other countries (either within or outside Europe), nor do the labor-exporting countries of South Asia send out a particularly large share of their workers.[2] Like public perceptions of the overall level of international migration, our perceptions of emigrant origins are swayed too easily by public discourse.

---

[1] Only Sweden, Ireland, the United Kingdom, and Norway allowed immediate access to workers from the 10 new member states in 2004. Every other EU member state introduced temporary restrictions, limiting migration from new member states for up to seven years (i.e., 2011). See Moses (2011b, 2011c).

[2] I do not mean to suggest that we will not find political development in the wake of these emigrant outflows. Indeed, from what we have learned thus far, we can expect to find relatively strong political effects in the Polish case, in which Polish workers find it relatively easy to leave (and return) home. Likewise, we might expect the political effects in the Asian labor-exporting countries to be mixed depending on how large is the exodus and how regulated its departure.

To avoid distractions such as these, it is important to keep one eye firmly on the data. In this respect, contemporary events actually offer promise (not just concern), because additional emigration data have been made available in recent years. The next section uses the EMIG 1.2 dataset to see if there is a connection between recent emigration patterns and a rough measure of democracy. Like earlier attempts, this rough cut at the data confirms that the relationship between these two variables is, at best, complex. This simple analysis also reveals a shortcoming in the EMIG 1.2 dataset: Many of the high-emigration states depend critically on a limited number of observations.

The third section then introduces a new dataset developed by the UN. This dataset is limited in time, but provides a very rich measure of national emigration rates, based largely on census (stock) data. Most significantly, this dataset includes a number of very small countries that have extremely high levels of emigration.

COMPARATIVE BASELINE: EMIG 1.2

We begin by comparing developments since 1976, using the same variables used in the preceding chapters. Table 7.1 provides an overview of emigration averages from 1976 to 2001. The full table is provided as Appendix V.

Before examining the nature of the relationship between emigration and political development, it is important to draw the reader's attention to an apparent shortcoming of more recent entries in the EMIG 1.2 dataset. As is evident in the "Count" column of Table 7.1, many of the high-emigration states depend very heavily on just a handful of observations. This should raise some cause for concern, because findings will then turn on what are likely to be outlier observations.[3] This problem was noted in previous chapters, but it seems to have worsened in the more recent data. Thus, the decade averages for Jamaica during this period draw from data from just 3 years (1976, 1977, and 1986) – leaving 23 years unaccounted.[4] On closer examination we find that many of the high-emigration states have only outlier observations from a handful of years:

---

[3] As explained in Chapter 5, the alternative is to discard the data or dilute it by averaging out over the entire decade. My main concern is to maximize the amount of data in play, because I suspect that missing data reflect reporting error, not the lack of emigration in a given year. At any rate, readers are advised of the potential problem.

[4] The 1976–7 figures are consistent with an earlier trend, for which we have data. Yet the 1986 figure is huge and irregular (it is not a typo, unless the *Demographic Yearbook* is

Only Sri Lanka, New Zealand, and Iceland draw from full datasets (with the Seychelles reporting a strong 23 observations).

With this important caveat in mind, what patterns do we see in Table 7.1? Four patterns are especially noteworthy. First, there seems to be a strong tendency for significant emigration from small states bordering the Caribbean and in Central America (Jamaica, Dominica, Nicaragua, El Salvador, and Dominican Republic), many of which are also islands. Second, we are beginning to see increased emigration from the more developed states (e.g., France, New Zealand, Switzerland, Ireland, and Iceland), which complicates any attempt to generalize across the developed–developing divide. In fact, we received some forewarning of this trend in Chapter 4, when a statistical analysis revealed a long and inverse lag between democratic development and emigration. Third, the break-up of the USSR increased opportunities for formal emigration from its former states, as evidenced by Kazakhstan and Kyrgyzstan. The last two patterns seem to be confirmed by examples in the medium-emigration group, in which we find other wealthy and former Soviet states (see Appendix V). Finally, the total number of countries included in the dataset has increased from 70 to 78, with most of the new countries in the high-emigration category.[5]

When we turn to the nature of the relationship between emigration and political development, we find scant supporting evidence. By examining a country's level of democracy in 2006, we see that the highest level of emigration is occurring from countries with lower democracy scores: The average democracy score for high-emigration countries was almost 20 (19.9) in that year, whereas the medium- and low-emigration countries enjoyed higher scores: 25 and 22, respectively. Given the large number of developed states experiencing emigration (in both the high- and medium-emigration groups), it is problematic to depict the relationship between emigration and political development in simple or linear terms. This complexity is also evident in the relationship between

---

wrong) and is extremely high (about 213/1000). In particular, 508,816 people were registered to have emigrated from Jamaica in 1986, at a time when the country's population was 2,390,000. This suggests either an accounting error in the original source or a very special circumstance.

5 In the most recent period, there are 78 total observations, 17 of which were categorized as high emigration, 16 as medium emigration, and 45 as low emigration (i.e., 17/16/45). In the postwar period (1947–76) analysis from Chapter 6, there were 71 observations (11/15/45), whereas in the prewar period analyzed in Chapter 5, there were only 27 total observations (6/8/13).

TABLE 7.1. *Summary of Emigration Flows and Political Development, 1976–2006, EMIG 1.2 Data (per mil, per annum, decade averages)*

	1976–85	1986–95	1996–2001	Period Average	Count	Level of Democracy 2006	Change in Democracy 1976–2006	Population 2005	Population Density 2005
						(19.9)	(6.2)	(10,647,529)	(173)
High Emigration									
Jamaica	15.64	212.89		114.27	3	13.1	2.3	2,668,000	243
Dominica		79.95	99.65	89.80	9	18.2	3.6	67,000	90
Nicaragua		45.21	79.69	62.45	11	24.8	21.6	5,455,000	42
El Salvador		45.51		45.51	3	18	6.1	6,059,000	288
Dominican Rep.	3.20	85.58		44.39	4	17.9	14.2	9,533,000	197
Syria	35.16			35.16	2	6.6	6.5	19,121,000	103
Burkina Faso		31.97		31.97	1	4.9	4.9	13,747,000	50
Seychelles	22.90	24.39	31.27	26.19	23	20.9	11.6	83,000	182
Bahrain			17.27	17.27	1	1.1	1.1	7,281,000	1,048
Kazakhstan		17.76	15.74	16.75	8	4	3.3	15,194,000	6
Sri Lanka	2.48	11.96	35.51	16.65	26	25.3	4.9	19,531,000	298
France	19.85	10.54		15.20	16	31.1	−2.2	61,013,000	111
Kyrgyzstan		12.74	13.05	12.89	10	4.1	1.7	5,221,000	26
New Zealand	15.18	10.23	12.41	12.61	26	32.7	5.1	4,111,000	15

Switzerland	7.89	13.74		10.82	20	41.4	−1	7,441,000	180
Ireland		12.55	7.6	10.08	15	34.1	10.5	4,187,000	60
Iceland	6.70	10.62	7.88	8.40	26	40.4	10.4	296,000	3

Medium Emigration (average)
N = 16   (25.0)   (5.0)   (20,071,813)   (1,463 [108]*)

Low Emigration (average)
N = 45   (22.0)   (9.0)   (62,659,295)   (171)

Notes: Per mil (o/oo) refers to the number of emigrants per 1,000 of the population in the sending (home) state. The Count column captures the number of annual observations recorded for a country during the period under consideration (the maximum count is 26 observations). The Level of Democracy indicator is the Vanhanen index in 2006. The Change in Democracy indicator takes the 2006 Vanhanen index and subtracts from it the 1976 index score. In short, I assume that the direction of change has been constant over the period, even though this was not always the case. For those countries that only came into being (or for which data were available) after 1976, I subtracted the first recorded year from the 2006 tally. *The average population density for medium-emigration countries includes two figures. The larger figure (1,463) is driven by Monaco, which is a serious outlier. When Monaco is removed, the group's average population density drops to 108 people per square kilometer. Bold figures refer to the decade averages that justify their inclusion in each grouping. See text in Chapter 5 for further clarification. See Appendix V for the complete table.

Sources: EMIG 1.2; COW (2002); Vanhanen (2007); and UNPOP (2008).

emigration and change in political development. When we use a measure that captures change in the Vanhanen (democracy) index from 1976 to 2006, we find that low-emigration states experienced the largest increase in political development over the period under consideration: Their democracy index increased nine points on average. Yet here too the relationship is not linear, because high-emigration states experienced a slightly higher increase in political development (6.2), on average, than did medium-emigration states (5.0). In short, there is no clear-cut relationship between political development and emigration in the EMIG 1.2 database.

In light of the initial observation that there are many small countries in the high-emigration group, it is prudent to consider the relationship between the size of the country and its exposure to emigration. As we have seen in earlier chapters, population density is an important contextual variable that can influence the effect of emigration on political development. The last two columns in Table 7.1 list a country's total population and its population density in 2005. Here we find that the high-emigration countries do tend, on average, to have smaller populations (with France as an important exception) and fairly high levels of population density (173, compared to 108 for medium- and 171 for the low-emigration countries).

Given our natural (and, as explained earlier, problematic) familiarity with recent developments, it is interesting to skim through the table and note apparent anomalies and curiosities. Doing so, we find that the labor-exporting countries in South Asia are scattered across the different emigration-level groupings: Only Sri Lanka is listed among the high-emigration countries (and I suspect that the reason for this is related as much to its civil war as to the emigration-encouraging policies of the government). As seen in Appendix V, Bangladesh, India, and Indonesia are ranked among the low-emigration countries (there are no statistics for Vietnam after 1942).

As we know, Europe experienced a significant liberalization of its migration laws during this period, driven mostly by the free-market ambitions of the EU. This change can help explain the number of European states now located in the high- and medium-emigration categories of Table 7.1. (Even though Switzerland, Iceland, and Norway are not members of the EU, they are subject to the same regulations and freedoms associated with the EU through their European Economic Area (EEA), or bilateral treaty, obligations.) In contrast, we might be surprised by the fact that Poland and Albania[6] did not score higher: Poland ranks among the lowest emigration countries, and Albania does not even show up in the EMIG 1.2 database (see Appendix V).

THE 2009 HUMAN DEVELOPMENT REPORT

Fortunately, alternative statistics are available for emigration in recent years, and the most accurate and extensive data have been assembled by the Department of Economic and Social Affairs at the United Nations (UN 2009). Although these data are remarkably thorough, the dataset has its deficiencies – and it is these deficiencies that originally prompted me to construct my own (EMIG) dataset.

In particular, the UN dataset comes packaged in five-year intervals and is limited to the period after 1950 (but with projections into the future). Just as importantly, the emigration figures are based on census data, so they capture emigrant stocks, not flows. These characteristics limit the dataset's utility in examining the effects of emigration over the long arc of history, but the dataset does enjoy several advantages when examining very recent trends. In particular, because the UN does not rely on the willingness of countries to report emigration data, the dataset is very complete: It reports data for each country in the world for a given year (181 observations in 2000/2002; see Table 7.2).

The recent (2009) UNDP Human Development Report (HDR) on Migration, *Overcoming Barriers: Human Mobility and Development*, uses only the most recent emigrant stock figures (around the year 2000) and breaks them down into sending and receiving countries (DRC 2007). Because these are stock figures derived from census data, we can use them to capture the aggregated effects of emigration in a given country at a particular point in time. Thus the 2000–2 emigration figures for a country include all the recent emigrants from that country: They indicate the number of people who are no longer in the country. In other words, the emigration figures in this database aggregate emigration effects and are less susceptible to annual fluctuations.

---

[6] Although the general public may be less aware of the Albanian exodus, it is probably the largest in Europe, even though much of it occurs beyond the view of immigration officials in Greece and the EU. For example, Erind Pajo (2008) suggests that as many as one-fifth of the Albanian population emigrated during the 1990s.

TABLE 7.2. *Summary of Emigration Stocks and Political Development, 1980–2006, UN Data*

Country	(1) Emigration Stock 2000–2, %	(2) HDI 2007	(3) Change in HDI 1980–2006	(4) Level of Democracy 2006	(5) Change in Democracy 1976–2006	(6) Political Rights 2009	(7) Change in Political Rights 1976–2009	(8) Population 2007
		(0.810)	(0.034)	(21.0)	(6.4)	(2.2)	(0.8)	(1,295,000)
High Emigration								
Antigua & Barbuda	45.3	0.868	0.008	25.8	13.4	3	−1	100,000
Saint Kitts & Nevis	44.3	0.838	0.006	22.3	3.5	1	1	100,000
Grenada	40.3	0.813	0.001	21.9	3.9	1	1	100,000
Dominica	38.3	0.814	0.000	18.2	3.6	1	1	100,000
Samoa	37.2	0.771	0.085	11.5	9.4	2	2	200,000
Suriname	36	0.769	0.010	21.2	4.8	2	0	500,000
Saint Vincent & Grenadines	34.4	0.772	0.009	25.7	13.1	2	0	100,000
Tonga	33.7	0.768	0.009	1.8	1.8	5	0	100,000
Guyana	33.5	0.729	0.007	18.7	4.9	2	1	800,000
Cape Verde	30.5	0.708	0.119	16.2	16.2	1	5	500,000
Barbados	29.8	0.903	0.013	18.3	−3.1	1	0	300,000
Jamaica	26.7	0.766	0.016	13.1	−2.3	2	−1	2,700,000

Bosnia & Herzegovina	25.1	0.812	0.008	27.8	−4.3	4	2	3,800,000
Saint Lucia	24.1	0.821	0.004	18.3	2	1	1	200,000
Occupied Palestinian Terr.	23.9	0.737	0.001					4,000,000
Malta	22.3	0.902	0.093	33.7	3.5	1	0	400,000
Albania	21	0.818	0.034	26.3	26.3	3	4	3,100,000
Armenia	20.3	0.798	0.067	20.9	4.3	6	−1	3,100,000
Trinidad & Tobago	20.2	0.837	0.099	22.9	9.9	2	0	1,300,000
Ireland	20	0.965	0.099	34.1	10.5	1	0	4,400,000
Medium Emigration N = 35		(0.780)	(0.043)	(16.8)	(6.4)	(3.5)	(0.4)	(6,432,353)
Low Emigration N = 126		(0.715)	(0.068)	(15.6)	(7.9)	(3.6)	(1.0)	(50,311,905)

Notes: The Level of Democracy and Change in Democracy columns employ Vanhanen's indicators as described in the notes to Table 7.1. The HDI and Population figures come from UNDP (2009). Change in HDI is the total change from the initial year of recording until the final recorded change in 2006. The Political Rights' score come from Freedom House (2010), where 1 is high and 7 is low. Change in Political Rights is the total change from the initial year of recording to the final recorded change in 2009. See Appendix VI for the complete table.

Sources: UNDP (2009, 2010); Vanhanen (2007); and Freedom House (2010).

Previous analyses employing the HDR data have found that emigration tends to come from richer rather than poorer countries: The median emigration rate in a country with low human development is below 4%, whereas the rate is more than 8% from countries with high levels of human development. We also know (and should not be surprised to find out) that more than three-quarters of international migrants move to a country with a higher level of human development (UNDP 2009: 2). Like most studies of this type, the 2009 Human Development Report examines the economic effects that trail in the wake of emigration, not the political effects per se (despite its broader mission to look at human development).

When these data are used to list countries in terms of the size of their recent emigrant stocks, as is done in Table 7.2, we see a pattern similar to what we found in Table 7.1: Emigrant-prone countries tend to be very small (often island) countries. The full table is found as Appendix VI. By grouping them into high (>20%), medium (10–20%), and low (<10%) emigration (stock) countries, we can begin to assess the relationship between emigration and a number of relevant variables.

Employing this measure of emigration, we find that the highest emigration states share an important characteristic with those in the EMIG 1.2 database: They are mostly very small countries. The relatively small overlap of high-emigration countries across datasets might be explained by the fact that the UN dataset contains data on many more countries, including very small countries (which were not included in the EMIG dataset). As anticipated, Albania is listed in the UNDP dataset as a high-emigration state, as are Dominica, Ireland, and Jamaica.[7] Rather remarkably, Sri Lanka ends up as a low-emigration country in the UN dataset.[8] In short, there is surprisingly little correspondence between the rankings provided by the EMIG and UN datasets, although they share one important characteristic: the tendency for the most emigration-prone countries to be very small in size.

Table 7.2 includes five columns capturing different aspects of political development. The second and third columns provide an indicator of a country's general level of human development using the Human Development Index (in 2007) and the recent change in that index (1980–2006).

---

[7] Many of the other high-emigration countries in the EMIG 1.2 ranking are found among the medium-emigration countries in the UN list: Kazakhstan, Seychelles, Bahrain, El Salvador, New Zealand, Iceland, and Kyrgyzstan.

[8] Along with Nicaragua, the Dominican Republic, Syria, Burkina Faso, France, and Switzerland.

The fourth and fifth columns report similar evidence in the form of Vanhanen's Democracy Index, as used in Table 7.1, and the sixth and seventh columns report another indicator of political development: the Freedom House's (2010) Political Rights index. The latter index only begins in 1972, so it was not used in the earlier analyses.

In the first set of indicators, which aim to capture the current level of political development, we find that high-emigration countries – on average – tend to enjoy more development than the medium- or low-emigration countries. In contrast, the high-emigration countries tend to have lower rates of development growth, on average, than either the medium- or low-emigration countries.[9] Careful readers will recall that this is different from the pattern described from the data in Table 7.1: Here the average relationships are more clear-cut, in the sense that we see higher levels of political development in those countries that have experienced the highest emigration rates (as a share of population).

To give a clearer indication of these relationships, Figures 7.1 and 7.2 provide scatterplots of national emigrant stocks (as a percentage of population) and the country's HDI (2007) and Level of Democracy (2006) score, respectively.[10] In both cases we see a weak but positive relationship, as indicated by the imposed regression lines and low R^2s, in which a higher emigrant stock level is associated with higher levels of political development.

---

[9] To ensure that the reader follows the analysis, let me spell this out. In general, high-emigration countries have a higher HDI score (0.810), Democracy score (21.0), and Political Rights score (2.2, where 1 is the highest) than medium (0.780/16.8/3.5) or low (0.715/15.6/3.6) emigration countries. They also experienced mostly slower development growth rates (0.034/6.4/0.8), than did the medium (0.043/6.4/0.4) and low (0.068/7.9/1.0) emigration countries. The same negative relationship between HDI growth and the size of emigration stock is evident when using the UNDP's "short-term annual average growth rate" (2000–7) and "Long-term annual average growth rate" (1980–2007) figures from appendix table G (UNDP 2009: 167–70). I did not use the UN-generated averages because these are peppered with missing data, and I think it is better to measure overall growth of the available data than to use annual averages with a smaller sample. Still, interested readers can note that the high-emigration countries averaged 0.57 (short-term) and 0.41 (long-term) annual HDI growth rates; the medium-emigration countries averaged 0.74 and 0.55, short/long respectively, and the low-emigration countries had the highest HDI growth rates, of 0.82 (short-term) and 0.75 (long-term).

[10] As the Political Rights index is not a continuous variable, but a seven-point index, I have not used it in the following graph-based analyses. However, it is also positively related with emigration (i.e., higher emigration rates correspond to higher levels of political rights [lower PR scores]).

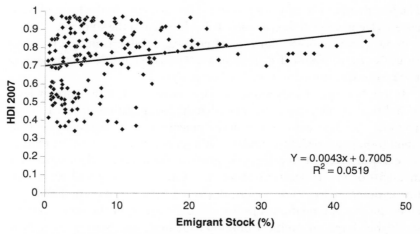

FIGURE 7.1. Emigrant Stock on HDI (2007), Scatterplot. *Source:* See Table 7.2 and Appendix VI.

As with the EMIG 1.2 dataset, we find that high-emigration countries tend to be much smaller, on average, than the medium- and low-emigration countries in the UN dataset. The average population size of the high-emigration countries was just over one million people! Because of

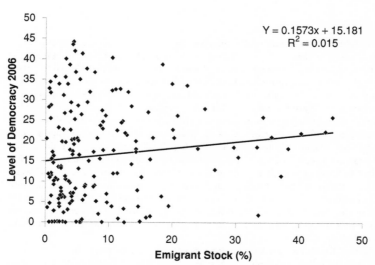

FIGURE 7.2. Emigrant Stock on Level of Democracy (2006), Scatterplot. *Source:* See Table 7.2 and Appendix VI.

their size, many of these countries are not included in the EMIG 1.2 database (or, for that matter, in the Polity governance dataset). For this reason, the next section considers the nature of the relationship between emigration and political development in states with very small populations.

SMALL-STATE EMIGRATION

The ten most emigration-prone states in Table 7.2 share a number of relevant characteristics. Each recently secured independence from a colonial power; the earliest was Samoa in 1962, and the latest was Saint Kitts and Nevis in 1983. Each has a very small population, totaling less than 500,000 people. Most of these states are small in size, with a land area of less than 1,000 square kilometers (386 square miles, with the exceptions being Suriname, Samoa, Guyana, and Cape Verde). Nearly all of these states (except Suriname and Guyana) are island states, and most are located in or near the Caribbean basin.

We might speculate that these countries, as small (mostly island) nations, share a number of economic features that can explain their high rates of emigration. For example, the 2009 Human Development Report notes that these small, high-emigration states tend to be underdeveloped (UNDP 2009: 80). The argument provided to explain this relationship is a reasonable one: Because poor small states tend to be overly dependent on a single commodity or sector and are too small to develop economies of scale (either with respect to economic activity or the provision of public goods), they are especially vulnerable to exogenous economic shocks. This vulnerability makes it more attractive for residents to pursue emigration, and many of the states involved seem to be aware of the positive impact of emigration on development and poverty reduction.

This interpretation is reasonable if we confine ourselves to looking at the relationship between levels of economic activity and rates of emigration: These countries are relatively poor (in GDP/capita terms) and have experienced high levels of emigration. Yet there can be several reasons for these countries being poor, and this simple correlation says little about the effects that emigration might have on their level of political development.

To answer this question, we need to be able to predict these countries' level of political development, given their level of economic development. We can then use this predicted value as a baseline to see whether states with high levels of emigration score better or worse than their predicted value. Quite simply, we can produce a model that predicts average relationships between economic development and political development for all the countries in the UN database and then compare that prediction against the actual position of the small countries in question. Figures 7.3 and 7.4 do this with two different indicators for political development.[11]

Consider the relationship between GDP per capita (in the year 2000, constant 2007 international dollars) and the Human Development Index (HDI) in 2007, as depicted in Figure 7.3. On that scatterplot is imposed a line that summarizes a positive but nonlinear (logarithmic) relationship between GDP/capita and HDI. We already know that several other (noneconomic) factors influence HDI, but this relationship is fairly robust, as indicated by the relatively tight fit of the data around the trend line. Yet when we locate the top ten emigration countries in the scatterplot, we find that each lies above the predicted relationship. In other words, these high-emigration countries tend to have a higher level of human development than their level of economic development alone would lead us to expect.

Figure 7.4 reveals the same general pattern, this time with reference to a country's level of democracy as indicated by the Vanhanen index in 2006. Here we see that nine of the ten top emigration countries are overperforming in terms of democratic accomplishment, given their level of economic development in the year 2000. The one exception is Tonga, where its semi-feudal system provided the monarch (and the indigenous royal family and aristocracy) with considerable power. Recent electoral reforms in that country, however, have expanded democratic influence, and we can expect Tonga to fall in line with the other high-emigration states in the future.

In closing, let me note that each of these ten countries experienced an improvement in its HDI score during the period under consideration. Given that this improvement was not limited to the high-emigration states (most states experienced an improvement in HDI scores in recent years), this is an interesting but not particularly significant observation.

---

[11] Because the Polity index does not include very small countries, most of the highest emigrant countries are not included in their governance score. For this reason, we limit ourselves to the Vanhanen and HDI indicators.

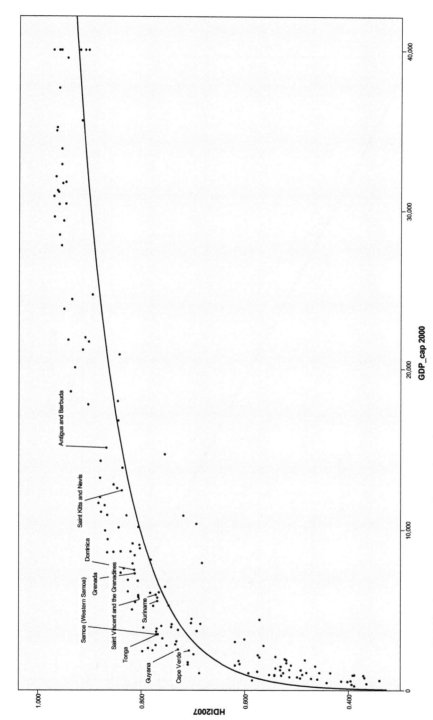

FIGURE 7.3. GDP/Capita on HDI, Scatterplot with High-Emigration States. *Source:* See Table 7.2 and Appendix VI.

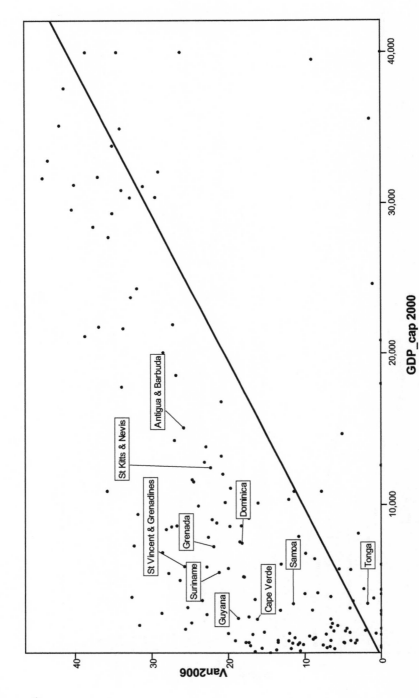

FIGURE 7.4. GDP/Capita on Democracy, Scatterplot with High-Emigration States. *Source:* See Table 7.2 and Appendix VI.

CONCLUSION

This chapter concludes the empirical study of international emigration and its relationship to national political development. Because this chapter covers more recent developments it has had access to alternative forms of data, and I have used this new information to look more critically at the nature of the political relationships and particular features of high-emigrant countries. Two important features are worth noting.

First, there is a remarkably large disconnect between public perceptions of international emigration and actual patterns. This disconnect concerns both the level of international migration (as a share of world population) and the largest source countries of emigration. Although the world's attention tends to be focused on refugee flows or the emigrant workers coming from Poland and South Asia, it is the smallest countries that are most exposed to the threat of massive emigration. These small countries do not always appear on the social scientist's radar, because they are not included in many of the more common datasets employed by social scientists.

This leads me to a second relevant observation: These very small states seem to be able to leverage their high levels of emigration to secure higher than expected levels of political development. Because many of these states are relatively underdeveloped (in terms of how they score on the HDI), the first impression may be that massive emigration is threatening or undermining their development potential. However, when we look at their level of political development relative to their level of economic development, these small emigrant countries do better than expected.

This suggests that some countries are still able to leverage political effects from emigration, even in a relatively restrictive international environment. For the ten small states considered at the end of this chapter, this leverage might be explained by their postcolonial status: The existence of earlier colonial ties opens up opportunities for international emigration that do not otherwise exist in a restrictive international environment. At this point, of course, the purported linkage is pure speculation, but it is interesting enough to warrant further study.

The last four chapters have examined international trends, in which the level of emigration tends to rise and fall with the global political climate. In the contemporary context, we have found that the nature of the international regime has some influence on the relationship between emigration and political development, but less than was originally expected. Another way to check for these sorts of regime effects is to compare development effects for (internal) out-migration within countries. After all, the political effects of emigration should also occur within countries as residents move from rural to urban sites or out of regions that have been politically less developed. The next chapter examines the nature of these internal relationships.

8

Internal Migration

This chapter takes yet another cut at the argument. Here we examine the development effects of emigration that occur *within* a given country. After all, the argument under study is a general one, and there is no reason to limit it to cases of international migration. We should expect to find the same sort of effects within countries, as migrants flee areas of underdevelopment in search of better lives.

In studying cases of internal (national) migration we are able to control for several features that otherwise vary in the international examples. Internal emigrants usually share the same language and overarching political context, which should facilitate mobility and integration. *Ceteris paribus*, the cost of exit should be smaller for internal emigrants than for international emigrants. Yet different countries, at different times, have regulated internal migration in ways that are similar to how the international community regulates and monitors international migration today. Thus, it is possible to compare the development lessons from internal migration regimes that are relatively liberal relative to those that are more regulated.

Most of this chapter considers the development effects from the largest population movement in U.S. history: the Great Migration from the South to the North in the fifty years after WWI. I show that there are good reasons to link the significant political gains won by African Americans after World War II – in the South and beyond – to the massive exodus to the North.

The second case is very different in that it examines the development effects of internal migration in contemporary China. In particular, I was curious to see if the political effects of emigration are more muted in the

Chinese case, given the relatively regulated nature of that migration. My findings are surprising in that in the Chinese case emigration is also linked to political development. Given space limitations (and recognizing that the Chinese case functions as a control), this case study is necessarily brief.

THE GREAT MIGRATION IN THE UNITED STATES

Migration has always played a central role in the political story that is American exceptionalism, whether it is with reference to the demographic composition of the country, the country's unique attitude to foreigners and citizenship, or its lack of a strong indigenous socialist movement.[1] This chapter looks at another, less studied way in which internal emigration affected political development in the United States: the political fallout from the Great Migration.[2]

This Great Migration of African Americans, or Blacks,[3] had an enormous influence on the demographic composition of the United States. In 1860, when slavery still limited black mobility, 88% of the black population of the United States resided in the South. Fifty years later, in 1910, that share was almost the same (85%), even though Blacks had been formally freed from slavery decades earlier.[4] After 1910, however, the demographic make-up of the country changed significantly, when almost

---

[1] For a disheartening example of the former, see Huntington (2004); for an elaboration of the second argument, see Moses (2009). The third argument can be explained with reference to the threat of exit wielded by American workers facing unreasonable employer demands. In contrast to Europe, where workers were forced to organize in response to employer pressure, American workers could always go out West when working conditions became unsatisfactory; this moderated employer attitudes, because they realized they could not demand too much (or risk losing workers), but it also made it difficult to radicalize the workers' movement in the United States. This argument has a long pedigree that can be traced to E. L. Godkin (1867).

[2] There have been numerous historical accounts describing the motivations underlying the Great Migration and its economic effects. For the former, see Grossman (1989), Lemann (1991), and Harrison (1991). For the latter, see Vickery (1977). However, I am unaware of any study that considers the political effects of that emigration.

[3] For the sake of brevity and convenience, and in contrast to reference to "White" emigrants, I employ the term "Black" when referring to African Americans in the text that follows.

[4] This is not to say that Blacks did not exploit the freedom of mobility that emancipation (briefly) entailed. Between 1870 and 1900, many Blacks took advantage of this freedom to move into growing urban areas in the South (Donald 1921, Gottlieb 1987) or to other (closer) rural areas in search of new landlords (Daniel 1985, Mandle 1978, Novak 1978, Ransom and Sutch 1977). Better known emigrant endeavors of the time are the relatively small, but still influential flight of southern Blacks into Kansas (the so-called Exodusters) and the emigration to Liberia, organized largely by the white-dominated

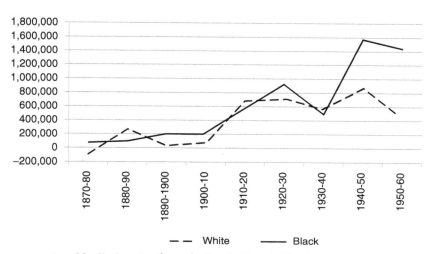

FIGURE 8.1. Net Emigration from the South, Decade Totals, 1870–1960. *Source:* Vickery (1977: 15). *Note:* Negative numbers indicate net immigration. The South includes the Confederate South plus West Virginia, Kentucky, and Oklahoma.

five million Blacks emigrated from the southern states. By 1960, only 55% of Blacks in the United States lived in the South (Vickery 1977: 11).

This exodus began, unofficially, in the spring of 1916, when the Pennsylvania Railroad Company ferried north a small contingent of black laborers to work on the rail lines. This small stream of workers grew into a torrent as southern Blacks flooded Harlem in Manhattan, the South Side of Chicago, Paradise Valley in Detroit, and other black centers in the urban North. In general, migrants chose from among three migration pathways: (1) from the southeast (e.g., Virginia–Florida), along the Atlantic coast, up to Pennsylvania, the mid-Atlantic states, and New England; (2) from Kentucky, Tennessee, Alabama, and Mississippi to the Midwest (i.e., Detroit and Chicago); and (3) from Texas, Louisiana, and Arkansas to the Pacific slope, especially California.

Figure 8.1 depicts the variance in these emigration trends over time, and we see a clear increase in the number of emigrants after 1910. This figure also shows that not only black workers were emigrating but also a sizable number of white workers were also leaving for greener pastures. At the end of this period (starting in the 1960s, but not depicted in the figure), Blacks began to return to the South en masse: The patterns are

American Colonization Society. See Hahn (2003: 320ff) and W. Cohen (1991a). However, as shown in Figure 8.1, these movements were too small to have much political effect.

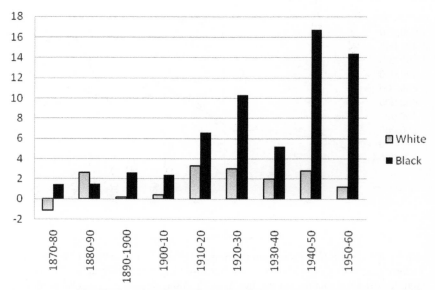

FIGURE 8.2. Net Emigration Rates from Southern States, 1870–1960, per Mil, Annual Averages. *Source:* Vickery (1977: 15). *Notes:* Rates of annual average emigration, per 1,000 average white/black population. The South includes the Confederate South plus West Virginia, Kentucky, and Oklahoma. Negative numbers indicate net immigration. Vickery's data are derived from Eldridge and Thomas (1964: 99); Lee (1957: 350, 352); and the U.S. Department of Commerce (1965: 26, 28).

largely the same as during the Great Migration, only in reverse (Jackson 1991: xvii).

When we weigh the figures by resident (black) population, as is done in Figure 8.2, we see that the rates of southern emigration exceeded all but the largest international migration figures. At the height of the black exodus, American Blacks were leaving their state of origin at a rate that was roughly twice that of the largest emigrant states before World War I. Whereas Norway was sending about 10 emigrants for every 1,000 residents at the height of its emigration (1880–9), the southern states were sending about 15 Blacks each year for every 1,000 black residents in the region during most of the early post-WWI period (1940–60).[5] In the

---

[5] It is likely that the southern emigration rates were even higher, because the numbers used here capture net (emigration–immigration) migration rates. Indeed, during the early years, some southern states experienced a rather large net immigration of Blacks (e.g., West Virginia, Arkansas, and Texas; see Table 8.1).

1910–20 and 1930–40 periods, black emigration rates were lower, but still large enough to wield political influence.

So that we can get a better feel for where the greatest emigrant pressure was felt, Table 8.1 breaks these figures down by state, as a percent of the local black population, over time. There is little point in breaking down these figures by level of emigration, as was done with comparable tables in earlier chapters, because only three states – Florida, Tennessee, and Texas – did not experience high rates of emigration (more than 10 mil or 10/1,000) during this period! In the postwar period, we find extremely high black emigration rates (around or more than 15 mil) in West Virginia, North Carolina, South Carolina, Georgia, Alabama, Mississippi, and Arkansas.

This massive emigration was driven by a unique constellation of events, affecting both push and pull factors. Before WWI, cheap European immigrant labor staffed northern industries. After the outbreak of the war, demand for industrial products grew, both from within the country and from beyond. Yet the supply of immigrant labor had been cut off, and the mobilization of armed forces in 1917 drained the North's potential labor pool even more. Northern factories could realize enormous profits only if they could find the workers needed to staff their factories. Their immediate, if temporary, solution was to open their factory gates to white women and black southerners.

Black southerners, in turn, had good reasons to be tempted northward. In addition to the deplorable political and social conditions under which they lived and worked, a series of economic setbacks (associated with boll weevils, storms, floods, tightening of credit, etc.) were limiting opportunities for rural employment and pushing Blacks to search for better jobs and living conditions in the North.

International migration levels never returned to their pre-WWI levels, and so the North's reliance on southern black migrant labor continued, as a new migration chain began to link southern rural areas to the urban North.

Political Development in the South

There is probably little need to elaborate on the nature of black repression in the post–Civil War South – the story is already well known and documented. Still, a short review can be useful. Following a brief period immediately after the war of Reconstruction during which Blacks made political and economic gains, the political position of southern Blacks

TABLE 8.1. *Net Black Emigration, per Mil Black Population, by State 1870–1960, Annual Averages*

	1870–80	1880–90	1890–1900	1900–10	1910–20	1920–30	1930–40	1940–50	1950–60
South Atlantic									
Virginia	−8.4	−10.1	−11.4	−8.9	−4.7	−20.7	−6.7	−5.4	−9.4
West Virginia	9.1	13.7	18.6	33.8	26.8	16.0	−3.5	−16.6	−38.6
North Carolina	−2.4	−8.6	−8.3	−5.5	−4.9	−2.5	−7.6	−14.9	−17.5
South Carolina	3.7	−3.6	−9.1	−10.8	−10.6	−29.5	−14.3	−23.7	−25.2
Georgia	−3.9	1.9	−1.8	−1.8	−7.3	−26.2	−9.6	−20.9	−17.8
Florida	1.9	13.4	16.6	19.4	1.9	18.0	12.8	1.7	13.7
Total	−2.6	−3.4	−5.3	−3.7	−5.7	−15.7	−6.9	−14.5	−13.1
East South Central									
Kentucky	−6.5	−10.1	−3.3	−9.2	−7.3	−8.3	−4.6	−12.2	−8.7
Tennessee	−8.5	−5.5	−3.3	−8.2	−7.2	−3.4	2.0	−8.5	−9.7
Alabama	−8.0	−1.1	1.3	−2.9	−9.1	−10.2	−7.6	−20.1	−21.5
Mississippi	4.0	−2.5	−0.1	−3.9	−15.4	−8.6	−6.5	−30.1	−31.9
Total	−4.0	−3.7	−0.7	−4.9	−10.9	−8.2	−5.2	−21.1	−21.7
West South Central									
Arkansas	19.2	21.8	−1.2	6.7	−0.4	−11.2	−7.9	−30.1	−33.0
Louisiana	0.2	1.3	−2.3	−2.6	−8.1	−4.1	−1.2	−15.6	−8.0
Oklahoma				63.7	0.7	1.3	−8.3	−28.9	−14.4
Texas	8.4	3.7	3.3	−2.0	0.7	1.8	0.5	−8.4	−1.2
Total	6.6	6.8	0.0	3.5	−2.6	−3.7	−2.3	−16.3	−9.5
TOTAL SOUTH	−1.4	−1.5	−2.6	−2.5	−6.6	−10.7	−5.1	−16.9	−14.5

Notes: Per mil (o/oo) refers to the number of emigrants per 1,000 of the population in the sending (home) state. These figures are derived by taking Vickery's net black migration rates, dividing them by the size of the non-white population for the given decade, multiplying this figure by the percent of the non-white population in each state that was Black at the end of the decade, times 1,000. The latter multiplication step is done to estimate the size of the black population in each state (by multiplying the share of Blacks in the state's non-white population times the size of the non-white population). These decade net black migration rates, per mil, were then divided by 10 to provide annual averages over the decades listed in each column, to facilitate comparison with the international emigration figures in previous chapters.

Source: Vickery (1977: 17, 157, and 159).

suffered significant setbacks. In W. E. B. Du Bois's famous expression, "[T]he slave went free; stood a brief moment in the sun; then moved back again toward slavery" (1977 [1935]: 30).

The Reconstruction Acts of 1867 secured black enfranchisement and promised that new southern state governments would be drawn up by men "of whatever race, color or previous condition of servitude" (Article XV, U.S. Constitution). Yet the ink had hardly dried on those acts before former slave states came to adopt a series of Black Codes, designed to restrict the political and civil rights of the freed slaves. Although these codes did provide Blacks with some rights (e.g., legalized marriage, ownership of property, and limited access to the courts), they denied them fundamental political rights (e.g., the right to testify against Whites, to serve on juries, or to vote) and economic liberties (e.g., the right to acquire land or to work in an occupation of their choosing).

As Whites regained control of southern state governments, they began a drawn-out process of black disenfranchisement. In the 1870s and 1880s, white legislators across the South introduced electoral qualifications and procedural requirements aimed to discourage Blacks from wielding the rights secured with the 15th Amendment. Later, after 1890, these states employed sophisticated legal means (e.g., literary tests, understanding requirements, poll taxes, and white-only primaries) to develop systems of disenfranchisement that were compatible with that amendment (Key 1984 [1949]: 536–7).[6]

As is well known, political repression was worst in the Deep South, where the black population was densest and the living conditions most oppressive.[7] In the pre-WWI period, the number of lynchings was on the rise, and the South's willingness and capacity to discriminate against Blacks only grew:[8]

For there was a willingness not just to disfranchise but to do so without any apology save for the fig leaf required by the Fifteenth Amendment. There was a

---

[6] See W. Cohen (1991a: 203–47) for an overview of state attempts to reintroduce the Black Codes.

[7] Remarkably, the states of Georgia, Alabama, Mississippi, and Louisiana contributed almost nothing to northward movement during the 1870–1910 period. At that time, most black emigrants were coming from the Upper South and border states (e.g., Virginia, North Carolina, Tennessee, and Kentucky). See Table 8.1.

[8] More than 2,800 lynchings were recorded between 1880 and 1914 (Zangrando 1980: 6–7). Subsequent research has documented how black emigration was highest in those areas exposed to high levels of racial violence. See, e.g., the work of Tolnay and Beck (1990, 1991, 1995).

willingness not just to lynch blacks publicly but to defend such behavior as just and moral. There was an insistence not just on the separation of the races but on formalizing and codifying the separation. . . . Indeed, it is difficult to avoid concluding that by 1907 southern legislators had come remarkably close to reenacting the black codes. By then the southern legal system was laden with vagrancy laws, enticement acts, contract-enforcement measures, and convict laws that, taken together, certainly look like the framework for a comprehensive system of involuntary servitude (W. Cohen 1991a: 246–7).

If the political and social conditions governing Blacks' lives were unique, the pre-WWI economic conditions of the South were similar to those that have characterized much of the developing world. In 1920, 57% of the South's population was still working in the agricultural sector; the North, by contrast, had passed that mark in 1850 (Marks 1989: 50). The South was the country's poorest region with an annual per-capita income of less than $400 (compared to more than $1,000 in the rest of the country), even though the South enjoyed the richest reserves of the country's natural resources: 96% of bauxite, 93% of phosphate rock, 69% of natural gas, and 63% of petroleum (Marks 1991: 38).

The role played by demographic factors in this long period of underdevelopment is disputed, except for a general consensus that the black population was consistently undercounted. Still, we know that black reproduction rates were very high throughout most of the antebellum period, but declined after the Civil War (although scholars tend to differ on why these rates fell). In the 1940s and 1950s there was a significant rise in black birth rates, combined with a large fall in black mortality rates. Thus, massive emigration from the South occurred without decimating the southern black population (Davis 1991: 12–13). In addition, emigration rates began to fall just as the birth/mortality rates began to flatten out in the 1960s. However, the relative bargaining power of Blacks would have fallen in the absence of emigration, because natural increases in population flooded the southern labor market.

In large part, the South's remarkable underdevelopment, in both political and economic realms, continued until the mid-1950s, when the region was rocked by a series of economic, social, and political eruptions. Almost without warning, the region threw itself into urbanization, the economy began to boom, and the Civil Rights Movement made significant inroads in breaking down Jim Crow laws.

After World War II the southern economy was transformed. Rural areas suffered severe population flight and with it a loss in political influence as congressional redistricting transferred power away from rural bastions of whitedom. After WWII, the Mississippi River Delta states lost five congressional seats because of demographic changes (Holley 2000: 192).

This population change was driven not only by emigration (as we shall see) but also by the mechanization of cotton harvesting and federal government attempts at land redistribution, born of the New Deal. These developments freed plantation farmers from relying on inefficient stoop (physically-demanding, bent-over and demeaning) labor and made cotton a more internationally competitive crop. In short, the dominant crop of the South switched from being labor-intensive to becoming capital-intensive, which had an enormous impact on the demand for local labor.

Mechanization meant that cotton farming no longer relied on a rural and repressed black peasantry. The South no longer needed cheap labor and with it the regressive social and legal framework that supported it (such as labor control laws and Jim Crow repression):

The end of the plantation system constituted an essential precondition that facilitated the civil rights movement of the 1950s. It was not accidental that Jim Crow began in 1890 as the postbellum plantation system took its final form in the waning century; nor was it accidental that the civil rights movement coincided with the collapse of the plantation system and agricultural mechanization (Holley 2000: 194).

From 1954 to 1968, a series of well-orchestrated marches, boycotts, nonviolent protests, and acts of civil disobedience focused attention on the plight of African Americans in the South. This political pressure resulted in a number of important court rulings (e.g., *Brown v. Board of Education* in 1954, which mandated the desegregation of public schools) and legislative gains, including the Civil Rights Act of 1965 (which banned discrimination at work and in public places), the Voting Rights Act of 1965 (which restored voter rights), and the Fair Housing Act of 1968 (which banned discrimination in the housing sector).

The results were evident quickly, as black candidates began to win elections and exercise the power of political office. A 1971 *Ebony* article celebrated the changes:

Perhaps in no facet of life in The South Today [sic] have blacks forced as significant change as in politics. Prior to passage of the Voting Rights Act of 1965 there were only 72 black elected officials in the eleven states of the old Confederacy. Today, according to March 1971 statistics of the Joint Center for Political Studies, there are 711 blacks holding elective offices in those states. They range from city councilmen and county commissioners to school board officials, justices of the

peace, mayors, sheriffs and state legislators. In some areas, political progress for
blacks has resulted from coalitions of blacks and progressive whites. But in most
instances, it has been the great political strength yielded by increasingly aware
blacks which has swept into office hundreds of black candidates. While only a
beginning has been made (there are, for example, only 40 blacks among the 1,805
state legislators in the South), not one former Confederate state is now without
blacks in important control positions in public life (*Ebony* 1971).

In conclusion, the century following the Civil War can be divided
into three periods. After experiencing some modest gains from Reconstruction, Blacks experienced little political relief until the mid-1950s;
only then did Southern Blacks experience significant political and economic development. The question before us is, What role did the Great
Migration play in bringing about the second Great Emancipation?

The March of the Impatient

As with international emigration, we can expect to see the political effects
of southern emigration channeled through individual emigrants, with the
money, ideas, hope, and skills that they introduced to the South – either
in the form of letters, remittances, or returning home after spending some
time in the North. Yet it is also at this level of analysis that we need to be
on the lookout for potential brain-drain effects.

Because internal migrants do not cross international borders it is more
difficult to track the size of remittance flows and the rates of return
migration. I am not aware of any study that has tried to document the
amount of money sent home to families that stayed in the South, and the
little work that has been done on return migration is referenced in this
section. However, there is abundant anecdotal evidence, which suggests
that the effects of southern emigration are very similar to what we saw
in the Norwegian experiences before WWI.

This evidence, as well as the existence of substantial white emigration
(see Figure 8.1), suggests that the motivation for most of the emigration
was probably economic in nature: There were better wages and working conditions to be gained by moving North. Yet even if the original
motivation had been primarily economic, the experience of living in the
North was bound to change political perceptions. When returning home
to visit, emigrants came across as rich and prosperous, and they were
full of stories about the world beyond the South. Through letters home,
emigrants changed perceptions about what was possible in the political
and social realm.

We can recognize these influences without glorifying the often deplorable conditions under which Blacks lived and labored in the North. My point is not to suggest that immigrant conditions in northern industrial towns were stellar – only that they represented a substantial improvement over what workers had experienced in the South. Indeed, in drawing attention to these relative differences, emigration served to engage new thinking about the role and the status of the southern black man:

> Back and forth along the chains flowed people, resources, and information about living conditions, job prospects, and the civil and political atmospheres. Letters, reverse migrations, and visitations alike told rural folk what they might expect and who might help them in Atlanta and Birmingham, Norfolk and Nashville, Harlem and Pittsburgh, Cleveland and Chicago. But the reverberations would also be heard through more extended circuits, new and old. Black railroad workers – sleeping car porters, cooks, dining car waiters, freight handlers, and track hands – employed by the Illinois Central, the Louisville and Nashville, the Southern, and the Seaboard Air Line railroads brought stories, handbills, and newspaper such as the *Chicago Defender* and the *Pittsburgh Courier*, which gained a growing readership in the South (Hahn 2003: 467).

Like the "America letters" from Norwegians in the United States, southern emigrants sent letters home that were read, discussed, and circulated widely:

> Chicago letters provided concrete images of not only the attractions of the city, but also the freedom and privileges enjoyed in the North. . . . A southerner might tear himself away more easily once he knew that his friend could "just begin to feel like a man" in Chicago where he "got some privilege. My children are going to the same school with the whites and I don't have to 'umble to no one. I have registered – Will vote the next election and there isn't any 'yes sir' and 'no sir' – it's all yes and no and Sam and Bill" (Grossman 1989:305).[9] The advantages of racial equality – unthinkable in the South – were thus presented in unmistakably attainable and personal terms. Integrated schools, respect, the franchise: if his friend could acquire such privileges, so could he (Grossman 1989: 90).

Even if much of the emigration was motivated by economic push and pull factors, it would be naïve to believe that none of the emigration was politically motivated. After all, "the Great Migration represented a refusal by one-half million black southerners to cooperate" (Grossman 1989: 38–9). Indeed, more than one chronicler of the Great Migration has noted how it symbolized "politically conscious migrants [who] 'voted with their feet' to reject their subordinate place in the southern social

---

[9] The internal quotes are from Scott (1919: 459).

order, moving to other regions in hopes of being able to exercise their citizenship rights" (de Jong 2005: 387).

Denied access to the normal democratic channels of political and social protest, migrating blacks voted with their feet, voted the only way they could, taking their talents, their energies, and their aspirations to a new promised land beyond the Ohio where, as generations of black expatriates dared to hope, the measure of human worth might be brains and character, not skin color (McMillen 1991: 86).

It is this politically motivated migration that has the potential to invoke images of brain drain. After all, before the turn of the twentieth century, when Blacks were enticed to settle in Liberia, concerns grew over "the migration of the talented tenth" because the first to go were often the most successful, best educated, and most outspoken Blacks who had borne the brunt of white violence (Woodson 2008 [1918]). From the census records we know that those with a high school education were more likely to leave and that migrants tended to be younger and in the prime of their productive life. As a result, the remaining population was surely burdened by a higher per-capita share of old people and young children.

Yet I have not found any evidence that the Great Migration drew disproportionately from the small southern black middle class:

Precisely because the exodus was the march of the impatient, precisely because it carried off many of those least satisfied with Jim Crow, too many have assumed that it drained the state of its best black stock, its most capable and intelligent black role models and community leaders.... Obviously, this kind of specula- tion is simply that: speculation – at best unprovable, at worst defamatory of nonmigrants (McMillen, 1991: 87).

What of returning migrants? From the census data we know that there was always a sizable number of northern black immigrants who returned to the South, and this figure increased significantly as conditions in the South improved. Taken as a whole, the South in the 1970s moved from a pattern of net black emigration to one of net immigration. This trend reflects both an increase in return migration and a decrease in emigration of Blacks from the region (Long and Hansen 1975: 611).

Relying on U.S. Census data, Campbell et al. (1974: 515–6) show how the share of returning black migrants increased from 27.4% in 1935–40, to 32.6% in 1955–60, and to 44.4% in 1965–70. Then, from 1970 to 1973 they find that the share exploded to 169.2%! In that period 117,000 Blacks moved from the South to the Northeast and North Central regions, whereas 198,000 Blacks moved from these areas back to the South.

On closer examination, they find that these migrant flows consisted mostly of return migrants who were remarkably young (almost half were between the ages of 15–29) and who enjoyed higher incomes, job skills, and education levels than the general population to which they returned (Campbell et al., 1974: 520–3). As for their motivation to return, the authors refer to another survey from the same period that found that a remarkably high percentage of the return migrants (52.3%) claimed social motivations for moving to the South, whereas just under 20% cited economic reasons (Campbell et al., 1974: 525).[10]

Most interestingly from our perspective is the authors' political interpretation of this large jump in return migration:

> The historical structures of the South created conditions that made it extremely difficult for Blacks to make social or economic progress. A large return movement would seem to indicate some positive changes in race relations. Of course, to some extent return migration is a response to a failure to realize expected life styles in the North. However, we feel that the successes of the Civil Rights movement, assisted by the Civil Rights and Voter Registration legislation in the 1960's, together with general economic development in the South, has contributed in making the regions increasingly attractive to Blacks (Campbell et al., 1974: 526).

A Declining Oversupply

As was already noted, the Great Migration made a significant impact on the demographic composition of the United States by reducing the concentration of the African American population in the rural South. This emigration brought with it indelible changes in the social and political make-up of the country, because "[m]any of the landmark political developments of twentieth-century America – electoral realignments, the New Deal, industrial unionism, the Great Society, and, of course, the battle for civil rights – would be difficult to imagine outside of this massive demographic shift that then continued, and accelerated" (Hahn 2003: 465). Yet the question before us is whether considerable black emigration led to a change in the balance of class power in the South that then strengthened the position of poor black farmhands relative to their white employers.

---

[10] Curiously, the rate of return migration was higher among Whites than among Blacks; see Long and Hansen (1975). Campbell et al. (1974) seem unaware of this fact. In the 1960s, there was a shift in the South from net emigration to net immigration among Whites. The Blacks' trend paralleled the one among Whites, but lagged by a decade (McHugh 1987: 173).

There is much anecdotal evidence to this effect. "As the trains and boats pulled out week after week and month after month, the South began to hurt from a loss of the black labor force, especially in the Deep South" (Henri 1975: 70). We know that white plantation owners and political officials adopted a number of coercive measures to intimidate and threaten workers who left (and the labor agents assisting them). Perhaps the best description of the situation was provided by a white southerner's account in Grossman (1991: 51): Emigration did not necessarily lead to a drastic shortage, but more of "a decline from an oversupply."

Some evidence of a change in class power was seen almost immediately. For example, black agricultural and industrial wages increased across the state of Mississippi by some 10–30% in the aftermath of WWI and into the 1920s. Planters offered better living conditions and greater autonomy; a number of communities across the state aimed to improve the educational opportunities and legal position of Blacks; and there was an increased awareness of the need to address black grievances (McMillen 1991: 93–4).

However, it is difficult to single out the effect of emigration alone on black wages, because the Great Emigration straddled two world wars and a revolution in the way that the region's most important crop, cotton, was harvested. The latter development is especially important for understanding how the South's balance of class power shifted radically in the 1960s, when the region switched from a labor-intensive to a capital-intensive form of farming, undermining its traditional need for a subservient, exploited peasantry. After a century of testing and experimenting, the mechanical cotton picker was finally ready to make its debut; by 1950, four companies had mechanical cotton pickers in commercial production. Just 20 years later, in 1970, the whole cotton crop of the South was being picked mechanically. In the intervening decades, an entire way of life, rooted in plantations and stoop labor, was eradicated.

These developments – mechanization, emigration, and the Second Emancipation – are clearly intertwined, and scholars have long argued the relative weight of each factor in the South's political and economic development. Following Holley's (2000: chapter 6) argument and evidence, it is clear that mechanization went hand-in-hand with emigration to create the ideal conditions for the economic and social transformation of the cotton-picking South.

If we can believe one of the first farmers to embrace this new technology, who was the long-time president of the National Cotton Council of America, the threat of emigration provided an additional incentive for

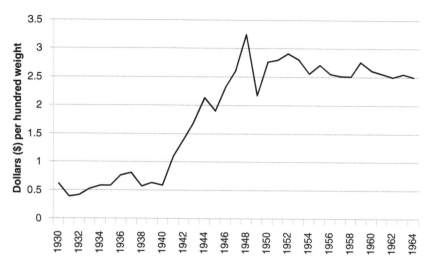

FIGURE 8.3. Average Wage for Picking Cotton, Mississippi, 1930–64. *Source:* USDA (1974: 86).

southern farmers to invest in the new machines that could harvest their crops:

Mechanization is not the cause, but the result, of economic change in the area. Most if not all of the migration of farmers and farm workers which has taken place during the past few years has resulted from factors other than mechanization itself. All over the South, tenant houses now stand vacant on farms where mechanization has not yet achieved considerable development (Johnston 1947: 37).

Contemporary historians arrived at the same conclusion:

[B]y and large, no serious labor displacement has been caused by the use of modern cotton production equipment. In most cases labor had already deserted the cotton fields and was no longer available in customary quantity so, where possible, the growers turned to mechanization. Machines have been adopted most readily when hand labor was scarce or relatively expensive.... The movement away from the farms has been a major factor in stimulating mechanization of the cotton fields. Since the farm population of the South is declining and since mechanization is progressing in a slow evolutionary manner, labor displacement does not seem to be a serious problem at the present time (Fite 1950: 28).

By examining wage developments for cotton pickers in Mississippi, as shown in Figure 8.3, we can clearly see the effect of World War II on the state's average wage level, which rose rapidly from 1941 to 1947. It is remarkable that the Mississippi cotton pickers' average wage did not fall immediately after the war, when northern factories laid off their black workers and returning soldiers resumed their prewar positions: Instead, the average wage for picking cotton remained stable, at a level five times what it was before the war. This is clear evidence that the region was not flooded with unskilled and desperate labor – but that other alternatives were available to the region's workers, both black and white.

In short, the Great Migration seems to have created incentives for farmers to adopt new (and expensive) harvesting techniques – techniques that would liberate these very same farmers from their need for cheap and oppressed labor. In the words of the historian Jay Mandle (1978: 118), "the emergence of the civil rights movement had its roots in the breakdown of the plantation economy." At the same time, the possibility of emigration seems to have functioned as a pressure-release valve; the region was able to avoid the serious social disruptions that many people expected with the introduction of labor-saving machines.

By reducing the supply of black labor, emigration helped improve the implicit bargaining power of those who remained: "In fact, much of the meaning of the Great Migration is to be found in the response of the nonmigrants, in the little-known history of those resourceful black southerners who found advantage in white disadvantage, who developed subtle but effective tools for black protest in an age when more confrontational forms of protest would have been virtually unthinkable" (McMillen 1991: 86).

If the relative position of black labor in the South was clearly strengthened by the Great Migration, that effect was not always evident to contemporaries. Leaders could be found on both sides of the color divide to support and discourage further black emigration from the region, and their positions changed over time.

Among black elites there seemed to be broad support, early on, for using emigration to secure political gain, because at that time plantation owners were completely dependent on cheap black labor to harvest their cotton.[11] Indeed Grossman (1989: 60–1, 297, emphasis in the original)

[11] Still, many black leaders were hostile to emigration, among them Frederick Douglass. Reacting to the early waves of emigration to Kansas, Douglass believed in holding the political and moral high ground. For him, emigration was "a surrender, a premature, disheartening surrender, since it would make freedom and free institutions depend upon migration rather than protection; by flight rather than by right; by going into a strange land, rather than by staying in one's own. It leaves the whole question of equal rights on the soil of the South open and still to be settled, with the moral influence of exodus against us; since it is a confession of the utter impracticality of equal rights and equal protection in any state, where those rights may be struck down by violence" (Douglass 1880: 15).

provides much evidence of this: whether with reference to William Cohen's survey of black southern newspapers, in which "virtually all" used the threat of exit as a bargaining chip, or the NAACP's Weldon Johnson's reference to the exodus as "tantamount to a general strike," or the encouragement by the editor of the *Christian Recorder*, Richard R. Wright, given to black southerners in 1917 to exploit the influence that was already being generated by the threat of exit: "IF ONE HUNDRED THOUSAND UNORGANIZED NEGROES CAN DO THIS WHAT COULD ONE MILLION ORGANIZED NEGROES DO?"

As Blacks began to gain political traction, however, elite opinion about the benefits of emigration began to wane; an opinion threshold seems to have been crossed. In the 1960s, civil rights leaders began to worry that emigration would threaten black voting majorities. Thus, Mississippi activist Lawrence Guyot explained, "[E]ven if Negroes get registered, we still have to worry about keeping them here" (de Jong 2005: 388). Similarly, Joseph Wheatley of Coahoma County, Mississippi, asserted, "Relocation is a dirty word to Negroes here in the Delta. The white politicians think it is the social remedy. Our people want to build decent homes and stay here." Likewise, the Alabama civil rights leader Roberts Strickland told a reporter, "The jack rabbits have stopped running." Those Blacks who lived in these areas intended to "stay put and fight for a better life" (de Jong 2005: 394).

An inverse trajectory is found in white elite opinion. In the early years of the exodus, plantation owners and white elites tried to restrict the emigration of African Americans. However, by the 1950s and 1960s, white elite opinion also crossed some sort of threshold, as many white southerners began to encourage black emigration as a means of limiting the effects of the civil rights movement and in a last-ditch attempt to preserve their traditional southern way of life (Alston and Ferrie 1993).

Thus, in the 1960s, there was a tidal change in perceptions about the utility of emigration. On the one hand, progress in the social and political spheres was making it more attractive for Blacks to remain in the South. On the other hand, it was increasingly important for Civil Rights leaders to use that progress to secure even greater gains. As the balance of class power shifted in favor of black labor, positions about emigration also shifted – on both sides of the color divide. White supremacists stopped trying to limit emigration, whereas black activists turned from supporting emigration to focusing black political influence on improving public services and economic development in the South.

In looking back on this second Great Emancipation, it is important to be cognizant of the difficulty Blacks had in organizing political activism and opposition, especially in the early years: In a political context steeped in violence, intimidation, and fear, traditional means of mass protest and political action were not available to black southerners. It is in this context that emigration was able to play such a powerful role in facilitating political development. By choosing to emigrate, Blacks were sending a strong signal that they rejected the economic and social status quo in the South:

In a time when blacks were almost powerless to affect government decisions, the Great Migration brought the possibility that they might be able to affect events after all by arguing that the migration was the outcome of southern racial oppression. If only the oppression would stop, so would the outflow of black labor. The theme appears everywhere, in editorials in black newspapers, in appeals for the President to act against lynching, and in appeals for the appointment of blacks to government posts (W. Cohen 1991b: 79).

Delivering Justice

Unlike nation-states in the international system, southern states had access to few formal instruments to stem the tide of emigration. Unable to issue travel documents or to control the flow of goods and people across state borders, southern state officials were mostly limited to using indirect incentives to discourage emigration.

In the early years of the Great Migration, as the number of emigrants increased rapidly, southern states realized the need to improve wages and living conditions or risk losing the stoop labor that they needed to bring in the cotton crop. Attempts to replace black with immigrant labor had proven unsuccessful, and mechanization was still not a viable option. In this context newspaper editors, business leaders, and political reformers pointed to the need to improve wages, working conditions, and overall treatment of Blacks.[12]

Thus, an Alabama church official, William Jones, explained to readers in a 1916 issue of the Montgomery *Advertiser* what was needed to keep the potential migrant at home:

He must be accorded better treatment, not only better schools, but better wages, better accommodations, better protection of life and in the pursuit of happiness.

---

[12] For example, Grossman (1989: 50–2) lists efforts by reformers to curb the activities of white mobs, improve educational offerings, establish charitable organizations, and increase wages.

He does not want to get into anyone's way, he does not want to crowd anyone out, he does not want to infringe on any person's rights. He wants to feel that he is wanted and he has friends. He knows that he has individual friends, but he wants to feel that society and the commonwealth are friendly toward him. In other words, he wants justice.[13]

Yet at least at the outset, providing justice was not in the cards. Wages and working conditions improved, but slowly. Instead, southern officials shifted their attention from addressing the underlying causes of emigration to limiting the damage that it could inflict. In particular, they used two related strategies: On the one hand, they used moral suasion and propaganda to deter emigration; on the other hand, they tried to restrict and intimidate emigrants and the labor agents hired to recruit them.

In a 1921 article in the *Journal of Negro History*, H. H. Donald described how southern newspapers and elites warned potential emigrants of the difficult labor market, climate, and living conditions they would find in the urban North. They warned that southern Whites understood the black laborer better than northern Whites, that many Blacks were returning home after experiencing unexpected hardships in the North, and that the northern trail was littered with ruthless agents waiting to exploit them. When this tactic proved ineffective, white political elites tried to restrict the reach of migrant/labor agents by, for example, requiring agents to reside locally, or by imposing exorbitant taxes/fees on them. Donald even refers to police raids on southern railway stations, in which hundreds of Blacks were rounded up and arrested on questionable charges; he describes how the tickets of potential emigrants were destroyed before they boarded northbound trains and how black emigrants were dragged from trains or otherwise prevented from boarding them (1921: 427).

Similarly, Grossman (1991: 59–60) tells how "[l]andlords deprived tenants of railroad fare by refusing to gin the whole cotton crop or make timely settlements. Southern railroads refused to honor prepaid tickets bought through northern carriers." In addition, southern Whites lobbied senators and congressmen; the Departments of Agriculture, Labor, Commerce, Justice, and War; and the War Labor Policies Board to protect them from the detrimental flight of their labor.

Similar pressure developed later during WWII, when labor was again in short supply because of the demands of the war. As in WWI, the wartime situation provided an opportunity for southern workers to obtain alternative employment in labor-deficit regions. Again, southern businessmen

[13] September 19, 1916. From Grossman (1989: 62).

and farmers responded by trying to restrict the influence of labor agents who were recruiting workers for northern factories. In addition, they provided draft deferments to workers who remained in the South and increased foreign immigration (through the Bracero Program) to fill labor needs in regions that might otherwise attract southern emigrants (Alston and Ferrie 2007: 499; see also Chapter 6).

Finally, because the Great Migration occurred within the borders of a single country, it is easier to see the way in which problems in both sending and receiving regions were linked. When a wave of urban riots swept the nation's cities in the 1960s, activists highlighted connections between urban migration and social unrest, "linking urban problems to the forced migration of displaced black southerners who stood little chance of finding employment in shirking northern job markets. In response, federal authorities stepped up rural antipoverty efforts and tried to prod southern governments into doing more to assist poor people in their communities" (de Jong 2005: 395). In this context, federal policy makers and northern political elites realized that, to deter future emigration, something needed to be done to improve conditions in the South. The existence of political linkages between North and South enabled elites in both places to realize the need to address the underlying problems motivating southern emigration, rather than simply trying to deal with the symptoms.

Conclusion

The Great Migration illustrates how important emigration can be in securing political development for repressed groups, which otherwise lack effective channels of political influence. A significant exodus of black workers from the South not only changed the South's underlying class balance but also the act of emigration was understood as a challenge to the legitimacy of the southern white order. Just as significantly, black emigrants sent home news from the North that influenced attitudes and expectations about the region's future political development.

Of course, emigration alone was insufficient to bring about these changes. Clearly, the South's political development was also propelled by the effect of two world wars (on local demographic trends and the attitudes of returning soldiers), the mechanization of the cotton harvest, and (last, but not least) a vibrant and effective southern freedom (or civil rights) movement. Yet the Great Migration played an important and complementary role in this potent mix for political reform.

This role is consistent with the one we have found in earlier chapters, when there were relatively free opportunities for international emigration and high (per-capita) levels of emigration. This correspondence spurred me to wonder whether (political) development effects are also generated by emigration within countries in which labor flows are more regulated or constrained. The following section considers just such a case.

THE GREAT MIGRATION IN CHINA

Internal migration in China offers an interesting and useful contrast to the American case. Obviously, the motivation for internal migration is different in the Chinese case: It is a more traditional case of demographic transformation, in which rural workers are drawn to urban centers in search of industrial jobs. Just as importantly, rural emigrants in China are not fleeing the same sort of political repression as were Blacks in the U.S. South. The Chinese case is interesting because the flow of labor is being influenced by regulations that effectively limit the opportunities available to migrants. These constraints are not as severe as we saw in the Mexican or Algerian cases in Chapter 6 or in today's international context (e.g., as seen in Chapter 7), but they are significant enough to influence the size of the potential migrant stream.

The *Hukou* System

There is a remarkable amount of public and academic attention focused on contemporary migration patterns in China. This makes sense, if only because the very size of these flows is breathtaking, and our awareness of them is increasing as China opens up to foreigners. As many as 130 million people are estimated to have left the Chinese countryside in search of work in the cities, making this the largest migration in history. Yet internal migration in China is not new, nor is it especially large when weighted as a share of the country's total population. What makes Chinese migration interesting and unique is the way that is regulated by the political authorities.

Although internal migration has been made easier in recent decades, it is important not to exaggerate the freedom of mobility that exists in China today.[14] It is clearly a restricted mobility regime. The *hukou* system was

---

[14] It is common, if somewhat misleading, to peg the start of modern Chinese internal migration to the reform policies of December 1978. Although the nature of contemporary

originally designed as a de facto internal passport system in the 1950s, following the example provided by Russians/Soviets to the north.[15] For an ordinary person without official connections, it is still very difficult – if not impossible – to receive a migration permit to move from a rural to an urban area or from a smaller city to a larger one. However, peasants can now migrate to take "temporary" jobs (i.e., they can move without obtaining local *hukou*). In doing so, however, they are not eligible for many benefits and rights enjoyed by ordinary local residents (Chan 2010: 2).

Nor is the level of internal migration in China especially high relative to other countries, considering that most countries go through an intense process of urbanization when modernizing their economies. A recent Human Development Research Paper ranked the intensity of Chinese internal migration as middle-of-the-road – significantly below the levels found in Latin America and much of the developed world (Bell and Muhidin 2009: 20–3). Using census-based stock data, they found that less than 3% of the population moved across the 31 provinces in China over the previous five years. Their findings are reproduced in Table 8.2. Still, given the enormous population of the country, this 3% involves a massive amount of people (more than 32 million)! In China, permanent or "lifetime" internal migration intensities are well below what we see in other countries (both more and less developed).

As has been well documented, most of the Chinese migrants leave for urban production centers located in Guangdong and Jiangsu Provinces, as well as the two metropolises, Shanghai and Beijing (Chan 2001: 136–7). This migration is an integral part of the government's development strategy, and subnational government officials manage the flow by using urban-based labor export offices. These offices provide assistance to potential migrants; for example, helping them obtain information about potential jobs, issuing family planning certificates, and providing legal advice. Yet most Chinese internal migrants retain strong connections with their home villages, returning for the holidays and maintaining legal ties to the land, to which they hope to return eventually.

migration has been strongly influenced by these reforms, there have always been massive migration movements, even in earlier communist periods, but they were driven largely by political and security issues and less by market-based motives (see Lary 1999).

[15] Under this system, each household is granted an occupation category (agricultural or nonagricultural) and a place of residence (*hukou*). The *hukou* designates a person as either a peasant or an urban resident, and this designation provides access to locally provided social goods such as housing, education, and health care. See Chan and Buckingham (2008) for details.

TABLE 8.2. *Internal Migration, Selected Countries, Province Level*

	5-Year		Lifetime	
	No. of Migrants	Intensity (%)	No. of Migrants	Intensity (%)
South Africa	1,704,363	4.3	6,717,270	15.4
China	32,347,800	2.7	73,087,300	6.2
Indonesia	3,954,104	2.2	42,341,703	4.1
India	n.a.	n.a.	16,729,095	8.4
Argentina	1,161,800	3.6	6,691,210	20
U.S. (interstate)	22,794,783	8.9	78,583,779	31.6

Note: See the original study for an explanation of terms and measures. These intensities are of a different magnitude from the emigration rates used in other parts of this book, because they capture stock data of the total number of settled emigrants over a given period of time.
Source: Bell and Muhidin (2009: 20–23).

Chinese Political Development

The regulated nature of its internal migration derives from China's unique path to political development. Western scholars and observers are surprised by the fact that Chinese Communist Party officials have managed a very successful economic reform and subsequent economic development without loosening their grasp on political power. This does not mean that China has avoided political development, but its development has not proceeded along the same trajectory as Western experience might have us expect.

Significant, broad-based development has been documented in a series of five Human Development Reports on China, the most recent of which was conducted in 2007 (HDR China 2007). Thirty years of spectacular reforms have transformed the Chinese economy, lifting hundreds of millions of people out of poverty and raising the country from low- to middle-income status. The very scope and speed of China's economic transformation are unique in the history of human development.

This economic growth has brought with it impressive improvements in the country's ability to provide basic public services, which are an essential element of any capabilities-based approach to development. Access to good health and education opportunities is an essential part of political development, but so too is the ability to enjoy political and social freedoms. For this reason, Chinese political development has been restricted by the continued dominance of a party-state apparatus that penetrates down to the grassroots level. This apparatus provides the Communist Party with incredible control, both vertically and horizontally, because local cadres are (in effect) representatives of the central state: The party endorses their appointments, and their work is regularly assessed by cadres from upper echelons.

Still, local officials do have some autonomy with respect to basic economic instruments. For example, the state entrusts township cadres with the authority to levy taxes and oversee quota purchases of agricultural produce, education, family planning, land use, public security, and social stability (Murphy 2002: 129). Indeed, since the early 1980s, village elections have been introduced, although their scope and democratic character have been disputed (O'Brien and Li 2000).

In short, there can be no question that China has experienced significant development over the last 30 years, and we can expect the level of development to vary across the country. In fact, unequal access to the fruits of development seems to be a major concern of the country's political elite. At the lowest (village) level, we can expect to find significant variance in political development, as locally elected officials try to respond to deficiencies with the limited tools available to them. Unfortunately, securing data at this level of analysis is quite difficult, and the variance in political development is likely to diminish at higher levels of aggregation (e.g., at the province level), where the data do exist.

In the sections that follow, we look at the nature of the relationship between emigration and political development at two levels of aggregation. At the province level, it is possible to document a relatively strong link between emigration and political development, as measured by a province's level of human development. Yet this correlation provides little evidence for the mechanisms by which emigration affects political development. Such evidence can be found at lower levels of aggregation, where the data are more sporadic and based on field research by scholars who are examining other aspects of internal migration.

Province Level. Much academic attention has been drawn to the economic effects of contemporary internal emigration, and the findings are generally as expected. Most studies have examined micro-level effects at the household level, showing how remittances contribute to the sending household's income and consumption levels (Du et al. 2005) and a decrease in its level of poverty (Zhu and Luo 2008).[16]

---

[16] For a brief introduction to the economic effects of internal Chinese migration and the supporting literature, see UNDP (2009: 52).

Although economists are able to obtain individual- and household-level data to measure the economic impact of emigration, a study of political development needs to draw from higher levels of aggregation. Ideally, we would like to secure comparable measures of political development across sending villages in China, but these data are not available. Instead, we must turn to a more conventional level of aggregation, at the province level, for which emigration and broader development data are available over time.[17]

Table 8.3 ranks Chinese provinces by their average level of emigration between 1995 and 2005. As in previous tables of this nature, I divided the provinces into three groups: high emigration, medium emigration, and low emigration.[18] Given the limited period of time for which Chinese data are available, I was not able to construct decade averages. Thus, the annual emigration-per-mil figures in Table 8.3 are based on five-year census data, rather than annual emigration figures averaged by decade. In other words, these figures are not directly comparable with the international emigration data in previous chapters, but they can be seen as close substitutes.

In Table 8.3 we find that recent inter-province emigration rates are of an order of magnitude similar to the (international) emigration rates we saw in some countries before WWI, but are lower than the very high rates of emigration from some southern states in the United States after WWII. In short, the highest emigration-sending provinces are losing about 10 emigrants per thousand residents a year (on average). These provinces tend to be centrally located and include Jiangxi, Chongqing, Sichuan, Anhui, and Hunan.

If we compare these numbers with the level of human development in 2006 (second column from the right), we find a clear and unsurprising trend in which emigration continues to flow from the least developed provinces. On average, low-emigration provinces enjoy a higher level of human development (0.785) than do high- or medium-emigration

---

[17] This is not an optimal level of aggregation for at least two reasons. First, China's 31 provinces are large, so that each province could experience significant variance in terms of both emigration and development within its provincial borders. Second, political officials at the province level have relatively few tools to secure political autonomy and hence relatively little room for political movement.

[18] The criteria for inclusion in each group are the same as before, in which high-emigration provinces experience more than 10 emigrants per thousand residents a year (on average); medium-emigration provinces experience between 5 and 10 per mil, and low-emigration provinces have less than 5 per mil. See Chapter 5 for details.

TABLE 8.3. *Inter-Provincial Emigration in China, per Mil, 1995–2005*

	1995	2000	2005	1995–2005 Average	HDI 2006	Change in HDI, 1990–2006 (%)
High Emigration					*(0.750)*	*(39.4)*
Jiangxi	2.21	12.95	11.49	8.88	0.744	40.64
Chongqing*		7.14	10.27	8.71	0.764	
Anhui	2.56	9.67	12.54	8.26	0.737	38.27
Sichuan	2.62	10.56	9.60	7.59	0.742	39.47
Hunan	2.10	10.13	10.52	7.58	0.762	39.31
Medium Emigration					*(0.749)*	*(35.2)*
Guangxi	2.37	8.19	9.11	6.56	0.755	37.77
Guizhou	1.66	6.99	9.47	6.04	0.659	40.21
Hubei	1.02	7.33	9.51	5.95	0.767	32.70
Henan	1.51	4.99	7.32	4.61	0.768	37.63
Heilongjiang	2.70	5.10	5.34	4.38	0.796	27.56
Low Emigration					*(0.785)*	*(30.0)*
Zhejiang	2.89	4.15	4.25	3.76	0.840	33.76
Qinghai	1.98	4.75	3.13	3.29	0.702	40.96
Jilin	2.03	3.88	3.92	3.27	0.795	30.54
Gansu	1.48	4.38	3.81	3.22	0.687	36.04
Shaanxi	0.99	3.99	4.45	3.14	0.756	37.45
Fujian	1.21	3.60	4.54	3.12	0.795	15.55
Inner Mongolia	1.46	3.71	3.50	2.89	0.779	36.43
Hainan	1.51	3.30	3.82	2.88	0.767	31.79
Jiangsu	1.23	3.34	3.55	2.71	0.830	30.09
Beijing	0.85	2.52	4.29	2.55	0.897	20.89
Shanghai	0.80	1.95	4.22	2.32	0.917	6.38
Ningxia	1.58	3.10	2.28	2.32	0.737	35.73
Hebei	1.34	2.59	2.89	2.27	0.797	33.28
Tibet	0.51	2.67	2.24	1.81	0.621	60.05
Yunnan	0.64	1.86	2.70	1.73	0.686	38.31
Shandong	0.83	1.93	2.43	1.73	0.815	30.40
Tianjin	0.75	2.08	2.05	1.63	0.881	10.40
Xinjiang	0.74	2.25	1.81	1.60	0.752	26.81
Shanxi	0.52	2.03	2.06	1.53	0.782	28.83
Liaoning	0.60	1.79	1.97	1.46	0.822	17.77
Guangdong	0.26	1.01	0.00	0.42	0.828	26.99

Note: The emigration data are based on five-year census out-migration data; see Chan (2010) for details. The demographic data are Chan and Wang's (2008) "de facto" population estimates, per province, in the closing year of each period (i.e., 1995, 2000, 2005). The resulting figures in the table are generated using province-level data in the simple formula: (Emigration/Population)*1,000. To make the figures comparable with the international figures presented in earlier chapters, I have divided the five-year period averages by the number of years (5) to get an estimate of annual average emigration, per mil. The bold figures represent five-year average highs that qualify the province for its ranking in a given category (high, medium, low). *Before 1996, Chongqing was included in the Sichuan province figures.

Sources: Chan (2010: 14); Chan and Wang (2008: 30); HDR China (2007: 139); and UNDP (1997).

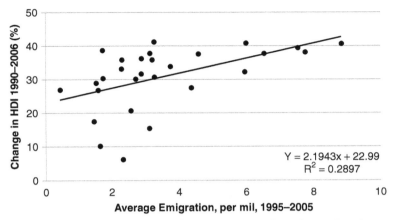

FIGURE 8.4. Emigration on Development, Scatterplot, Chinese Provinces, 1990–2006. *Sources:* See Table 8.3. *Note:* Tibet (outlier) and Chongqing (missing data) are removed. With Tibet included, the relationship is captured by the equation: $y = 1.776x + 25.614$, $R^2 = 0.1445$.

provinces (0.750 and 0.749, respectively). Clearly, the most developed provinces are attracting migrants, not shedding them. The only exception to this rule is Tibet (and possibly Yunnan), which has a remarkably low level of human development, given it is a low-emigration province.[19]

In the far-right column in Table 8.3, I listed the percentage change in a province's Human Development Index (HDI) score from 1990 to 2006. This score can be used as an indicator for broad-based political development, even though it lacks an explicitly political component (see Chapter 2 for elaboration). When we take the (high, medium, low) emigration group average for change in HDI, we find that those provinces with the highest levels of recent emigration also experienced the highest rates of development (39.4%); medium-emigration provinces had, on average, a little slower rate of development (35.2%), whereas low-emigration provinces experienced the lowest average change in development (30%).

To get a feel for the nature of the relationship, Figure 8.4 uses the data in Table 8.3 to map the level of emigration across provinces onto

[19] Obviously, Tibet finds itself in a unique position relative to the central Chinese authorities, and many Tibetans have fled China after its 1959 annexation of Tibet. The first wave of displacement occurred in 1959, when 85,000 Tibetans are said to have followed the Dalai Lama into exile in India. A second wave started in the early 1980s, when Tibet was opened up to trade and tourism. I do not have access to recent refugee/emigrant flows, but it is not unreasonable to expect that the level of inter-provincial migration between Tibet and the rest of China is affected by this political history.

the change in development over the same period of time (1990–2006). In this figure, Tibet and Chongqing are removed (the former because of its outlier status, the latter because of a lack of data). Here we find that about 29% of the variance in broad-based development across Chinese provinces is explained by the level of emigration.

It should not be necessary to point out that this is a very simplistic depiction. We know that the HDI is an imperfect indicator for political development and that other factors can also explain political development across provinces in China. We are also aware that using the province level of aggregation conceals as much as it reveals about the nature of the relationship linking emigration to political development. However, the quality of the data requires that we keep the analysis very simple, and our current objective is limited to exploring the potential relationship between emigration and political development. In light of these caveats, there are sufficient grounds to suspect a link between emigration and development across provinces in China – these grounds are strong enough, at least, to warrant further study.

Local Level. Although these findings are interesting, they do not provide us with any evidence that the threat of emigration is affecting a province's level of political development. To find this sort of evidence, we need to examine the motives of actors at lower levels of aggregation (and the instruments they have at their disposal). As was hinted earlier, it is at the village level that we might expect to find local – perhaps even elected – officials under pressure to improve political development in the face of growing emigration pressures.

Given access problems, there has been relatively little statistical work done at the regional or village level. The one important exception is a detailed statistical study, using village-level panel data, which finds that emigration communities first experience a drop in income equality, but that over time emigration generates strong income-inequality–reducing effects in the sending region (Ha et al. 2009: 5). More common are field studies conducted by sociologists and anthropologists interested in the general effects of emigration on local communities. Rachel Murphy's (2002, 2009) work is exemplary of this sort of fieldwork, and her findings are consistent with those found in the earlier mentioned statistical study:

[M]igration remains central to any explanation of change in the Chinese countryside.... [R]ural people's mobility and increased control over resources afford them a stronger bargaining position with respect to other members of society (including officials), and many are deploying their resources and achieving goals that are transforming the countryside politically, socially, and economically (Murphy 2002: 51).

Students of internal Chinese emigration note many of the same sorts of pressures that we have found in the international studies, even though their focus is seldom aimed at the political effects of that emigration. Several have observed the role that emigration plays in introducing new ideas and norms to the local village community. For example, Murphy (2002: 220) notes that "labor mobility exposes rural people (both villagers and officials) to new values and possibilities while at the same time increasing the resources available to them for pursuing personal, family, business, and development goals." Likewise, Chan (2001: 145–6) holds that "[t]he circularity of movements has generated a reverse flow not only of wealth (remittances) but also of progressive attitudes and modern, technical skills to the peripheral areas.... It is very likely that exposure to the outside world and especially non-agricultural skills have a more lasting impact on the local development of rural communities than do remittances."

Davin (1999: 89) observes how urban immigrants are influenced by the ideas and lifestyles of the city, taking these back to the villages when they return. For example, male construction workers are forced to learn about the hardships of women's lives when they need to fetch their own water, prepare their own meals, and wash and mend their own clothes. This experience can change their attitudes and behavior in ways that facilitate subsequent political and social development. Similarly, women who stay at home can end up inheriting jobs that were traditionally reserved for men: They too learn a new way to look at life and might enjoy more independence. Women who immigrate to the city (e.g., as maids) can observe and experience different models of marriage and family interaction. They come to expect and enjoy the benefits of running water, flush toilets, refrigerators, proper drainage, and the like.

Finally, family members remaining at home are often forced to become functionally literate in new ways: For example, they must now go to banks and post offices and learn how to use bank accounts (often for the first time) to deposit the remittances being sent home from loved ones abroad.

Tiebout-like effects have also been noted; for example, Murphy (2002: 180ff) speaks about how emigration improves the political environment for business: "[R]eturnees tend to compare the developed economies of the coastal cities with their rural home towns, explaining the differences in terms of local-level policies and government behavior." Indeed, Murphy (2002: 181) quotes a migrant to this effect:

My boss asked me why all the Jiangxi country cousins (*laobiao*) come to work in Guangzhou. I told him that it is all to do with the policies. Your policies are open and ours are backward. At home they tell us to run but tie our legs. If your policies were like ours and ours were like yours then Guangzhou people would be coming to work in Jiangxi.

Although this quote references the business environment, we might expect to find the same sentiment applied to other assets of local politics. Indeed, Murphy points to a Yudu (a county in Jiangxi Province) Party Committee brochure that seems to confirm as much, when it assures emigrants that "we are going to further liberate our thought, become more open, formulate preferential policies" (Murphy 2002: 184).

A Hirschman effect, of voice intertwined with the threat of exit, is also evident in many of these accounts, in which migration provides rural households with a means to bypass the power of political authorities in the sending area. Thus households without local political contacts or traditional skills find new opportunities for generating (nonfarm) incomes:

[M]igration reduces the influence of local patronage in the allocation of off-farm earning opportunities to households. The political elite tend to control local off-farm earning opportunities, but migration creates an extended social and economic network, thereby allowing villagers to circumvent the political monopoly over off-farm opportunities (Murphy 2002: 52).

Conclusion

Although we cannot explore the Chinese case in any detail because of a lack of data, the initial findings are illuminating. Despite burdensome regulations on internal migration, the threat of emigration seems to be increasing the level of political development, broadly conceived, in sending regions. Those provinces that are experiencing the highest rates of emigration are those that are, on average, experiencing the largest improvements in human development in recent years.

Anecdotal evidence from the village level seems to support a direct link between emigration and political pressure for change, but the nature and scope of the data are insufficient to reach a conclusion with any certainty. It could be that the level of political development is an indirect result of the economic development that we know is being generated by emigration. Still, the existence of a general relationship between emigration and economic and political development is particularly interesting in the Chinese context, in which we tend to assume that political development is stifled by the central authorities.

These are curious findings worthy of further investigation. The effects are stronger than expected (compared to the aggregate international comparisons in earlier chapters), given that the Chinese regime is regulated and the per-capita level of emigration is not especially high. In light of our earlier findings, two speculative thoughts come to mind in trying to explain this outcome. The first concerns demographic pressure. Given China's strong commitment to its one-child policy, the overall demographic context of limited growth may be amplifying the emigration effect in China. This effect may be similar to what we saw in the European guest-worker programs in Chapter 6. In addition, the lack of alternative venues for affecting political change in China may make the threat of exit an especially effective tool for signaling political dissatisfaction (as we saw earlier in the U.S. case study). I hope that future work might begin to study these posited relationships in more detail.

CONCLUSION

The two case studies in this chapter remind us that the political effects of emigration are not confined to international migration; Indeed, migration within countries has always played an important role in the political and economic development of most nations. In both domestic and international cases, emigration seems to facilitate political development by affecting people's expectations and their ability to transform political conditions at home.

The American and Chinese cases vary in several ways: in the motivation driving each of their great migrations, the degree of regulation of each migration, and their political and cultural contexts. They also differ in terms of the relative size of each emigration: Southern black rates of emigration in the United States, especially after WWII, were substantially higher than what we find in contemporary China (as a percent of population). Despite these important differences, both cases reveal a clear relationship between emigration from specific regions and the subsequent political development of those regions.

What does this say about the effects of systemic regulation on emigration? In these cases, it would seem that even semi-regulated migration flows can generate political development in the sending region. Emigration in China is constrained by a regulatory system that prohibits undocumented migrants from accessing social services and benefits. As such, the Chinese internal migration regime is not all that different from the international regulatory regime today, in which irregular migrants chase down jobs in the developed world, without benefits, and at the constant risk of deportation.

Having found the relationship between emigration and political development to exist at the national level of aggregation, it is time to conclude the empirical analyses in this book by looking at the individual-level effects of emigration. This is the subject of the following chapter.

9

Fellow Travelers

In the half century before World War I, the world experienced massive international migration. As we know, during that time it also experienced the first and largest wave of democratization. In the preceding chapters we have learned that the relationship between emigration and political development cannot be characterized simply: It is a relationship influenced strongly by a number of contextual variables and linked by complex causal mechanisms.

This, in itself, is not surprising. After all, the general literature is filled with a host of competing and more established variables than emigration for explaining democratization and political development. The most common of these draw on the political and economic pressures emanating from an organized working class in the heat of industrialization – when established political elites extended the suffrage and relinquished political authority in the face of a growing and increasingly radical working class.

Indeed this first wave of democratization was propelled by a vibrant internationalist socialist movement that became increasingly radical and revolutionary before World War I. The threat of revolution hung in the air as sundry national and international movements grew in power and influence. This influence was evident in the rise of the First and Second Internationals – organizations of socialist and labor parties – before WWI and a Moscow-led internationalist movement after the Bolshevik Revolution in 1917. This specter of revolution motivated many democratic reforms, as political elites scrambled to maintain power by addressing the escalating demands of workers.

The concomitant rise in international migration, revolutionary socialism, and democratization is not accidental. Much of the nascent labor

movement in Europe was driven by leaders of a threatened craft tradition – a tradition that embraced migration and mobility as part of its
apprenticeship training. When traveling around Europe and learning their
trades, workers became connected with and informed about the struggles
of fellow workers.

Indeed, the etymology of terms used for types of workers at the turn
of the last century is itself revealing. Consider the position of a journeyman, a fully qualified worker who has finished his apprenticeship in a
particular trade or craft but who still works in the employment of others.
Traditionally, journeymen traveled to build up their résumés and working
experience. The word *journée* – from the French – means the period of
one day. Thus a "journeyman" might be understood in terms of the right
to charge a fee for a day's labor, as well as the travel (the journey) often
associated with the position. It is also interesting to note that some of the
most radical labor organizations are linked to the traveling trades: in
the United States, the Longshoremen and Teamsters; in other countries,
the (often temporary and mobile) construction trades.

In this chapter I examine the links between political radicalization and
migration in light of the experiences of individual migrants. Indeed, it is
at this level of analysis that we expect much of the political effects of
emigration to be evident. I begin by taking another look at the rise of
the Norwegian Labor Party (DNA) and one of its guiding stars, Martin
Tranmæl, first examined in Chapter 5. I conclude that it is reasonable to
generalize from Tranmæl's experience because a significant proportion of
important political reformers/revolutionaries had emigrant backgrounds.

MARTIN TRANMÆL: "THE STORMY PETREL OF NORWEGIAN LABOR"[1]

Martin Tranmæl is not well known outside of Norway, and he is almost
forgotten by the modern Norwegian labor movement.[2] However, in his

---

[1] This heading comes from a phrase in Hovde (1934: 273).

[2] As far as I know, there is no English biography of Tranmæl. The Norwegian biographies
are all dated and strongly influenced by their respective political positions. As Jorunn
Bjørgum (1998: 15–16) notes, Tranmæl is usually depicted in one of three ways: as a
hero by followers of the DNA (e.g., Zachariassen, 1939; Lie, 1988, 1991); as a villain
by those affiliated with the Norwegian Communist Party (e.g., Olsen 1991); and in a
mocking or scornful way by followers of a left-communist splinter group, *Mot Dag* (e.g.,
Maurseth 1979). Even more surprising is the lack of English references to the history of
the Norwegian labor movement. To date, the best English reference remains Galenson
(1949).

time, Tranmæl was a force to be reckoned with. Although he shied away from elected positions, he was a member of the DNA's central board (1918–63) and editor of the party's newspaper *Social-Demokraten* (later *Arbeiderbladet*) from 1921–49. He was the Labor Party Secretary from 1918–23, served on the Norwegian Workers' National Trade Organization (AFL/N, subsequently LO) Secretariat (1920–45), and was a long-time member of the "cooperation committee," which coordinated the activities between the LO and the DNA (1927–59).

Labor activists and chroniclers writing in the 1970s–90s were well aware of his influence.[3] Per Maurseth (1979: 4) called him "the most powerful man in the Norwegian labor movement" during the interwar period, whereas Håkon Lie (1991) referred to him simply as the pathfinder. Even Nikolai Bukharin – when leading a Comintern committee whose (ultimately unsuccessful) task was to return the DNA to the Internationalist fold – is said to have called Tranmæl "invincible" (Gabrielsen 1959: 86).

Tranmæl's influence is evident in both the political and union wings of the Norwegian labor movement. In addition to being one of the main architects of the modern DNA, he piloted the party as it navigated the treacherous political waters of the interwar period. With Tranmæl at its helm, the Norwegian Labor Party became one of the most radical in Europe. His influence on the LO was just as pronounced: "The internal history of the Norwegian Federation of Labor [LO] during the next decade [1910–1920] can be written largely in terms of the struggle between the craftsmen and this new group of unskilled workers, between social democracy and semi-syndicalism. The struggle revolved around Martin Tranmæl, the most controversial figure in Norwegian labor history" (Galenson 1949: 20).

What makes Tranmæl interesting for this study is his experience as an emigrant: He spent more than four of his most formative years in the United States, working with, organizing, and studying the American labor movement during a very tumultuous time in its history. These experiences made a deep impression on the young Tranmæl.

Before examining his early life more closely, let me point out that Tranmæl's experiences were not unique. Norway's political development (and that of Europe, more generally) is replete with similar stories, because

[3] Any historian will marvel at the list of leading labor leaders with whom Tranmæl came into contact. In my reading, I have found evidence of him meeting the following individuals: Nikolai Bukharin, Eugene Debs, Seth Höglund, Mother (Mary Harris) Jones, Karl Kautsky, V. I. Lenin, Karl Liebknecht, Gustav Möller, Karl Radek, Fredrik Ström, Leon Trotsky, and Grigory Zinoviev. This list is not meant to be exhaustive.

many Norwegian activists cut their teeth on American political practice. For example, the Chicago accountant (and Tranmæl's later nemesis), Erling Falk, returned to Norway to become editor of the radical labor paper, *Mot Dag* (Toward Daybreak), which played a key role in the 1920 infighting between the Communist Party and the Labor Party (Derry 1973: 315). Similarly, Olav Kringen returned home in 1897, after working in leftist labor politics in the United States, aligning his Minnesota-based Norwegian-language newspaper, *Gaa Paa* (Press Forward), with the Norwegian Labor Party's moderate reform wing (Wyman 1993: 156). Norway's feminist movement was bolstered by the return of the writer and painter, Aasta Hansteen, who had emigrated in 1880. After nine years in the United States, she came home to help lead Norway's campaign for women's rights (Wyman 1993: 156). These experiences could be multiplied to fill an entire chapter, but doing so would not allow us to examine them in any detail.

For this reason, I focus attention on Tranmæl's experience, because he made such an enormous impact on the Norwegian Labor Party during its foundational and most tumultuous years. Tranmæl's influence on the party and subsequently on Norway's political development can be traced to five particular twists and turns in the DNA's path to political dominance.

1. In 1911, he led an oppositional movement from Trondheim, around the so-called Trondheim Resolution, which challenged the reformist nature of the DNA on several fronts. Although this program was never realized in full, the resolution became an important symbol in the struggle for the DNA.

2. In 1918, Tranmæl's oppositional faction took over the effective leadership of the party (Tranmæl was elected to serve as Labor Party Secretary from 1918–23) and turned the DNA sharply to the left. In 1920, Tranmæl's influence can be seen in the LO's "new direction," when it agreed to many of the organizational reforms proposed by the Trondheim opposition.

3. The radicalization of the Norwegian labor movement resulted in the DNA joining the Comintern in 1919 and initially agreeing to many of the constraints that membership entailed, including a growing level of influence from Moscow – although with important (albeit often forgotten) reservations.

4. In the early 1920s, Tranmæl began to pull the DNA back from the communist abyss, as he came to realize the amount of Soviet control and influence. In 1923, he orchestrated the party's split with the

Comintern and began to deal with the organizational consequences: the splintering of the political wing of the Norwegian labor movement into three parties: (1) the DNA; (2) the Norwegian Social Democratic Labor Party (*Norges Sosialdemokratiske Arbeiderparti*, NSA), which had already split off from the DNA in 1921 in response to DNA's membership in the Comintern, but would return soon to the DNA; and (3) the Norwegian Communist Party (*Norges Kommunistiske Parti*).

5. In 1927, Tranmæl used his position as editor of the *Arbeiderbladet* to encourage the DNA's rehabilitation as a responsible, mainstream political party (Malme 1979: 89). The DNA mended its bridges with members of the NSA, resulting in a unified and reform-minded DNA. This new strategy delivered impressive electoral results. In 1928, the DNA enjoyed its first, if very fleeting, stint in government: The Hornsrud government lasted just 18 days in office. Yet the DNA had showed that it could act as a responsible governing party and play by parliamentary rules. By 1933, the DNA fully returned to the reformist fold, attracting massive voter support. In 1935, with the election into office of the Nygaardsvold government, the DNA began its long bout of electoral hegemony.

From the mid-1930s, both the DNA and Tranmæl became mainstream. After WWII, Tranmæl appeared to be a different man: He became staunchly anticommunist and a strong supporter of Norway's subsequent membership in NATO. In those ideological shifts Tranmæl reflected a transformed Labor Party; he was no longer leading it. By the time of Tranmæl's death, in 1967, the revolutionary roots of the DNA were buried deep in the party's history.

It is not controversial to argue that the DNA had a significant influence in directing Norway's political development in the interwar and immediate postwar period nor that Tranmæl held a leading and influential position in the party during its formative years. What may be controversial is my contention that much of Tranmæl's early vision of a radicalized Norwegian labor movement was colored by his experiences as an immigrant to the United States. To trace these connections, we need to take a closer look at the life of Tranmæl, the emigrant.

The Emigrant

Martin Tranmæl was born in 1879 and grew up on a small farm in Melhus, just outside of Trondheim. Although Melhus did host a local

Thrane movement in the 1850s,[4] Tranmæl's most immediate political influences were from the left (*Venstre*, the party that attracted his father's avid support) and the temperance movement, both of which were firmly established in Melhus. A child of the time, Tranmæl grew up hearing the stories of emigrants: Three of his uncles had left for the United States when he was still a child, and three of his four siblings would later do the same – all of whom settled in Wisconsin.

Tranmæl went to work at an early age: At 15 he found work with a local painter, and in 1896 he moved to Trondheim to begin work as an apprentice. There he joined the local painters' apprentice union. Yet it was not until he began to travel as a journeyman, first to Bergen and then to Kristiania (now Oslo), that his union membership delivered any political returns. In the capital city, the local hall of the painters' apprentice union was affiliated with the DNA, and Tranmæl began to campaign for the party there, before returning to Trondheim later in the same year (Kokkvoll 1979: 12). His political talents were clearly appreciated: In the following year, 1899, he became part of the editorial committee of a new labor newspaper in Trondheim (*Ny Tid*) and was elected to the board of the painters' apprentice union (Bull 1976: 79).

Immediately thereafter, in the spring of 1900, Tranmæl emigrated to America with his sister. They went first to Wisconsin, to live with their two brothers who had emigrated earlier and to learn English. After a year, Tranmæl traveled westward, writing a series of travelogues that were printed in *Ny Tid*,[5] many of which concerned the American labor struggle. In San Francisco, for example, he witnessed a violent strike involving sailors and longshoremen that ended with the police beating back the protestors. Settling in Los Angeles, he joined the Brotherhood of Painters and came into contact with Eugene Debs' nascent Socialist Party of America (SPA), eventually becoming a member. This first trip ended in the spring of 1902, when he returned home to Trondheim. This was not meant to be permanent, because he had already made plans to meet someone at the 1905 World's Fair in St. Louis (Gabrielsen 1959: 32). Even though he planned to return to America in a few years, Tranmæl jumped headfirst into Norwegian politics.

At this point, I should note that emigration may not be the correct word to describe Tranmæl's adventures, because several of his biographers

---

[4] See Chapter 5 for a brief description of Marcus Thrane and his movement.
[5] See, for example, his *Ny Tid* travelogues on May 16 and October 9, 1900, and January 9 and February 4, 1902.

argue that Tranmæl never intended to settle in the New World (e.g., Bjørgum 1998: 515; Zachariassen 1939: 31; and Gabrielsen 1959: 27).[6] However, the exact choice of words is unimportant, because the period itself lent itself to fluid perceptions. Most "emigrants" of the time had a relatively open-ended attitude about leaving home: They were going to give the New World a shot, to get a little taste of the world outside, and then return home. Yet the plans of many travelers changed while they were abroad: Many became emigrants with time, and conversely many declared emigrants eventually returned home. The point is that during this time the lack of formal restrictions on exit and entry allowed workers this latitude. It was possible to explore and learn from the world outside and then to bring back that experience to help shape conditions at home. For our purpose, it matters little whether Tranmæl intended to settle permanently in the United States when he first left. What matters is that he went there for some time, experienced life and work abroad, and returned home with those experiences.

In his letters home, Tranmæl actually advised against emigration: Even if the wages were attractive, it was often difficult to secure permanent work, and he predicted a future economic crisis that would make conditions worse (Bull 1976: 80). However, this did not stop him from using emigration as a political lever. During his short trip home to Trondheim, Tranmæl wrote mockingly about Norwegian emigration: "One hears people crying, high and low, that mother Norway is being let down. Which mother are they talking about?" (*Ny Tid*, April 22, 1902). In this account we can already hear an internationalist accent: "One should defend his country. But whose country is this?" In May he returned to the subject. "Since I've returned home," Tranmæl noted, "nearly every paper I pick up is filled with deplorable letters regarding massive emigration. And it is tragic, and true. But what has been done in the form of social support?" He noted how the country was willing to build fortifications against the Swedes; build warships and torpedoes and cannons; and even extend the draft for young recruits, but it could not afford to improve the social conditions that were forcing out its talented workers: "The only way to defend against emigration is to build a just social system. Let us hasten its arrival" (*Ny Tid*, May 6, 1902).

---

[6] By contrast, Edvard Bull (1976: 79) describes Tranmæl as someone who "travelled over as an emigrant, and worked at his profession in America, but did not set his roots in any one place."

In October 1903, Tranmæl returned to the United States. As he did
on his first trip, he settled in Los Angeles, but also traveled around the
country – visiting Chicago, Seattle, and a number of other places. From
his letters home to *Ny Tid*, we learn of his efforts to engage the American
labor struggle more and more, on both political and economic fronts.

His points of connection to the American socialist movement were
many and varied: He became secretary of a socialist group while in Seattle (Gabrielsen 1959: 33); worked for the Scandinavian section of the
SPA while in Chicago (Bull 1976: 81), chairing one of its committees and
editing *Socialisten* for Scandinavian readers in Chicago (Andersen 1975:
212); and took evening classes in economics from the Los Angeles branch
of the SPA (Zachariassen 1939: 47). Tranmæl's travel accounts reveal
a deep admiration for Eugene Debs,[7] whom Arlow William Andersen
(1975: 212) credits with having taught Tranmæl "the wisdom of employing parliamentary methods rather than the direct-action approach of the
Industrial Workers of the World."

Yet it was probably Tranmæl's study of American industrial relations
that made the biggest impact on him. He reported on many American
strikes in *Ny Tid*, and became convinced of the need to conduct the
workers' struggle on both economic and political fronts. In one American
strike after another, Tranmæl witnessed how the state came to the aid
of employers in repressing worker demands: The police protected strikebreakers, the military was called in to protect employer property, and
union members were frequently arrested and deported:

In America he learned how the struggle could be much more ruthless than he
knew from his European experience. It was commonplace for strikes to be beaten
down with the greatest brutality. Workers were forced to meet this ruthlessness
with strength and resolve.... But the most important and valuable lesson that
he learned was the strong impression of courage, enthusiasm and a spirit of
self-sacrifice that revolutionary socialists in America brought to the struggle for
workers' interests (Zachariassen 1939: 52).

Tranmæl reasoned that developments in America were a precursor of
what would occur in Norway. As capital became more and more concentrated in large concerns, and as industrialization facilitated the hiring
of many unskilled workers, it would become increasingly difficult to use
strikes and boycotts to gain concessions for workers. When the state

[7] To Gabrielsen (1959: 31), Tranmæl recollected that Debs had made "an indelible impression on him...a magnificent speaker, clear and convincing, and genuine through and
through."

was captured by employer interests, and all the power of the state was employed to quash worker actions, strikes and boycotts would become all the more ineffective. Worse still, workers were being taught that their own power should be limited to the economic struggle, with strong barriers being erected between union and party organizations.

This realization directed Tranmæl's focus on the form and strategy of different worker organizations. On joining the Brotherhood of Painters he had gained some experience with the American Federation of Labor (AFL/US), to which it was affiliated. This experience was anything but positive. He felt that Samuel Gompers and the AFL's leadership had sold their soul: By supporting class cooperation, the AFL split workers from one another and made it difficult to organize workers as a class:

The old conservative union federation, the "American Federation of Labor" ... has far from satisfied the requirements of a modern union organization. First of all, it is based on a heresy, that workers and capitalists share common interests. In addition, its very form of organization divides workers. The high entry dues of most of its component unions are used to secure its monopoly position: they protect already organized workers and hinder the great masses outside from joining the organization (*Ny Tid* December 27, 1905).

His experience with the AFL/US convinced Tranmæl that the greatest shortcoming of the American labor movement was the lack of a strong political organization or party. In Norway, by contrast, the political organization tended to dominate over the union organization. Yet in both cases, Tranmæl came to recognize the need for labor's political and union organizations to stand hand in hand.

When an alternative labor organization, the Industrial Workers of the World (IWW, or Wobblies) was established in the summer of 1905, Tranmæl was especially excited about its potential. Indeed, he attended its convening congress in Chicago. Because Tranmæl was a member of an AFL/US-affiliated union, he could not establish a formal affiliation with the new organization, but his excitement was evident in his letters home:

The new organization is clearly the most focused and modern movement we have yet seen on the economic front. It is for this reason that its principles and methods should attract international attention. It is broad enough to include all workers, but focused enough to exclude reactionaries and misguided compromisers from its midst (in Zachariassen 1939: 51).

The IWW was designed to break down the organizational barriers that separated workers into discrete trades. It was organized into 13 industrial departments, and its membership fees were kept purposively low. Most of all, Tranmæl appreciated the political inclinations of the early IWW: It had established direct connections to both of the U.S. socialist parties at the time.[8]

The Agitator

Tranmæl returned to Trondheim for Christmas in 1905. He then set his mind to building an oppositional labor movement in Norway, one that was better prepared to meet the struggles ahead. In many respects, the early IWW was a prototype for his movement: It was struggle-oriented, encouraging the use of strikes, demonstrations, sabotage, and violent actions to make its point; it was organized along industrial lines to create a stronger sense of class identity and to minimize the (trade) differences that might separate workers in their common struggle; it embraced unskilled workers with low membership dues and a willingness to take up their cause; and it realized the need to secure political power, through a socialist political movement, to ensure that it would reap the rewards of their struggle.

In 1907 Tranmæl was ready to launch this new movement. In a *Ny Tid* article entitled "Our Fighting Spirit," Tranmæl fired a broadside at the mainstream labor movement in Norway. That movement, as directed by the AFL/N, focused its attention on securing binding wage agreements. Tranmæl took issue with this strategy, arguing that miniscule wage increases and binding agreements often had the effect of placating or pacifying workers. Over time, these workers would end up losing their appetite for and interest in the organization and its struggle. This was the greatest threat to the labor movement: Temporary setbacks resulting from unsuccessful conflicts were less damaging than a membership uninspired by small and numbing wage gains, born of binding centralized agreements.

In the same year, in a debate at the 1907 Trade Congress in Oslo, Tranmæl justified this position with reference to the successful tactics he had observed in America:

In America, several trade unions were trying to avoid binding wage agreements, as they often had the effect of limiting the larger liberation struggle. By participating

---

[8] Both Eugene Debs's SPA and Daniel De Leon's Marxist-oriented Social Labor Party (SLP) were vying for influence during the initial meetings of the IWW. De Leon, who thought that the political and economic wings of labor should work closely together, was later expelled from the IWW (in 1908), when the movement became more syndicalist and antiparliamentarian.

in these sorts of agreements, the employer appears to be relinquishing some of his gain, but in actuality these concessions are most often used to tie the workers' hands (Zachariassen 1939: 71-2).

Three years later, at a 1910 congress of the Federation of Labor, Tranmæl formally proposed that the AFL/N should reorganize along industrial lines, similar to the IWW. He later elaborated on this need in a 1912 document summarizing the organizational needs of workers in the 20th century:

The natural boundary for each union should be industry, not the trade or branch. With the development of machines and the concentration of employers, existing trade-based barriers will be broken down. *Trade* unions stand as a testimony to a time that has passed us by. But a fighting organization such as ours cannot afford to maintain such memorials. By following developments closely, we shall persevere (Tranmæl, 1912, emphasis in original).

Tranmæl's 1910 proposal failed to gain majority support (not by a long shot), and he returned to Trondheim to rethink his strategy. In 1911, at the Trondheim Central Trade Council meeting, Tranmæl formulated what became known as the "Trondheim Resolution." This resolution called for rebuilding the labor movement on more radical foundations and included three specific proposals: (1) Binding collective wage agreements should be abolished and union insurance funds discontinued; (2) trade unions should rely on strikes, boycotts, obstruction, sabotage, and worker coops to secure their demands; and (3) the AFL/N should become an industrial-based (not a trade-based) organization, with central trades councils being established at the local level.[9]

Each of these three proposals can be directly traced to Tranmæl's experiences in the United States and to his admiration of the early IWW. Indeed, the result of Tranmæl's Trondheim Resolution was a more radical Norwegian labor movement that came to embrace decentralization, reject narrow parliamentarianism, and use revolutionary tactics. On each of these fronts, Tranmæl's position was clearly informed by his experiences with a nascent American labor movement. This interpretation is, at any rate, consistent with the one found in the official history of the DNA (Koht 1939: 77).

---

[9] Not surprisingly, it was the focus on sabotage that especially caught the media's critical attention, and much of Tranmæl's (rather dicey) reputation was established when he suggested the following to a 1912 meeting of the Kristiania Labor Party: "[W]hat if some sticks of dynamite happened to be left in the drill holes which only the striking workers were aware of: don't you think that the strikebreakers would think again before beginning to work?" (Bull 1947: 224). When a striking worker was subsequently shot by a strikebreaker in 1913, Tranmæl was blamed by most of the mainstream media.

Emigrant Influence

The preceding section aimed to link an individual emigrant's experiences with subsequent political developments in his homeland. My attempt is necessarily tentative, if only because the causal chain under scrutiny includes three separate links: (1) the effects that emigration had on Tranmæl's own perceptions and actions, (2) the effect that Tranmæl had on the formative years of the DNA, and (3) the effect that the DNA had on subsequent political developments in Norway.

Because I do not think that the latter two links are particularly weak or controversial, I focused attention on the first. However, because this link concerns the perceptions of a historical figure, we must not expect it to bear too heavy a load. Perceptions are difficult enough to trace among living contemporaries, with whom we can at least discuss the matter.

With this caveat in mind, there is a remarkable amount of overlap between Tranmæl's written and reported evaluations of the nascent American labor movement and the specific form of critique/opposition that he leveled at Norway's labor elites on returning home. Each of the main elements in his oppositional platform – his advocacy for industrial, as opposed to trade, unions; his embrace of mass actions and sabotage as tools for securing labor victories; his preference for revolutionary over reformist approaches; his critique of binding wage agreements at the expense of mass actions; and his emphasis on fighting both economic and political fronts simultaneously – can be traced to what the young Norwegian labor activist saw and experienced in the United States. It is difficult to imagine that Tranmæl would have developed this particular form of opposition had he not emigrated to the United States and studied developments there.

However, it is also easy to exaggerate the effects of his emigrant experiences. Clearly, these experiences are insufficient in themselves to explain Norway's subsequent political development. Tranmæl could have immigrated to the United States, experienced what he did, and returned to a Norwegian context that was ill prepared to embrace those experiences. Tranmæl seems to have been the right man, at the right place, at the right time.

Indeed, Tranmæl himself was reluctant to emphasize the effect of his experiences in the United States in any simple fashion:

In his later years, he [Tranmæl] claimed that the IWW had not been a model in his work to renew the Norwegian labor movement. That may be right: it was impossible to copy the IWW onto Norwegian conditions. The IWW was a child of America's Wild West. But we can be fairly certain that his fundamental political view and his work in the years that followed was deeply influenced by his impressions of the American labor movement (Lie 1988: 83).

Clearly, other international influences had an important effect on Tranmæl's vision – remember Tranmæl was politically active at a time of heated discussions in Germany, a failed 1905 revolution in Russia, the debates of the First and Second Internationals, and the 1917 Bolshevik Revolution. Just as importantly, Tranmæl continued to travel around Europe and even visited Canada after returning from America.[10]

Yet his trip to the United States happened at a more formative time in his life than did these other events – and he spent more time there than in other European countries and Canada. It is for these reasons that the American experience made such a deep impression on Tranmæl. In effect, Tranmæl left a small farming village and a relatively docile labor movement in Trondheim to travel to a world apart – that was in a storm of political agitation. He first left Norway as an impressionable 21-year-old and stayed in the United States, more or less, until he was 26. Even those who are reluctant to emphasize the impact of the emigrant experience on Tranmæl's political development recognize that those experiences had made an indelible mark. In the words of Jorunn Bjørgum (1998: 515),

It was first and foremost the capitalists' extreme brutality and ruthless suppression of every workers' struggle that made an impression. In addition, he saw the ability of capitalists to employ the state's instruments of violence in the form of the police and military. I believe that Tranmæl's experiences led him to conclude that this was the true face of capitalism – and it wasn't very pretty.

EMIGRANT REVOLUTIONARIES

It would be fruitless to generalize on the basis of one man's experience. For every story about Martin Tranmæl, there is another emigrant account

---

[10] Between 1907 and 1912 Tranmæl visited like-minded socialists in Stockholm and Copenhagen and in Hamburg and Berlin, Leipzig, Frankfurt, Köln, and Dresden. He also visited Belgium, the Netherlands, Paris, Prague, and several places in Italy. After this trip, Tranmæl reflected on the need for external stimulus and reflection. In one of his articles, he wrote,

> *Those who travel abroad return with new ideas with respect to their trade and culture.... We [the Norwegian labor movement] could also benefit from mingling more with the outside world. A young journeyman is particularly well-suited for the task. All that is needed is a little resolve and thought"* (referenced in Zachariassen 1939: 75).

that ends in little or no political effect. Such is the nature of individual accounts. However, in examining Tranmæl's experience, we are able to see the particular human mechanisms that can link emigration to political development. This places the larger argument in a context and level that resonate with us as individuals.

Even though we cannot legitimately generalize from Tranmæl's account, we can establish whether his experiences were unique by examining whether emigration experiences are common among those who lead revolutions or important political transformations. To do so, I decided to search published lists of influential politicians, reformers, and revolutionaries. By drawing from an already existing sample, I hoped to avoid any suspicion of biased sampling on the dependent variable. I also assumed that the revolutionaries included in previously published studies could not have been chosen with an eye on their emigrant status.

The decision of which list to choose was much easier than expected, because there are few published lists of important people who have changed the political world. Thus, I was both relieved and excited when I came across a copy of Jack A. Goldstone's (1999) *Who's Who in Political Revolutions: Seventy-Three Men and Women Who Changed the World*. This selection of 73 influential individuals was drawn from his larger (1998) *The Encyclopedia of Political Revolutions*; however, no explicit criteria are mentioned for inclusion in the *Who's Who* listing.[11] Still, a brief glance at the biographies (see Table 9.1) makes it clear that this is a geographically and chronologically diverse group of individuals, stretching in time from Martin Luther (1489–1546) to Rigoberta Menchú Tum (1959–).

To measure the degree to which these individuals had had significant emigrant experiences, I read each of the Goldstone biographies in search of references to time spent aboard before their "revolutionary" (or otherwise noteworthy) activity. I operationalized this foreign experience in terms of an individual spending more than one year living in a foreign country, whether it was time spent pursuing an education, in exile, and/or working. This measure did not include experiences with internal exile (e.g., Stalin in Siberia; Sukarno in Sumatra) or time spent abroad as part of military service, even though these experiences may have had similar effects.

---

[11] In the preface to the *Encyclopedia*, we learn that members of the Editorial and Advisory Boards "commissioned a small number of essays on revolutionary leaders and thinkers, particularly those whose influence has spread beyond the boundaries of their own societies" (Goldstone 1998: vii).

TABLE 9.1. *Foreign Experience of Successful Reformists/Revolutionaries*

Revolutionary	Foreign Experience	Revolutionary	Foreign Experience
Adams, John	No	Lumumba, Patrice	No
Adams, Samuel	No	Luther, Martin	No
Anthony, Susan B.	No	Luxemburg, Rosa	Yes
Atatürk, Kemal	No	Madison, James	No
Biko, Steven	No	Mandela, Nelson Rolihlahla	Yes
Bolívar, Simón	Yes	Mao Zedong	No
Buonarroti, Filippo Michele	Yes	Martí, José	Yes
Burke, Edmund	No	Marat, Jean-Paul	Yes
Cabral, Amílcar	Yes	Marx, Karl	Yes
Castro, Fidel	Yes	Menchú Tum, Rigoberta	Yes
Chiang Kai-shek	Yes	Mosaddeq, Mohammad	Yes
Cromwell, Oliver	No	Mugabe, Robert Gabriel	Yes
Deng Xiaoping	Yes	Mussolini, Benito	Yes
Engels, Friedrich	Yes	Nasser, Gamal Abdel	Yes
Fanon, Frantz Omar	Yes	Nehru, Jawaharlal	Yes
Franklin, Benjamin	Yes	Nkrumah, Kwame	Yes
Gandhi, Mahatma	Yes	Nyerere, Julius Kambarage	Yes
Garibaldi, Giuseppe	Yes	Orwell, George	Yes
Gorbachev, Mikhail	No	Paine, Thomas	Yes
Gramsci, Antonio	Yes	Robespierre, Maximilien	No
Guevara, Ernesto "Che"	Yes	Rousseau, Jean-Jacques	Yes
Havel, Václav	No	San Martin, José Francisco de	Yes
Henry, Patrick	No	Sandino, Augusto César	Yes
Hitler, Adolf	Yes	Sorel, Georges	No
Ho Chi Minh	Yes	Stalin, Joseph	No
Hong Xiuquan	No	Sukarno	No
Jefferson, Thomas	No	Sun Yat-sen	Yes
Jinnah, Mohammad Ali	Yes	Tito, Josip Broz	Yes
Juárez, Benito	Yes	Tocqueville, Alexis de	Yes
Kenyatta, Jomo	Yes	Trotsky, Leon	Yes
Khomeini, Ayatollah Ruhollah	Yes	Walesa, Lech	No
		Washington, George	No
Kim Il Sung	Yes	William of Orange	Yes
King, Martin Luther, Jr.	No	William the Silent	Yes
Lafayette, Gilbert du Motier de	Yes	Zapata, Emiliano	No
Lechín Oquendo, Juan	No	Total	73
Lenin, Vladimir Ilyich	Yes	Number with foreign experience	47
Locke, John	Yes		
L'Ouverture, Francois-Dominique Toussaint	No	Percentage with foreign experience	64%

Source: Goldstone (1999).

A remarkably large number of the Goldstone biographies made reference to foreign experience. Of those that did not, I conducted an additional Internet search. In both sources (whether Goldstone or the Internet), we can assume that the nature of the foreign experience (education, exile, emigration) had to be significant before it would be mentioned in otherwise very brief accounts. This represents a fairly high threshold, because more detailed biographical accounts (in any number of different languages) could still provide evidence of significant emigrant experience, but be beyond the scope of my search. In short, I assumed that the emigrant experience mattered if it was mentioned in otherwise very brief biographies.

Of the 73 people included in Goldstone's list, 47 (or 64%) had a significant emigrant experience *before* they became influential. Indeed, in 41 cases, this foreign experience was noted in the quite short (usually less than two pages) Goldstone biographies. This in itself is an indication of the importance that the biographer placed on the individual's foreign experience. In the six other cases, evidence of significant foreign experience was easily tracked down on the Internet and is generally well known.[12]

Sixty-four percent is a strikingly high proportion, given the otherwise very different backgrounds of these influential individuals. Indeed, other studies of revolutionary leaders (e.g., Rejai and Phillips 1979) find them to be surprisingly diverse: Revolutionary leaders do not tend to distinguish themselves, relative to more conventional political leaders, in terms of unique personal experiences/characteristics.[13] Therefore it is especially interesting to find that many revolutionaries share a common experience of living abroad. This surprisingly strong finding also made me suspicious that the sample might suffer from bias. After all, these 73 individuals were successful in changing the world, but it may be that unsuccessful revolutionaries have a different emigrant experience.

---

[12] The six Goldstone biographies where foreign experience was not explicitly noted (but that was subsequently found on the Internet) are of Engels, Marx, Mussolini, Nasser, Nyerere, and Rousseau. A more extensive documentation of the foreign experience of these six is available by contacting the author.

[13] Of the 64 revolutionaries in their study, Rejai and Phillips (1979: 77) find that only 23% had *not* traveled abroad before their revolutionary activities. Of the 49 revolutionaries who had international experience, 60% had spent at least a year abroad, whereas 42% had spent four or more years abroad.

For this reason, I broadened the scope of the investigation to look at all potential revolutions and rebellions, failed and successful. On the Internet, it is possible to find two such lists, one provided on the *All-Experts* site and another on *Wikipedia*.[14] Both of these lists were quite long, so the search was restricted to the post-1850 period. Although the *Wikipedia* site was more exhaustive, it also included a great many war-related resistance movements. Given the significant overlap across the two datasets, I chose to conduct an extensive Internet survey of the *AllExperts* revolutions/rebellions between 1850 and 2005.

I began by trying to associate a given individual (sometimes more than one) as a leader to the movement in question. Sometimes a leader was mentioned in the *AllExperts* list, but often this was not the case. I then needed to link the movement with a particular leader or set of leaders (see Table 9.2). With this done, I tracked down Internet biographies for each of the candidate revolutionaries, to search for relevant emigrant experience.[15] In this search, I operationalized emigrant experience in the same way as described in the Goldstone study earlier. The results are shown in Table 9.2.

The proportion of leaders of these 115 events who had foreign experience is remarkably similar to what we found in the Goldstone collection: about 65%. Although there is some overlap between the two datasets, this is not sufficient to explain the similar proportions. Clearly, foreign experience is an important common element that many revolutionaries share. Of course, these lists include leaders of notorious and sometimes wicked political movements – I do not mean to suggest that emigrant experiences will only lead to positive political developments. Yet to the extent that we associate political development with political change, and to the extent that it is legitimate to operationalize this change in terms of a list of notable revolutions and rebellions, then it seems that foreign experience, of the type enjoyed by most emigrants, is an important influence on individuals who subsequently bring about revolutionary political changes.

---

[14] The *AllExperts* list was downloaded from *http://en.allexperts.com/e/l/li/list_of_revolutions* on January 19, 2010; the *Wikipedia* list was downloaded from *http://en.wikipedia.org/wiki/List_of_revolutions* on February 2, 2010.

[15] An Excel file with the documentation and reference supporting the choice of a particular leader and his or her "foreign experience" claims is available by contacting the author.

TABLE 9.2. *Foreign Experience of Leaders for Important Rebellions and Revolutions, 1850–2009*

Year	Event/Place	Leader/Candidate	Foreign Experience
1851	Taiping Rebellion (China)	Hong Xiuquan	No
1857	Indian Rebellion (Sepoy Mutiny)	Lakshmibai, the Rani of Jhansi	No
1858–61	Reform War (Mexico)	Benito Juárez; Melchor Ocampo & Juan Álvarez	Yes
1865	Morant Bay Rebellion (Jamaica)	Paul Bogle	No
1866–8	Meiji Restoration (Japan)	Sakamoto Ryoma	No
1868	Glorious Revolution (Spain)	Juan Prim	Yes
1868	Grito de Lares (Puerto Rico)	Ramón Emeterio Betances & Segundo Ruiz Belvis	Yes
1871	Paris Commune (France)	Louis Auguste Blanqui	Yes
1871–76	Porfirio Diaz Rebellion (Mexico)	José de la Cruz Porfirio Díaz Mori	No
1885	Ancash Peasant Revolt (Peru)	Pedro Pablo Atusparia & Pedro Cochachin	No
1885	North-West Rebellion (Canada)	Louis Riel	Yes
1893	Mosquito Coast Annexation (Nicaragua)	José Santos Zelaya	Yes
1895	Liberal Revolution (Ecuador)	Eloy Alfaro	Yes
1895	Coup against Cáceres (Peru)	Nicolás de Piérola	Yes
1896–98	Revolution (Philippines)	Andrés Bonifacio	No
1904	Liberal Uprising (Paraguay)	Benigno Ferreira	Yes
1905	1905 Revolution (Russia)	George Gapon	No
1908	Young Turks (Turkey)	Murad Bey, Ahmed Riza, Damad Mahmud Pasha, & Prince Sabaheddin	Yes
1910	Mexican Revolution	Francisco I. Madero	Yes
1910	Republican Revolution (Portugal)	Machado Santos	No
1910–11	Sokehs Rebellion (Micronesia)	Somatau	No
1911	Xinhai Revolution (China)	Sun Yat-sen	Yes
1916–23	Irish Revolution	Michael Collins	Yes

TABLE 9.2 *(continued)*

Year	Event/Place	Leader/Candidate	Foreign Experience
1917	October Revolution (Russia)	V.I. Lenin	Yes
1918–19	German Revolution	Emil Barth, Richard Müller, & Georg Ledebour	No
1918–19	Student Reform Movement (Peru)	Víctor Raúl Haya de la Torre & José Carlos Mariátegui	No
1918–21	Ukrainian Revolution	Nestor Makhno	No
1918–22	Third Russian Revolution	Stepan Petrichenko	No
1919	Hungarian Soviet Republic	Béla Kun	Yes
1921–24	Mongolian Revolution	Damdin Sükhbaatar	No
1926	28 May Revolution (Portugal)	Manuel Gomes da Costa	No
1926–9	Cristero Rebellion (Mexico)	René Capistrán Garza	No
1927–33	Nicaraguan Uprising	Augusto César Sandino	Yes
1930	Brazilian Revolution	Getúlio Dornelles Vargas	No
1932	Aprista Revolt (Trujillo, Peru)	Víctor Raúl Haya de la Torre	Yes
1932	Siamese Coup (Thailand)	Prayoon Phamornmontri & six other students	Yes
1933	Revolt against Gerardo Machado (Cuba)	Fulgencio Batista	No
1936	Febrerista Revolution (Paraguay)	Rafael Franco	Yes
1936	Spanish Civil War	Francisco Franco	No
1936	Anarchist Revolution (Spain)	Buenaventura Durruti	Yes
1936–9	Military Uprising (Bolivia)	Germán Busch Becerra	Yes
1938–48	Zionist Revolution	David Ben-Gurion	Yes
1942	Cocos Islands Mutiny (Sri Lanka)	Gratien Fernando	No
1944	Guatemalan Revolution	Juan José Arévalo	Yes
1944	Albania	Enver Hoxha	Yes
1944	Glorius May Revolution (Ecuador)	Velasco Ibarra	Yes
1944–7	September 9 Coup (Bulgaria)	Kimon Georgiev Stoyanov	Yes
1945	August Revolution (Vietnam)	Ho Chi Minh	Yes

(continued)

TABLE 9.2 *(continued)*

Year	Event/Place	Leader/Candidate	Foreign Experience
1945	Coup for Democracy (Venezuela)	Rómulo Ernesto Betancourt	Yes
1947	Civil War (Paraguay)	Rafael Franco	Yes
1947–52	Albanian Subversion	Albanian expatriates were used as agents	Yes
1948	Birth of North Korea	Kim Il Sung	Yes
1949	Communist Transformation (Hungary)	Mátyás Rákosi	Yes
1949	Communist Revolution (China)	Mao Zedong	No
1952	National Revolution (Bolivia)	Víctor Paz Estenssoro	Yes
1952	Rosewater Revolution (Lebanon)	Fuad Shihab	Yes
1954–62	War of Independence (Algeria)	Ahmed Ben Bella	Yes
1955–70	Union of the Peoples of Cameroon	Ruben Um Nyobé	No
1956	Hungarian Revolution	Imre Nagy	Yes
1958	Coup (Venezuela)	Wolfgang Larrazábal	No
1958	July 14 Revolution (Iraq)	Abd al-Karim Qasim	Yes
1959	Cuban Revolution	Fidel Castro	Yes
1959	Rwanda	Grégoire Kayibanda	Yes
1960	Independence Struggle (Congo)	Patrice Émery Lumumba	No
1961–75	War of Independence (Angola)	Holden Roberto	Yes
1962	Independence Struggle (Yemen Arab Rep., or N. Yemen)	Abdullah al-Sallal	Yes
1962–74	Independence Struggle (Guinea-Bissau)	Amílcar Cabral	Yes
1963–7	Independence Struggle (People's Dem. Rep. Yemen, or S. Yemen)	Qahtan Mohammed al-Shaabi	Yes
1964	Zanzibar Revolution	John Gideon Okello	Yes
1964	October Revolution (Sudan)	Joseph Lagu	Yes
1964–75	Independence Struggle (Mozambique)	Eduardo Mondlane	Yes
1966–80	Rebel Movement (Chad)	Ibrahim Abatcha	Yes

TABLE 9.2 *(continued)*

Year	Event/Place	Leader/Candidate	Foreign Experience
1967	Revolution (Anguilla)	Ronald Webster	Yes
1968	Revolution (Congo)	Mobutu Sésé Seko	Yes
1968	May '68 Revolt (France)	Daniel Cohn-Bendit	Yes
1968	Coup (Peru)	Juan Velasco Alvarad	No
1968	Prague Spring (Czechoslovakia)	Alexander Dubček	Yes
1969	1968 Uprising (Pakistan)	Usman Baloch	No
1969	Coup/Uprising (Libya)	Mahmud Sulayman al Maghrabi	Yes
1969	Uprising (Somalia)	General Mohamed Siad Barre	Yes
1971	Liberation War (Bangladesh)	Sheikh Mujibur Rahman	No
1972	Coup/Revolution (Benin)	Mathieu Kérékou	Yes
1972	Coup/Revolution (Malagasy Republic)	Didier Ratsiraka	Yes
1973	Bloodless Coup (Afghanistan)	Mohammad Daud	Yes
1973	Violent Demonstrations (Thailand)	Sanya Thammasakdi	Yes
1974	Revolution (Ethiopia)	Mengistu Haile Mariam	No
1974	Carnation Revolution (Portugal)	Costa Gomes	Yes
1975	Revolution (Cambodia)	Pol Pot	Yes
1975	Revolution (Laos)	Kaysone Phomvihane	No
1975	Independence (Cape Verde)	Aristides Pereira	Yes
1976	Violent Demonstrations (Thailand)	Tanin Kraivixien	Yes
1978	Saur Revolution (Afghanistan)	Nur Muhammad Taraki	Yes
1979	New Jewel Movement (Grenada)	Maurice Bishop	Yes
1979	Marxist Revolution (Nicaragua)	Daniel Ortega	Yes
1979	Iranian Revolution	Grand Ayatollah Ruhollah Khomeini	Yes
1979	Cambodian Liberation	Son Sann	Yes
1980	Santo Rebellion (New Hebrides)	Walter Lini	Yes
1983	Coup (Burkino Faso)	Thomas Sankara	Yes
1984–5	Revolt (New Caledonia)	Jean-Marie Tjibaou	Yes

(continued)

TABLE 9.2 *(continued)*

Year	Event/Place	Leader/Candidate	Foreign Experience
1986	People Power Revolution (Philippines)	Corazon Aquino	Yes
1988	Re-Independence (Estonia)	Edgar Savisaar	No
1988	Re-Independence (Latvia)	Anatolijs Gorbunovs	No
1988	Re-Independence (Lithuania)	Algirdas Mykolas Brazauskas	No
1989	*Caracazo* Riots (Venezuela)	Hugo Rafael Chávez	No
1989	Revolution (Romania)	Ion Iliescu	Yes
1989	Velvet Revolution (Czechoslovakia)	Václav Havel	No
1996	Taliban Control (Afghanistan)	Mullah Mohammed Omar	Yes
1998	Bolivarian Revolution (Venezuela)	Hugo Rafael Chávez	No
1998	Indonesian Revolution	Megawati Sukarnoputri	No
2000	Bulldozer Revolution (Yugoslavia)	Vojislav Koštunica	No
2001	EDSA Revolution (Philippines)	Gloria Macapagal-Arroyo	Yes
2003	Rose Revolution (Georgia)	Mikheil Saak'ashvili	Yes
2004	Orange Revolution (Ukraine)	Viktor Andriyovych Yushchenko	No
2005	Cedar Revolution (Lebanon)	Michel Naim Aoun	Yes
2005	Tulip Revolution (Kyrgyzstan)	Kurmanbek Saliyevich Bakiyev	No
TOTAL			115
Number with foreign experience			75
Percentage with foreign experience			65%

Sources: AllExperts and various Internet sites. See text for elaboration.

CONCLUSION

In the last empirical chapter in this book, I have drawn our attention to the nature of the emigration–development relationship at the lowest possible level: in the life of individual emigrants. Such a focus is surprisingly uncommon in a study of this type, because social scientists tend to embrace larger, more structural determinants of social change. Indeed, most studies of revolution or even of piecemeal democratic change focus on systemic factors for explaining outcomes (e.g., the struggle among classes, ethnic groups, or political factions; rapid social and economic change; the failings of old regimes; or the impact of international conflicts).

By focusing on the individual effects, I do not mean to suggest that these other factors are irrelevant. Far from it! Instead, my objective was to focus on the individual incentives and effects that always lay beneath the larger structural explanations. It is at this level of analysis that we often posit these effects to occur, and it is here we need to find them. Of course, the effect of this foreign experience on political development depends on the extent to which these experiences are aggregated across contexts that include important structural determinants. Yet what is interesting about emigration is its capacity to affect these other factors. Not only does emigration have the potential to change the underlying balance of political power but it can also amplify these changes by introducing foreign ideas and voices that can help articulate how those changes can be brought about. It is this two-edged nature of the effects of emigration that makes it so difficult to measure, but also so important for understanding political development.

10

Conclusion

My objectives in this study have been twofold: to understand (1) the general nature of the relationship that links emigration to political development and (2) the underlying causal mechanisms. The first objective lends itself to an aggregate statistical study covering the full span of contextual variations; the second objective is better met with in-depth and comparative case studies that can trace the mechanisms as they play out in particular contexts over time. This, in a nutshell, describes my modus operandi.

Neither objective can be secured easily. The complex nature of the underlying relationship, the multitude of contextual influences, the difficulty in capturing the dependent variable, and the paucity of data on the independent variables combine to challenge any statistical attempt to map the relationship over time. Unfortunately, these same characteristics problematize any attempt to compare results across cases.

These problems are anything but unique. For the social scientist, interesting questions are usually difficult questions. Still, we cannot stop trying to answer important questions just because they are complex or because we lack adequate data. Rather, we forge ahead cautiously – and modestly – clearing paths that we hope will tempt others to follow.

As every new student to science learns, correlation is not causation. History is chock-full of correlations and coincidence, and I think social scientists do well by assuming coincidence as their point of departure. Yet when coincidences start to add up, we need to search harder for the underlying mechanisms that link them. Because these relationships are often quite complex, it may be difficult to pin them down with certainty – but we can use theory and method to corner them, carefully, in the realm of the plausible. When we have a good theoretical story that can explain why two variables are correlated, and we find evidence that the manner of connection is as posited (i.e., we find the smoking gun), then we are probably on the right causal track.

I believe this has been done in the preceding chapters. The survey of more than 150 years of history has uncovered numerous examples – at different levels of analysis, at different times, in different places – in which emigration is related to political development. Having stumbled over the first such example, say the East German case described in the introduction, we might chalk it up as coincidence. After all, it is not unreasonable to assume that political development would have occurred in East Germany without a high level of emigration.[1] Yet when these coincidental relationships start to stack up – when we see them in Norway, in Spain and Portugal, in the southern United States, in the sending provinces of contemporary China, and in the experiences of a number of small, relatively underdeveloped states in the world today – we should begin to suspect that the pattern is more than coincidental. The theoretical framework outlined in Chapter 3 provides sufficient reason to expect that emigration can play an important (if supporting) role in political development. Several of the posited mechanisms linking emigration to political development were found in the various analyses that followed.

This concluding chapter retraces that investigative journey while focusing on its two component elements. The first part of the chapter surveys the evidence found to justify the existence of a relationship between emigration and political development. The second part zeroes in on the posited causal mechanisms. I then close the chapter by considering what this research can mean for policy makers in a world that is still characterized by limited international mobility.

EMIGRATION AND POLITICAL DEVELOPMENT

The first task of this project was to establish whether emigration is associated with political development (whether for individuals, communities/states, or for the system at large) and, if so, how that relationship develops over time (i.e., the length of the lag).

---

[1] In fact, the actual size of the East German exodus is relatively small in a comparative context, roughly 1.9 emigrants per mil.

Individual

At the lowest level of aggregation, the relationship is most evident, even self-evident. Clearly, emigration is emancipating for the individual. By moving across the country or around the globe, migrants increase the number of real opportunities available to them. The proof of this is evident in the choice made by the individual emigrant: Individuals migrate because they expect to find better opportunities in the host community than they have at home.

This is not to belittle the often significant costs associated with migration; in emigrating, individuals and families experience significant hardship and alienation. Rather, it places those costs in a comparative context – one of opportunity costs – and forces us to think about the way that individual development is too often limited by contextual factors that are beyond the individual's capacity to affect. To the extent that development is freedom (to paraphrase Sen), then emigration facilitates the development of individuals by offering more opportunities and capabilities with which to develop. Surely, political development cannot be furthered by constraining an individual's freedom of movement; this is the antithesis of freedom (and the foundation for slavery) and is justly criticized when employed within states (whether apartheid South Africa or the Soviet Union).

Because this relationship is so self-evident, I have not aimed the empirical investigation in its direction. Indeed, analyses designed to capture correlation rely on aggregate statistics that conceal individual decisions. Still, this individual relationship between emigration and freedom lies beneath all the aggregate findings in the preceding chapters – it motivated the crofters who emigrated from Norway at the turn of the last century, just as it motivates young Chinese workers on the move today. However, it is most evident in the one migrant life that we did examine in any detail: the life of Martin Tranmæl (Chapter 9).

Community/State

It is at the next level of aggregation – the state or community level – where it is easiest to establish an empirical link between emigration and political development. Most of the statistical indicators are aggregated at this level, and datasets with extended time series allow us to monitor the strength of the relationship as it changes over time.

The TSCS statistical analyses in Chapter 4 mapped out the nature of aggregate correlations and established the length of the lag between a country's experience with emigration and its subsequent increase in political development. While being aware of the limits to the data and method, we can cautiously conclude that emigration is associated with political development after a significant lag (13 years when measured by the Polity indicator, 41 years when measured by the Vanhanen indicator), when controlling for economic growth.

By documenting the temporal lag, we can be confident about the direction of the relationship: We know that emigration is influencing subsequent development (not only that development affects emigration). However, as the temporal lag stretches across decades we need to be leery of the posited effects. This is why it is comforting to find political development kicking in after decades of emigration in the two most extensive case studies: Norway and the U.S. South. However, the length of the posited lag might also explain why it was difficult to find any clear relationships in the aggregate tables found at the beginning of Chapters 5, 6, and 7: These tables could only capture a loosely defined and relatively short-term lag (e.g., political development at a specific point, shortly after the emigration occurred).

When we look at the results from the individual case studies, it is more difficult to establish a specific lag period, but the correlations are just as evident. Emigration and political development occurred together in most of the case studies, including Norway, the U.S. South, China today, southern Europe immediately after WWII, and several small island states in recent years. This work has also uncovered cases that should motivate us to look deeper at the contextual context: Emigration did not seem to facilitate political development in Mexico, Algeria (and the Maghreb, more generally), or Yugoslavia after WWII.

The evidence suggests that there are community-level effects from emigration, but certain underlying conditions need to be in place. After all, we know that political development occurs in countries that have not experienced significant emigration – and that the process of political development is complex and multifaceted. Yet, when the statistical and case studies are combined, it suggests that certain contexts are more prone to encouraging political development, and these contexts highlight three variables: (1) the size of the emigrant stream as a share of the country's population; (2) the surrounding migration regime type (i.e., liberal or restricted); and (3) the rate of the community's underlying demographic growth. Because these factors help explain the particular mechanism that links emigration to political development, they are discussed later in more detail.

This evidence indicates that emigration is related to the process of political development, but it does not allow us to determine whether the correlation is spurious, or driven by other (e.g., underlying or endogenous) variables. Although the statistical studies were able to control for the effect of economic development, a number of other relevant variables could still be influencing the outcome.

Regime/System

Of all the results, the most surprising was the degree of variation found to exist across migration regimes. Although a clear regime pattern is evident in the aggregate analyses, individual communities and/or states still found room for political development even under fairly restrictive migration regimes.

As with the state-level results, the statistical analyses in Chapter 4 set the stage for tracking the system-level relationships. Here we found distinct regimes clearly evident in the global data. In particular, it seems fairly clear that global emigration levels correspond with Huntington's three waves of democratization. This finding suggests that the political effects of emigration are stronger under more liberal regimes than under more restricted regimes, presumably because the threat of exit is more acute (real/actual) or because important underlying factors are driving both political development and emigration at the global level. More precisely, the analysis documents a statistically significant relationship between changes in the global emigration level and subsequent (global) political development. As in the national studies, this effect came after a lag (8 years in the Polity indicator, 25 years in the Vanhanen indicator), so we can be confident that global political development followed in the wake of increased emigration.

This type of regime effect was also evident in several of the case studies. For example, political officials in Mexico were able to exploit the highly regulated nature of international migration to channel emigrant streams in ways that bled off political pressure in unstable areas, and lined the pockets of political allies in the sending community. This seems to be also what was occurring in recent Yugoslav history, as well as in the Maghreb states surveyed in Chapter 6 (especially Algeria).

Yet other cases suggest that communities can still enjoy political benefit from emigration, even under restrictive regimes. In these cases the results stand in contrast to initial expectations: (1) Spain, Portugal, and Greece were able to secure political development under a highly regulated international regime and rather circumscribed bilateral migration agreements (Chapter 6); (2) emigration-prone provinces in China secured higher levels of human development under a very restricted system of internal mobility (Chapter 8); and (3) small states have been able to secure relatively higher levels of political development (given their level of economic development), under today's restrictive international migration regime.

This evidence is both surprising and hopeful: It suggests that emigration might be used to stimulate political development, even in a context with significant constraints on migration. Yet this evidence also suggests that we need to know more about the specific contexts that facilitate the relationship.

ON THE NATURE OF THE RELATIONSHIP

Whereas the statistical studies were designed to map the general nature of the relationship, the case studies aimed to trace the particular causal mechanisms that might link emigration to political development.

When we take a closer look at the nature of a community's political development and the sort of causal connections outlined in Chapter 3, our confidence in the relationship grows. When we see how the threat of continued emigration is often used in contemporary debates or when we see how political elites find it necessary to address the threat of a hemorrhaging population, we know that emigration plays a role in facilitating political development – although it is not always clear how large that role is or what development would have looked like in the absence of significant emigration.

Indeed, the parallels across cases are fascinating. Compare, for example, the lesson generated from the most detailed case studies (in Norway and the southern United States). In both instances significant emigration of repressed classes (the crofters from Norway, Blacks from the South) served as an important impetus for subsequent economic and political reform. In Norway, the flight of crofters instigated important social and political reforms, because it raised the price of peasant labor back home on the farm and encouraged a modernization of Norwegian farming techniques (and land distribution). In the U.S. South, where the political transformation was even more remarkable, a black exodus forced a mechanization of farming that brought about subsequent (and radical) political and social changes. In both the Norwegian and American cases, we see emigration affecting a change in the class balance – a change that facilitated subsequent economic and political development.

These cases, as well as the Tranmæl biography in Chapter 9, document the important role played by individual migrant accounts in introducing information in the sending community about real alternatives to the status quo. We see how the hope provided by these alternatives can motivate changes at home and how the threat of further emigration can be used to leverage political debates and shift the underlying balance of class power. Although the study of Europe's postwar guest-worker programs did not go into the same level of detail, what we find there is consistent with this sort of class-balancing effect, as political development only occurred in those states that were experiencing relatively low rates of demographic growth.

In short, when a significant proportion of people leaves a given community, especially when that community's population is growing slowly, we find that the workers and peasants who remain enjoy a stronger political position from which they can advance their political demands. With the threat of increased emigration, political elites find it necessary to address perceived injustices. In effect, emigration is found to be a catalyst that can instigate political (and sometimes economic) transformation.

This sort of connection was most evident in the Norwegian case, but it is consistent with what we found in the European examples (Spain, Portugal, Italy, and Greece) in Chapter 6 and in the southern states of the United States in Chapter 8, and it may explain the higher levels of political development found in the very small states examined in Chapter 7. Finally, this connection may be the reason that emigration is influencing political development in the Chinese provinces, where demographic pressure is held in check by stringent regulations aimed at limiting family size and where residents have relatively few channels to employ voice.

This finding puts a twist on mainstream or conventional accounts of democratization and political development. In those accounts, political development is secured by a growing number of workers (or a growing middle class) who exert their influence on the political process. By contrast, the lesson derived from this study is that class power is important, but is not solely a function of size. Rather, the political influence of workers and farmers rests on their relative bargaining power vis-à-vis landed and capitalist interests. Emigration actually weakens the numerical base of the working classes – but, in doing so, it strengthens their bargaining position relative to other classes. When emigrants leave en masse, in a context with relatively slow demographic growth, the workers and farmers who remain can demand better conditions. This lesson is somewhat counterintuitive, but it was not lost on labor organizers caught up in a context of massive emigration (whether it was Marcus Thrane in Norway, or black activists in the southern United States).

Clearly, demographics matter in questions related to emigration: Emigration will be more attractive to people from communities that are otherwise overpopulated, and emigration can influence the subsequent political development of those communities. In places experiencing massive demographic growth, emigration can moderate the most regressive impacts of that growth and the effect that population growth has on relative class power. In communities with slow demographic growth, emigration can strengthen the political hand of the labor force that remains. In both cases, emigration increases the power of labor (as decreed by the laws of supply and demand): Labor's position would be demonstrably worse in the absence of emigration.

Here too, however, the relationship is complex. Emigration-driven development can occur in contexts characterized by significant population growth, as was arguably the case in the U.S. South and even in Norway. As a consequence it is impossible to predict a specific threshold of population growth over which emigration does not facilitate political development. There are no hard-and-fast rules here. Rather, we find that emigration seems to have a stronger influence in contexts with lower levels of demographic growth, and we know there are good reasons for expecting this to be the case.

This change in relative class power can affect the attractiveness of alternative means (and systems) of production. For example, we have seen how it can spur producers to adopt more capital-intensive (less labor-intensive) technologies. In the southern United States, emigration helped force a radical transformation in the form of production, which brought about significant changes (both economic and political). As a result, there was no longer any real demand for an oppressed black peasantry. The same effect was visible in Norway before WWI and in the wave of democracies that washed across postwar Europe. Emigration became an important additional impetus that helped (in connection with other factors) facilitate economic transformations that brought about subsequent political development.

Yet these demographic and contextual conditions are not always in place. When they are missing, political authorities can exploit the lure of emigration to siphon off troublemakers, to release political pressure in tense areas, and to strengthen the political position of elites in emigrant-sending regions (as we saw in the case of Mexico and perhaps in Algeria). A restrictive migration regime does not make political development impossible, but it provides a context that makes it easier for repressive political authority to exploit emigration and protect the status quo from challenges otherwise posed by the threat of emigration.

In short, the two most important contextual variables – demographic growth and the surrounding regime – are neither necessary nor sufficient conditional agents. Political development can occur in the absence of emigration, demographic growth, and a liberal migration regime. Yet these three factors together tend to increase the chances that workers and peasants are able to use the threat of exit to secure better political conditions at home.

The Role of Economic Development

Economic factors shadow the analysis in nearly every case study, although not always in the same way. As with the other relationships described earlier, the relationship between emigration and economic development is complex. In most of the cases, emigration preceded both economic and political development, but here too the relationships vary across contexts, so it is difficult to speak about hard-and-fast rules.

Although the statistical analyses in Chapter 4 provided a rough measure of control, the detailed case studies provided a better opportunity to consider how emigration was related to both economic and political development. In the Norwegian case, the relationship was complicated in that the country had secured a fairly high level of political development before it achieved significant economic development. Then, at the end of the 19th century, we find a mad dash of intertwined variables: Political and economic developments occur concomitantly in the aftermath of significant emigration. Something similar occurred in the U.S. South, where emigration spurred a radical economic and political transformation.

In the Mexican case, the country was experiencing significant economic growth – a Mexican Miracle, no less – at the same time as it was participating in the Bracero Program. Yet this combination of economic growth and emigration did not produce political development – indeed, both trajectories seem to have contributed to support the status quo and continued political apathy. The same lukewarm relationship was found in those areas that supplied Europe's guest workers after WWII: Economic growth was a poor predictor of political development (although political development was related to wealth). In these contexts, the threat of emigration was contained, and the dominant interests were able to maintain the status quo.[2]

In a brief examination of several small states that have recently experienced massive emigration (in Chapter 7), we found that they enjoyed a relatively higher level of political development, given their (relatively low) level of economic development. Yet the superficial nature of the study does not shine any light on the way that political and economic development are linked (or not) in these cases.

Clearly economic development facilitates political development, because it is easier to redistribute pieces of a growing pie. Yet in this study, there is no clear rule that can be derived from the case study evidence. Although the statistical studies tell us that emigration contributes to political development (with a varying lag) after controlling for economic activity (at both national and global levels), the most detailed case studies (e.g., Norway and the U.S. South) suggest that political and economic development are both spurred by emigration. Other examples confirm that the relationship is anything but black and white. We are aware of communities that have experienced emigration and economic development, but not political development (Mexico), as well as communities that have experienced emigration and political development, but not economic development (East Germany).

Summing Up

The cases in this study were selected to control for a number of contextual features, including variation in both dependent and independent variables. Because this was an investigatory study, I employed Mill's indirect method of difference to test the most likely explanatory variables. A simplified results table is presented in Table 10.1.

---

[2] Parenthetically, I might note that in East Germany, the combination of exit and voice resulted in radical political transformation, with the eventual collapse of the regime – but the (now unified) country paid a significant economic price. Economic development did not immediately accompany East Germany's political development (this may be the result of an improper exchange rate between eastern and western currencies at the time of unification, but this is another matter).

TABLE 10.1. *Results Table*

Case	Political Development	High Per-Capita Emigration	Prior Economic Development	Limited Demographic Growth	Liberal Regime
Norway	Yes	Yes	No	No	Yes
U.S. South	Yes	Yes	No	No	Yes
China	Yes	Yes	No	Yes	No
Small states	Yes	Yes	No	–	No
Spain, Portugal, Greece	Yes	*No*	Yes	Yes	*No*
Mexico	No	No	Yes	No	No
Yugoslavia (postwar)	No	No	Yes	Yes	No
Algeria	*No*	Yes	Yes	*No*	*No*

By presenting the results in this way, we can see the contingent nature of these relationships, but we can also detect some distinctive patterns. Three of these patterns are particularly noteworthy. First, there is a clear pattern linking high (low) levels of emigration to political development (or the lack of such). The pattern is evident in the first two columns. Yet this table also shows that emigration is neither necessary nor sufficient to secure political development, because countries like Spain, Portugal, and Greece experienced political development without high levels of emigration (East Germany would also fall into this category), whereas Algeria experienced a high level of emigration, but without significant political development. These two groups of exceptions to the rule are italicized in the table.

Second, the table reveals a consistent pattern between political development, per-capita emigration, and prior economic development. Those cases that experienced political development and high levels of emigration did *not* enjoy prior economic development (e.g., Norway, the U.S. South, Chinese provinces, and the small states), whereas Mexico and Yugoslavia enjoyed economic development, but not political development (accompanied by relatively low levels of emigration). As with the first pattern, Spain, Portugal, Greece, and Algeria are exceptions to the pattern.

Finally, the liberal nature of the migration regime and limited demographic growth did not appear as consistently relevant factors for explaining political development – even though individual cases seem to highlight the importance of underlying demographic pressures.

WHAT DOES THIS MEAN?

In closing, I would like to reflect briefly on what these findings mean for the real world around us. We began this investigation by pondering the role that emigration had on a number of specific emigration-prone states, such as China, India, and Pakistan. I conclude by using what we have learned to comment on the role that emigration might play in the political development of the states listed in Table 1.1.

Given the design of this study, the reader will not be surprised to find that three different types of lessons can be drawn from this inquiry – lessons that correspond to different levels of analysis. At the *regime* level, we need to be more aware of how immigration policies in the developed world affect the potential for political development of other states in the system. Repressive states know that it is in their interest to limit mobility, and the current international context facilitates this capacity. By making it easier for people to move out of repressive political contexts, the international community can actually encourage political development. Conversely, by maintaining significant barriers to migration, we are limiting the development possibilities of others.[3]

The *individual*-level lessons parallel those found at the regime level. It is very unlikely that political development could be improved by limiting an individual's opportunity to emigrate. The only apparent beneficiaries of a restrictive international (or national) migration regime are those who benefit from the status quo (whether they are elites in repressive regimes or the affluent voters of today's developed states). Political brain drain, or the flight of potential opposition, is unlikely, and a restrictive international migration regime only plays into the hands of repressive regimes that are able to channel emigration in ways that strengthen their own positions of power.

It is at the *community* or state level that the most relevant lessons can be found. Emigration provides a very important complement to more traditional tools of political development, because it leverages the influence of those that are otherwise disenfranchised. Emigration is often an act of desperation; in emigrating, this desperation comes to the surface,

---

[3] On the flip side, we can take some comfort in realizing that political development is still possible even under restrictive (regime) conditions.

forcing a response from the political authorities. Just as significantly, the act of emigration – if engaged in by large numbers of people – can change the underlying class balance in ways that can bring about political development. For emigration to have this effect, however, it has to be sufficiently large (as a percentage of the home population) or sufficiently focused (either in terms of skill type, region, or political message).

To illustrate this effect, we can consider again whether emigration can help or deter the political development of the states listed in Table 1.1. The reader will recall that this table listed the most emigrant-prone states in the world today and showed that they included both free and unfree states. In the Introduction we found no evident relationship between the absolute size of the emigrant stream and the state's freedom status. In light of this analysis, however, we now know to focus on the relative (not the absolute) size of the emigrant stream. When we do so, we find that the average rate of emigration is higher among the unfree states (averaging 3.5 per mil) than among the free and partly free states (2 and 3.3 per mil, respectively).

What does this tell us? The most interesting lesson is that none of these states are experiencing very high rates of emigration when examined from a historical and/or comparative perspective. Not a single one of these states rises above the "high-emigration" criteria (10 per mil) used in the preceding chapters. Thus, the likelihood of emigration playing a role in subsequent political development is limited in all of these countries (even though the overall numbers of emigrants tend to impress).

The second lesson concerns the importance of paying attention to the nature of the data and its temporal context. Because the emigration and development statistics in this table are from the same time period, they reflect the motivation for emigration more than the state's response to emigration. By contrast, the more detailed analyses in this book have been designed to provide a clear temporal buffer between the emigration and political development statistics, to ensure that we have captured the correct causal sequence. In short, the statistics in Table 1.1 do not provide this buffer, so we can only see that people are more likely to flee from repressive states than from freer states. This is consistent with the underlying argument of this book, but it is somewhat peripheral to the main point.

Finally, we have learned that the relationship between emigration and political development is so complex that it is impossible to use emigration alone to predict the development path of any given country. Whether Pakistan, for example, will enjoy political development depends on much more than the number of people who emigrate each year. Yet we have learned that emigration – if sufficiently large as a percentage of the population – can play an important role in changing the balance of class power within states and that this change can play an important role in facilitating rapid political (and economic) transformation.

We can also be sure that limiting emigration does little to encourage political development. Indeed, it would seem that today's international migration regime, which places a number of significant barriers in the way of international migrants, mostly deters political development around the world. Denizens of repressive states need to enjoy a greater opportunity of exit before they can exploit the potential that emigration has to influence political change.

APPENDICES

Appendix I: Case-Selection Matrix

	Study Type	Examples	Relevant Chapters
Testing Relationships			
Across countries	Aggregate, case	TSCS stats; Norway; Mexico; Mediterranean basin; very small states	4; 5; 6; 7
Over time	Aggregate, case	Global stats; waves of democratization; Tables 5.1, 6.1, 7.1, and 7.2	4; 5; 6; 7
Within countries	Case	U.S. South; China	8
Temporal lag	Aggregate	TSCS stats; global stats	4
Testing Mechanisms			
Indirect effects	Case, aggregate	Statistical studies and in-depth cases (Norway, U.S. South)	4; 5; 8
Individual effects	Case, aggregate	Tranmæl; emigrant stories in case studies; surveys of revolutionaries	5; 8; 9
Group effects	Case	Norway; Mexico; U.S. South	5; 6; 8
Community-competition effects	Case	Norway; Mexico; U.S. South	5; 6; 8
Negative effects	Case, aggregate	TSCS stats; Mexico; Algeria; China	4; 6; 8
Testing Explanatory Variables			
Emigration	Case, aggregate	All	All
Regime type	Case, aggregate	Global stats; waves of democratization; U.S. South versus China	Compare across chapters
Demographics	Case	Each case considers demographic trends	5; 6; 7; 8
Economic development	Case, aggregate	Controlled in statistical studies; considered in each case	4; 5; 6; 7; 8

Appendix II: EMIG 1.2 Overview

Country	Years	Sources Used
Afghanistan	1979–81	UN *Demographic Yearbooks*
Algeria	1893–1924, 1956–74	Ferenczi & Willcox (1929); UN *Demographic Yearbooks*; Adler (1985: 267)
Angola	1972–3	UN *Demographic Yearbooks*
Antigua & Barbuda	1959–65	UN *Demographic Yearbooks*
Argentina	1871–1957	Mitchell; UN (1958); UN *Demographic Yearbooks*
Armenia	1980, 1985–2007	ILO (2009); CIS (1996); NSS-Armenia (2002: 61–2); Armenia (2008)
Aruba	1972–2006	CBS Aruba (2009)
Australia	1904–2007	Ferenczi & Willcox (1929); Mitchell; UN (1979); UN *Demographic Yearbooks*; ILO (2009); ABS (2008)
Austria	1850–1913, 1921–37, 1947–75, 1996–2008	Mitchell; UN (1958); UN *Demographic Yearbooks*; Statistics Austria (2009)
Azerbaijan	1980, 1985–92, 1999–2007	CIS (1996); ILO (2009)
Bahamas	1911–18, 1956–63	Ferenczi & Willcox (1929); UN *Demographic Yearbooks*
Bahrain	2001	CIO Bahrain (2002: table 1207.1)
Bangladesh	1976–2008	BMET (2009)
Barbados	1913–21, 1923–4, 1957–63	Ferenczi & Willcox (1929); UN *Demographic Yearbooks*

Country	Years	Sources Used
Belarus	1980, 1985–2003	CIS (1996); ILO (2009)
Belgium	1850–1913, 1919–95, 2000–8	Ferenczi and Willcox (1929); Mitchell; UN (1958); UN (1979); UN *Demographic Yearbooks*; Statistics Belgium (2009)
Belize	1953–64, 1966–9, 1974–5, 1980–2000	UN *Demographic Yearbooks*; CSO-Belize (2000: table C5)
Bermuda	1904–16, 1918–24, 1989–93	Ferenczi & Willcox (1929); UN *Demographic Yearbooks*
Bolivia	1941–5, 1947–9, 1967–73	UN (1958); UN *Demographic Yearbooks*
Botswana	1971	UN *Demographic Yearbooks*
Brazil	1904–12, 1935–43	Ferecenzi & Willcox (1929); UN (1958); UN *Demographic Yearbooks*
British Virgin Islands	1973–5	UN *Demographic Yearbooks*
Brunei	1963–4	UN *Demographic Yearbooks*
Bulgaria	1893–1902, 1931–43, 1953–64, 1966–75, 1990–6	Ferenczi & Willcox (1929); Mitchell; UN *Demographic Yearbooks*; ILO (2009)
Burkina Faso	1991	UN *Demographic Yearbooks*
Burma	1968, 1971–5, 1980–3, 1987–8, 2001–2	UN *Demographic Yearbooks*; ILO (2009)
Cameroon	1923	Ferenczi & Willcox (1929)
Canada	1903–17, 1919–20, 1949–50, 1952–2008	Ferenczi & Willcox (1929); UN (1958); Statistics Canada (2009)
Cape Verde	1912–20, 1922–3	Ferenczi & Willcox (1929)
Cayman Islands	1975–6, 1981–2	UN *Demographic Yearbooks*
Chile	1908–23, 1936–47, 1967–72, 1974–5	Ferenczi & Willcox (1929); UN *Demographic Yearbooks*
China	1850–1940	McKeown (2009 and 2010)
Christmas Island	1967–8	UN *Demographic Yearbooks*
Colombia	1930–47, 1949–69, 1980–1	UN (1958); UN *Demographic Yearbooks*
Costa Rica	1936–47, 1949–50	UN *Demographic Yearbooks*; UN (1958)
Croatia	1991–2006	ILO (2009)
Cuba	1993	UN *Demographic Yearbooks*

(continued)

Country	Years	Sources Used
Cyprus	1953–89, 1993–4, 2002–7	UN *Demographic Yearbooks*; Republic of Cyprus (2009: 170, table 117)
Czechoslovakia	1920–38, 1950–2007	Ferenczi & Willcox (1929); UN (1958); CZSO (2007)
Denmark	1869–2008	Ferenczi & Willcox (1929); Statistics Denmark (2009)
Djibouti	1968	UN *Demographic Yearbooks*
Dominica	1955–67, 1993–2003	UN *Demographic Yearbooks*; MTICDA (2009)
Dominican Rep.	1960–4, 1966, 1968–70, 1972–3, 1985–6, 1993–4	UN *Demographic Yearbooks*
Ecuador	1978–2008	UN *Demographic Yearbooks*; INEC (2004, 2009)
Egypt	1968–73, 1987	UN *Demographic Yearbooks*
El Salvador	1937–50, 1952–3, 1988–9, 1992	UN (1958); UN *Demographic Yearbooks*
Estonia	1920–4, 1927, 1929–37, 1946–99, 2004–7	Ferenczi & Willcox (1929); Statistics Estonia (2009)
Ethiopia	1966–9	UN *Demographic Yearbooks*
Fiji	1973–2003	FIBS (2009)
Finland	1882–2008	Ferenczi & Willcox (1929); Mitchell; UN *Demographic Yearbooks*; Statistics Finland (2009)
France	1857–1924, 1948–88	Ferenczi & Willcox (1929); Mitchell; UN *Demographic Yearbooks*
Gambia	1960–1	UN *Demographic Yearbooks*
Germany	1850–1917, 1919–39, 1950–2007	Ferenczi & Willcox (1929); Mitchell; UN (1958); UN *Demographic Yearbooks*; SBD (2009)
Ghana	1949–50, 1956–64, 1967–70	UN *Demographic Yearbooks*
Greece	1850, 1851–4, 1856–7, 1859–67, 1869–1929, 1931–40, 1946–77	NSSG (2009); UN (1958)
Grenada	1957–65	UN *Demographic Yearbooks*
Guatemala	1945–7, 1951–5	UN *Demographic Yearbooks*
Guyana	1869–81, 1959–64, 1966, 1969–76, 1982–99, 2005	Ferenczi & Willcox (1929); UN *Demographic Yearbooks*; BOS-Guyana (2009)

Country	Years	Sources Used
Haiti	1968–75	UN *Demographic Yearbooks*
Hong Kong	1981–2008	SB-Hong Kong (2009)
Hungary	1871–1913, 1921–42, 1946–8, 1973–6, 1979–87, 1990–2002	Mitchell; UN *Demographic Yearbooks*; INSEE (2005: 35)
Iceland	1961–2008	Statistics Iceland (2009)
India	1850–1947, 1953–2007	Davis (1951: 100); UN *Demographic Yearbooks*; Ministry of Labour (2003); Ministry of Labour and Employment (2004); Ministry of Overseas Indian Affairs (2009); MPI (2009)
Indonesia	1976–2002	Wickramasekera (2002: 15); ILO (2009)
Ireland	1851–1921, 1924–39, 1941–54, 1956–63, 1987–2008	Ferenczi & Willcox (1929); UN (1958); UN *Demographic Yearbooks*; CSO (2008: 2)
Isle of Man	1976	UN *Demographic Yearbooks*
Israel	1935–46, 1948–72, 1984–6, 1988–90, 1992–2001	UN (1958); UN *Demographic Yearbooks*; ILO (2009)
Italy	1869–1942, 1946–96, 1998–2000, 2002–7	Ferenczi & Willcox (1929); UN (1958); Mitchell; UN *Demographic Yearbooks*; ILO (2009); ISTAT (2009)
Jamaica	1902–5, 1908–24, 1945–52, 1960–2, 1975–7, 1989	Ferenczi & Willcox (1929); UN *Demographic Yearbooks*
Japan	1898–1924, 1946–50, 1954–2006	Ferenczi & Willcox (1929); UN *Demographic Yearbooks*; JSY (2005, 2009)
Kazakhstan	1980, 1985–8, 2003	CIS (1996); ILO (2009)
Kenya	1909–14, 1948–76	Ferenczi & Willcox (1929); UN *Demographic Yearbooks*
Korea, Rep. of	1962, 1983–2002	UN *Demographic Yearbooks*; ILO (2009)
Kyrgyzstan	1980, 1985–2000, 2003–5	CIS (1996); ILO (2009)
Latvia	1919–23, 1991–2008	Ferenczi & Willcox (1929); Latvijas Statistika (2009)
Lesotho	1908–14, 1920–4	Ferenczi & Willcox (1929)

(*continued*)

Country	Years	Sources Used
Liberia	1970	UN *Demographic Yearbooks*
Liechtenstein	1981–4, 1986–8	UN *Demographic Yearbooks*
Lithuania	1988–2008	ILO (2009); Statistikos Departmentas (2009a and 2009b)
Luxembourg	1936–9, 1946–7, 1953–74, 1979–95, 2000–8	UN *Demographic Yearbooks*; UN (1979); STATEC (2009)
Macao	1981, 1995, 2000–6	UN *Demographic Yearbooks*; ILO (2009)
Macedonia	1994–6, 1998–2006	ILO (2009)
Madagascar	1921–4	Ferenczi & Willcox (1929)
Malawi	1913–17	Ferenczi & Willcox (1929)
Malaysia	1891–1900, 1913–24, 1936–8, 1946–7, 1953–8	Ferenczi & Willcox (1929); UN *Demographic Yearbooks*
Malta	1912–16, 1919–24, 1936–8, 1940, 1943–7, 1950–2003	Ferenczi & Willcox (1929); UN *Demographic Yearbooks*; UN (1979); ILO (2009)
Mauritius	1900–24, 1936–47, 1953–94	Ferenczi & Willcox (1929); UN *Demographic Yearbooks*; CSO-Mauritius (2000: table 3.2)
Mexico	1850–2009	DHS (2009 and 2008); UN 1958; Mitchell
Moldova	1980, 1985–96, 2000–7	CIS (1996); ILO (2009)
Monaco	1968–72, 2000–8	UN *Demographic Yearbooks*; Monaco (2008)
Morocco	1955–60, 1962–4, 1966–73, 1980	UN *Demographic Yearbooks*
Mozambique	1952–4, 1956–61	UN *Demographic Yearbooks*
Namibia	1953–62	UN *Demographic Yearbooks*
Nauru	1922–4, 1962–5, 1967, 1996–9, 2006	Ferenczi & Willcox (1929); UN *Demographic Yearbooks*; BOS-Nauru (2009)
Netherlands	1850–2008	Mitchell; Statistics Netherlands (2009)
New Guinea	1936–41, 1962–5, 1967–75, 1980–1, 1983–9, 1995	UN *Demographic Yearbooks*; ILO (2009)
New Zealand	1853–2008	Ferenczi & Willcox (1929); UN (1958); Mitchell; UN *Demographic Yearbooks*; Statistics New Zealand (2009)

Country	Years	Sources Used
Nicaragua	1937–47, 1989–99	UN *Demographic Yearbooks*; ILO (2009); INEC-Nicaragua (1994: 84)
Nigeria	1953–7, 1959–62, 1966–70, 1972–3	UN *Demographic Yearbooks*
Niue	1967–71	UN *Demographic Yearbooks*
Norfolk Island	1980	UN *Demographic Yearbooks*
Norway	1850–1940, 1945–2008	SSB (2009a, 2009b); UN *Demographic Yearbooks*
Pakistan	1972–98	Wickramasekera (2002: 15)
Palestine	1922–4, 1936–47	Ferenczi & Willcox (1929); UN *Demographic Yearbooks*
Peru	1936–46, 1960–4, 1976, 1990–2007	UN *Demographic Yearbooks*; INEI-Peru (2008: 21)
Philippines	1850–74, 1878–97, 1899, 1901–7, 1909–30, 1932–41, 1945–7, 1962–8, 1970, 1972–6, 1981–2008	McKeown (2009, 2010); UN *Demographic Yearbooks*; Wickramasekera (2002: 15); CFO Philippines (2009)
Poland	1890–1904, 1907–12, 1920–4, 1926–9, 1931–8, 1955–65, 1973–6, 1978–2006	Ferenczi & Willcox (1929); UN (1958); UN *Demographic Yearbooks*; ILO (2009); CSO-Poland (2008)
Portugal	1866–1988, 1992–2005, 2007	Ferenczi & Willcox (1929); Mitchell; UN *Demographic Yearbooks*; Statistics Portugal (2007a, 2007b); EUROSTAT (2009)
Romania	1920–4, 1926–43, 1986–2006	Ferenczi & Willcox (1929); UN (1958); ILO (2009)
Russia	1850–1915, 1967–2008	Ferenczi & Willcox (1929); HIAS (2009); UN *Demographic Yearbooks*; FSSS-Russia (2008, 2009)
Rwanda	1967–8	UN *Demographic Yearbooks*
Samoa	1922–4, 1975–6	Ferenczi & Willcox (1929); UN *Demographic Yearbooks*
San Marino	1960–2007	UN *Demographic Yearbooks*; ILO (2009); UPECEDS-San Marino (2009)
Serbia	1889–99, 1901–8	Mitchell

(continued)

Country	Years	Sources Used
Seychelles	1900–24, 1964–87, 1990, 1992–2008	Ferenczi & Willcox (1929); UN *Demographic Yearbooks*; NSB-Seychelles (2009: 5)
Sierra Leone	1951–2	UN *Demographic Yearbooks*
Singapore	1850–73, 1922, 1951–2	McKeown (2009, 2010); UN *Demographic Yearbooks*
Slovak Rep.	1990–2007	INSEE (2005: 30); UN *Demographic Yearbooks*; Slov-Stat (2009)
Slovenia	1989–2007	ILO (2009); SORS (2009)
Somalia	1908–10, 1912, 1920–4, 1972	Ferenczi & Willcox (1929); UN *Demographic Yearbooks*
South Africa	1910–22, 1924–2003	Ferenczi & Willcox (1929); UN (1958); Mitchell; UN *Demographic Yearbooks*; Statistics South Africa (2009)
Spain	1882–2005	Ferenczi & Willcox (1929); UN (1958); UN *Demographic Yearbooks*; INE-Spain (2009)
Sri Lanka	1878–1900, 1911–24, 1936–45, 1955–8, 1960–4, 1966–71, 1975–2007	Ferenczi & Willcox (1929); UN *Demographic Yearbooks*; Wickramasekera (2002: 15); Gunatilleke (1998); SLBFE (2009)
St. Helena	1900–24, 1953–8, 1960–9, 1972–3, 1977–86	Ferenczi & Willcox (1929); UN *Demographic Yearbooks*
St. Kitts & Nevis	1961–4, 1966–71	UN *Demographic Yearbooks*
St. Lucia	1954–64, 1967–8	UN *Demographic Yearbooks*
St. Vin. & Grenadines	1963	UN *Demographic Yearbooks*
Suriname	1898–1900, 1903–10, 1912–14, 1919–21, 1981–2, 1985–7	Ferenczi & Willcox (1929); UN *Demographic Yearbooks*
Swaziland	1908–10, 1913–16, 1921, 1923–4	Ferenczi & Willcox (1929)
Sweden	1851–2008	SCB-Sweden (2009)
Switzerland	1868–1995, 2004–7	Mitchell; UN (1958); UN *Demographic Yearbooks*; Swiss Statistics (2009)
Syria	1980–1	UN *Demographic Yearbooks*
Taiwan	1953–8, 1966–7	UN *Demographic Yearbooks*
Tajikistan	1980, 1985–94	CIS (1996); UN *Demographic Yearbooks*

Country	Years	Sources Used
Tanzania	1953–68	UN *Demographic Yearbooks*
Thailand	1850–1931, 1956–60, 1973–2003	McKeown (2009, 2010); UN *Demographic Yearbooks*; Wickramasekera (2002: 15); ILO (2009)
Timor, East	1956–8	UN *Demographic Yearbooks*
Togo	1923–4	Ferenczi & Willcox (1929)
Tonga	1997–8	ILO (2009)
Trinidad & Tobago	1918–23, 1955–9, 1964–87	Ferenczi & Willcox (1929); UN *Demographic Yearbooks*
Turkey	1850–1924, 1951–2, 1956–75	Ferenczi & Willcox (1929); UN *Demographic Yearbooks*; Ebiri (1985: 216)
Turkmenistan	1980, 1985–92	CIS (1996: 46)
Uganda	1958–74	UN *Demographic Yearbooks*
Ukraine	1980, 1985–98, 2000–6	CIS (1996); ILO (2009)
United Kingdom	1850–1938, 1946–2007	Mitchell; UN (1958); UN *Demographic Yearbooks*; National Statistics-UK (2009)
United States	1868–95, 1898–1902, 1908–57	Ferenczi & Willcox (1929); UN (1958), UN *Demographic Yearbooks*
Uruguay	1879–1940, 1943–4	Mitchell; UN (1958)
Uzbekistan	1980, 1985–92, 1994–5	CIS (1996: 46); UN *Demographic Yearbooks*
Venezuela	1919–21, 1924, 1936–47, 1957–64, 1966–71, 1974, 1979–82, 1985–91	Ferenczi & Willcox (1929); UN *Demographic Yearbooks*
Vietnam	1936–42	UN *Demographic Yearbooks*
Wallis & Futuna Islands	1969	UN *Demographic Yearbooks*
Yemen	1968–70	UN *Demographic Yearbooks*
Yugoslavia	1889–1908, 1919–38, 1955–8, 1960–5, 1967–70, 1976–7, 1992–3	Ferenczi & Willcox (1929); Mitchell; UN *Demographic Yearbooks*
Zambia	1964–6	UN *Demographic Yearbooks*
Zimbabwe	1954–96	UN (1979); UN *Demographic Yearbooks*; Mitchell

Appendix III: Countries with No Emigration Data (and hence excluded from final version)

Albania; Anguilla, Benin; Bhutan; Bosnia and Herzegovina; Burundi; Cambodia; Central African Republic; Chad; Comoros, Dem. Republic of Congo; Republic of Congo; Côte d'Ivoire; Equatorial Guinea; Eritrea; French Antilles; Gabon; Georgia; Guadeloupe; Guinea; Guinea-Bissau; Honduras; Iran; Iraq; Jordan; Kiribati; Dem. Republic of Korea; Kuwait; Laos; Lebanon; Libya; Maldives; Mali; Mauritania; Micronesia, Federated Islands of; Mongolia; Montserrat; Nepal; Netherlands Antilles; Niger; Oman; Palau; Panama; Paraguay; Qatar; Sao Tome and Principe; Saudi Arabia; Senegal; Solomon Islands; St. Martin; Sudan; Tunisia; United Arab Emirates; U.S. Virgin Islands; and Vanuatu.

Appendix IV: Lagging Pattern, Newey-West Models, Truncated TSCS Data

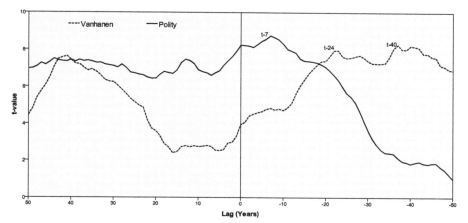

Note: See comments associated with Figure 4.7 for an explanation. This is the lagging pattern when the pre-statehood data from Norway (pre-1905), Ireland (pre-1922), and India (pre-1947) were excluded from the dataset.

Appendix V: Emigration Flows and Political Development, 1976–2006, EMIG 1.2 Data

	1976–85	1986–95	1996–2001	Period Average	Count	Level of Democracy 2006	Change in Democracy 1976–2006	Population 2005	Population Density 2005
High Emigration						(19.9)	(6.2)	(10,647,529)	(173)
Jamaica	15.64	212.89		114.27	3	13.1	2.3	2,668,000	243
Dominica		79.95	99.65	89.80	9	18.2	3.6	67,000	90
Nicaragua		45.21	79.69	62.45	11	24.8	21.6	5,455,000	42
El Salvador		45.51		45.51	3	18	6.1	6,059,000	288
Dominican Rep.	3.20	85.58		44.39	4	17.9	14.2	9,533,000	197
Syria	35.16			35.16	2	6.6	6.5	19,121,000	103
Burkina Faso		31.97		31.97	1	4.9	4.9	13,747,000	50
Seychelles	22.90	24.39	31.27	26.19	23	20.9	11.6	83,000	182
Bahrain			17.27	17.27	1	1.1	1.1	7,281,000	1048
Kazakhstan		17.76	15.74	16.75	8	4	3.3	15,194,000	6
Sri Lanka	2.48	11.96	35.51	16.65	26	25.3	4.9	19,531,000	298
France	19.85	10.54		15.20	16	31.1	–2.2	61,013,000	111
Kyrgyzstan		12.74	13.05	12.89	10	4.1	1.7	5,221,000	26
New Zealand	15.18	10.23	12.41	12.61	26	32.7	5.1	4,111,000	15
Switzerland	7.89	13.74		10.82	20	41.4	–1	7,441,000	180
Ireland		12.55	7.6	10.08	15	34.1	10.5	4,187,000	60
Iceland	6.70	10.62	7.88	8.40	26	40.4	10.4	296,000	3
Medium Emigration						(25.0)	(5.0)	(20,071,813)	(1,463 [108])*
Monaco			9.65	9.65	2			32,000	21,781
Australia	6.72	7.46	8.42	7.54	26	33.9	0.6	20,395,000	3

(continued)

249

	1976–85	1986–95	1996–2001	Period Average	Count	Level of Democracy 2006	Change in Democracy 1976–2006	Population 2005	Population Density 2005
Bulgaria		7.38	7.42	7.40	7	32.3	32.3	7,739,000	70
Uzbekistan		7.23		7.23	4	2.1	−5.2	26,320,000	59
Germany	6.29	6.24	8.39	6.98	26	37	5.4	82,409,000	231
Philippines	4.53	6.11	9.37	6.67	26	22.8	22.8	85,496,000	285
Denmark	5.49	6.31	7.37	6.39	22	43.5	1.2	5,417,000	126
Estonia		9.42	2.75	6.09	9	24.7	−14.7	1,347,000	130
Fiji	4.14	6.69	6.73	5.86	26	0	−13.3	828,000	45
Armenia		8.47	3.16	5.81	11	20.9	4.3	3,065,000	103
Guyana	5.28	9.52	1.75	5.52	19	18.7	4.9	764,000	4
New Guinea	3.28	6.31		4.80	10	31.6	12.3	6,118,000	13
Latvia		5.65	3.72	4.69	11	27.4	1	2,292,000	35
Norway	3.68	4.68	5.28	4.55	26	38.6	3.4	4,635,000	12
Venezuela	5.56	3.27		4.41	11	16.1	−3.8	26,726,000	29
Korea, Rep. of	0.88	5.24	4.46	3.53	19	26.8	26.8	47,566,000	478
Low Emigration						(22.0)	(9.0)	(62,659,295)	(171)
Japan	3.69	4.98		4.34	20	32.8	3.6	127,449,000	337
Ukraine		4.88	3.01	3.95	10	32.6	10.3	46,936,000	78
Israel	3.02	3.76	3.54	3.44	16	31.9	3.1	6,692,000	302
Sweden	3.05	3.02	4.03	3.37	26	40.1	2.2	9,066,000	20
San Marino		3.30	2.28	2.79	10			30,000	496
Lithuania		3.97	1.19	2.58	11	23.9	−1.9	3,416,000	52
Portugal	2.14	2.48	2.80	2.48	23	27.2	1	10,547,000	115
Finland	2.66	1.52	2.53	2.24	26	37.6	24.4	5,244,000	16
Kenya	2.16			2.16	1	9.4	9.4	35,817,000	62

Country									
Mexico	1.25	3.35	1.76	2.12	26	23.1	21.4	105,330,000	54
Thailand	0.92	2.01	3.23	2.05	26	0	-3.8	65,946,000	129
Moldova		2.01	2.10	2.05	8	20	12.4	3,539,000	111
Greece	1.95	1.64		1.95	2	36.9	11.9	11,064,000	84
Canada	2.41	1.64	1.61	1.89	26	29.1	5	32,307,000	3
Trinidad & Tobago	2.64	0.65		1.65	12	22.9	9.9	1,318,000	257
Malta	3.67	0.89	0.22	1.59	26	33.7	3.5	403,000	1,274
Cuba	1.39			1.39	1	0	0	11,193,000	101
Colombia	1.32			1.32	2	9.9	0	43,049,000	38
Cyprus	2.29	0.26		1.28	16	38.7	23.7	836,000	90
Belize	1.34	1.25	1.20	1.26	20	15.5	0.6	282,000	12
Mauritius	0.88	1.63		1.26	19	22.1	-1.4	1,252,000	614
Bangladesh	0.51	1.23	1.85	1.20	26	17.3	17.3	153,122,000	1,063
Romania		1.60	0.72	1.16	16	20.6**	19.8**	21,635,000	91
Pakistan	1.49	1.04	0.93	1.15	23	5.7	-10.4	165,816,000	208
Italy	1.48	1.04	0.83	1.12	24	35.1	-5	58,645,000	195
Belarus		1.06	1.05	1.05	11	11.1	5.2	9,816,000	47
Indonesia	0.29	0.63	2.07	1.00	26	28.7	24.6	219,210,000	115
Zimbabwe	2.26	0.41	0.32	1.00	21	8.8	-5.3	12,475,000	32
Croatia		0.93	1.00	0.97	10	24.5	18.8	4,443,000	79
Azerbaijan		0.69	1.14	0.91	5	17.3	14.3	8,453,000	98
Russia	0.50	0.94	0.70	0.71	26	17.3	17.3	143,170,000	8
Slovenia		0.88	0.54	0.71	10	28.5	3	2,001,000	99
Czechoslovakia	0.59	0.78	0.72	0.69	21	33.9	33.9	10,195,000	129

(continued)

	1976–85	1986–95	1996–2001	Period Average	Count	Level of Democracy 2006	Change in Democracy 1976–2006	Population 2005	Population Density 2005
Poland	0.70	0.67	0.55	0.64	20	20.7	20.3	38,198,000	118
Spain	0.38	0.58	0.62	0.53	26	35.6	35.6	43,060,000	85
Yugoslavia	0.54	0.50		0.52	4				
Afghanistan	0.50			0.50	3	12	12	24,507,000	38
Turkey	0.45			0.45	5	20.4	11.7	71,169,000	91
Slovak Rep.		0.69	0.20	0.44	9	20.9	−6.5	5,386,000	110
Turkmenistan		0.41		0.41	2	0	−0.9	4,843,000	10
India	0.38	0.38	0.41	0.39	26	25.6	10.6	1,130,618,000	344
Hungary	0.14	0.37	0.63	0.38	22	27	26.7	10,078,000	108
Burma	0.26	0.32	0.47	0.35	7	0	0	48,345,000	71
South Africa	0.50	0.23	0.26	0.33	26	10.8	18.8	48,073,000	39
Macedonia	0.19	0.19	0.38	0.29	7	22.6	10	2,035,000	79

Notes: Emigration flows are measured in per-mil (o/oo) terms, where per mil refers to the number of emigrants per 1,000 of the population in the sending (home) state. The Count column captures the number of annual observations recorded for a country during the period under consideration (the maximum count is 26 observations). The Level of Democracy indicator is the 2006 Vanhanen index in 2006 (**except for Romania, which is for 2002). The Change in Democracy indicator takes the 2006 Vanhanen index and subtracts from it the 1976 index score (**except for Romania, which ends in 2002). In short, I assume that the direction of change has been constant over the period, even though this was not always the case. For those countries that only came into being (or for which data were available) after 1976, I subtracted the first recorded year from the 2006 tally. *The average population density for medium-emigration countries includes two figures. The larger figure (1,463) is being driven by Monaco, which is a serious outlier. When Monaco is removed, the group's average population density drops to 108 people per square kilometer. Bold figures refer to the decade averages that justify their inclusion in each grouping. See text in Chapter 5 for further clarification.

Sources: EMIG 1.2; COW (2002); Vanhanen (2007); and UNPOP (2008).

Appendix VI: Emigration Stocks and Political Development, 1980–2006, UN Data

Country	Emigration Stock 2000–2002, %	HDI 2007	Change in HDI 1980–2006	Initial HDI Year	Level of Democracy 2006	Change in Democracy 1976–2006	Political Rights 2009	Change in Political Rights 1976–2009	Initial Political Rights Year	Population 2007
High Emigration	*(0.810)*	*(0.034)*			*(21.0)*	*(6.4)*	*(2.2)*	*(0.8)*		*(1,295,000)*
Antigua & Barbuda	45.3	0.868	0.008	2006	25.8	13.4	3	−1	1981	100,000
Saint Kitts & Nevis	44.3	0.838	0.006	2005	22.3	3.5	1	1	1981	100,000
Grenada	40.3	0.813	0.001	2005	21.9	3.9	1	1	1976	100,000
Dominica	38.3	0.814	0.000	2005	18.2	3.6	1	1	1978	100,000
Samoa	37.2	0.771	0.085	1985	11.5	9.4	2	2	1976	200,000
Suriname	36	0.769	0.010	2005	21.2	4.8	2	0	1976	500,000
Saint Vincent & Grenadines	34.4	0.772	0.009	2005	25.7	13.1	2	0	1979	100,000
Tonga	33.7	0.768	0.009	2000	1.8	1.8	5	0	1976	100,000
Guyana	33.5	0.729	0.007	2005	18.7	4.9	2	1	1976	800,000
Cape Verde	30.5	0.708	0.119	1990	16.2	16.2	1	5	1976	500,000
Barbados	29.8	0.903	0.013	2005	18.3	−3.1	1	0	1976	300,000
Jamaica	26.7	0.766	0.016	2000	13.1	−2.3	2	−1	1976	2,700,000
Bosnia & Herzegovina	25.1	0.812	0.008	2005	27.8	−4.3	4	2	1992	3,800,000
Saint Lucia	24.1	0.821	0.004	2005	18.3	2	1	1	1979	200,000
Occupied Palestinian Terr.	23.9	0.737	0.001	2005						4,000,000
Malta	22.3	0.902	0.093	1985	33.7	3.5	1	0	1976	400,000
Albania	21	0.818	0.034	2000	26.3	26.3	3	4	1976	3,100,000

				Year					Year	Population
Armenia	20.3	0.798	0.067	1990	20.9	4.3	6	−1	1991	3,100,000
Trinidad & Tobago	20.2	0.837	0.099	1980	22.9	9.9	2	0	1976	1,300,000
Ireland	20	0.965	0.099	1980	34.1	10.5	1	0	1976	4,400,000
Medium Emigration		(0.780)	(0.043)		(16.8)	(6.4)	(3.5)	(0.4)		(6,432,353)
Kazakhstan	19.4	0.804	0.026	1990	4	3.3	6	−1	1991	15,400,000
Cyprus	18.4	0.914	0.065	1990	38.7	23.7	1	2	1976	900,000
Georgia	18.3	0.778	0.039	2000	6.6	−10.6	4	2	1991	4,400,000
Seychelles	17	0.845	0.004	2000	20.9	11.6	3	−2	1976	100,000
Kuwait	16.6	0.916	0.071	1980	1.5	1.5	4	2	1976	2,900,000
Belize	16.5	0.772	0.067	1990	15.5	0.6	1	0	1981	300,000
Portugal	16.1	0.909	0.099	1980	27.2	1	1	1	1976	10,600,000
Bahrain	15.9	0.895	0.071	1980	1.1	1.1	6	0	1976	800,000
Belarus	15.2	0.826	0.031	1990	11.1	5.2	7	−3	1991	9,700,000
Fiji	15	0.741	−0.003	2005	0	−13.3	6	−4	1976	800,000
Congo	14.7	0.601	0.004	1990	4.1	4.1	6	−1	1976	3,600,000
Equatorial Guinea	14.5	0.719	0.064	2000	7.8	7.8	7	−1	1976	600,000
Azerbaijan	14.3	0.787	0.031	2005	17.3	14.3	6	−1	1991	8,600,000
El Salvador	14.3	0.747	0.099	1980	18	6.1	2	1	1976	6,100,000
Moldova	14.3	0.72	−0.014	1990	20	12.4	3	2	1991	3,700,000
Serbia	13.6	0.826	0.029	2000	28.6	3.4	2	1	2006	9,800,000
Sao Tome & Principe	13.5	0.651	0.012	2005	14.2	14.2	2	3	1976	200,000
Israel	13.1	0.935	0.083	1980	31.9	3.1	1	1	1976	6,900,000

(continued)

Country	Emigration Stock 2000–2002, %	HDI 2007	Change in HDI 1980–2006	Initial HDI Year	Level of Democracy 2006	Change in Democracy 1976–2006	Political Rights 2009	Change in Political Rights 1976–2009	Initial Political Rights Year	Population 2007
Lebanon	12.9	0.803	0.003	2005	21.5	21.5	5	–1	1976	4,200,000
Liechtenstein	12.6	0.951	0.001	2006			1	3	1976	
Eritrea	12.5	0.472	0.041	2000	0	0	7	–1	1993	4,800,000
Mali	12.5	0.371	0.099	1980	3.4	3.4	2	5	1976	12,400,000
Mauritius	12.5	0.804	0.086	1990	22.1	–1.4	1	2	1976	1,300,000
Estonia	12.2	0.883	0.066	1990	24.7	–14.7	1	1	1991	1,300,000
Croatia	12	0.871	0.055	1990	24.5	18.8	1	2	1991	4,400,000
New Zealand	11.8	0.95	0.071	1980	32.7	5.1	1	0	1976	4,200,000
Jordan	11.6	0.77	0.099	1980	1	1	6	0	1976	5,900,000
Tajikistan	11.4	0.688	–0.019	1990	12.1	9.7	6	–3	1991	6,700,000
Macedonia	11.3	0.817	0.035	1995	22.6	10	3	0	1992	2,000,000
Ukraine	10.9	0.796	0.041	2000	32.6	10.3	3	0	1991	46,300,000
Bahamas	10.8	0.856	0.004	2005	17.7	6.3	1	0	1976	300,000
Afghanistan	10.6	0.352	0.005	2005	12	12	6	1	1976	26,300,000
Iceland	10.6	0.969	0.005	2005	40.4	10.4	1	0	1976	300,000
Bulgaria	10.5	0.84	0.083	1980	32.3	32.3	2	5	1976	7,600,000
Kyrgyzstan	10.5	0.71	0.037	2000	4.1	1.7	6	–1	1991	5,300,000
Low Emigration		(0.715)	(0.068)		(15.6)	(7.9)	(3.6)	(1.0)		(50,311,905)
Burkina Faso	9.8	0.389	0.071	1980	4.9	4.9	5	0	1976	14,700,000
Andorra	9.7	0.934	0.001	2006	6.9	–1.8	1	1	1976	100,000
Hong Kong	9.5	0.944	0.005	2005			1		1993	6,900,000
Luxembourg	9.5	0.96	0.004	2005	26.2	–7.9	1	1	1976	500,000

Country										
Dominican Republic	9.1	0.777	0.099	1980	17.9	14.2	2	2	1976	9,800,000
Latvia	9.1	0.866	0.063	1990	27.4	1	2	0	1991	2,300,000
Nicaragua	9.1	0.699	0.071	1980	24.8	21.6	4	1	1976	5,600,000
Mexico	9	0.854	0.099	1980	23.1	21.4	2	2	1976	108,000,000
Cuba	8.9	0.863	0.024	2005	0	0	7	0	1976	11,200,000
Guinea-Bissau	8.6	0.396	0.099	1980	15.6	15.6	4	2	1976	1,500,000
Lithuania	8.6	0.87	0.042	1990	23.9	−1.9	1	1	1991	3,400,000
Uzbekistan	8.5	0.71	0.024	2000	2.1	−5.2	7	−1	1991	26,900,000
Slovakia	8.2	0.88	0.053	1995	20.9	−6.5	1	2	1993	5,400,000
Morocco	8.1	0.654	0.099	1980	5.1	5.1	5	0	1976	31,200,000
Greece	7.8	0.942	0.071	1980	36.9	11.9	1	1	1976	11,100,000
Comoros	7.7	0.576	0.083	1980	8.9	8.9	3	2	1976	600,000
Haiti	7.7	0.532	0.099	1980	11.3	11.3	4	2	1976	9,700,000
Russia	7.7	0.817	−0.004	1990	17.3	17.3	6	−3	1991	142,000,000
Benin	7.5	0.492	0.071	1980	8.7	8.7	2	5	1976	8,400,000
Uruguay	7	0.865	0.099	1980	31.8	31.8	1	5	1976	3,300,000
Paraguay	6.9	0.761	0.099	1980	15.1	10.1	3	2	1976	6,100,000
Finland	6.6	0.959	0.071	1980	37.6	24.4	1	1	1976	5,300,000
United Kingdom	6.6	0.947	0.099	1980	29.5	−2.2	1	0	1976	60,900,000
Guinea	6.3	0.435	0.009	2005	6.6	6.6	7	0	1976	9,600,000
Singapore	6.3	0.944	0.071	1980	9	−0.6	5	0	1976	4,500,000
Algeria	6.2	0.754	0.126	1985	8.7	8.4	6	0	1976	33,900,000
Laos	5.9	0.619	0.100	1995	0.7	0.7	7	0	1976	6,100,000

(continued)

257

Country	Emigration Stock 2000–2002, %	HDI 2007	Change in HDI 1980–2006	Initial HDI Year	Level of Democracy 2006	Change in Democracy 1976–2006	Political Rights 2009	Change in Political Rights 1976–2009	Initial Political Rights Year	Population 2007
Tunisia	5.9	0.769	0.099	1985	5.5	5.5	7	–1	1976	10,100,000
Panama	5.7	0.84	0.071	1980	26.7	26.7	1	6	1976	3,300,000
Switzerland	5.6	0.96	0.071	1980	41.4	–1	1	0	1976	7,500,000
Angola	5.5	0.564	0.023	2005	0	0	6	0	1976	17,600,000
Austria	5.5	0.955	0.083	1980	35.1	4.3	1	0	1976	8,300,000
Burundi	5.4	0.394	0.083	1980	16.5	16.5	4	3	1976	7,800,000
Italy	5.4	0.951	0.099	1980	35.1	–5	1	1	1976	59,300,000
Ecuador	5.3	0.806	0.099	1980	20	20	3	3	1976	13,300,000
Honduras	5.3	0.732	0.099	1980	13.2	13.2	4	2	1976	7,200,000
Turkmenistan	5.3	0.739	0.001	2006	0	–0.9	7	–1	1991	5,000,000
Slovenia	5.2	0.929	0.077	1990	28.5	3	1	1	1991	2,000,000
Poland	5.1	0.88	0.074	1990	20.7	20.3	1	5	1976	38,100,000
Brunei Darussalam	4.9	0.92	0.083	1980	0	0	6	0	1976	400,000
Guatemala	4.9	0.704	0.099	1980	8.3	2	4	0	1976	13,400,000
Germany	4.7	0.947	0.083	1980	37	5.4	1	0	1976	82,300,000
Netherlands	4.7	0.964	0.083	1980	42	3.2	1	0	1976	16,500,000
Sri Lanka	4.7	0.759	0.083	1980	25.3	4.9	4	–2	1976	19,900,000
Romania	4.6	0.837	0.051	1990	20.6	19.8	2	5	1976	21,500,000
Bangladesh	4.5	0.543	0.099	1980	17.3	17.3	3	4	1976	158,000,000
Ghana	4.5	0.526	0.032	2000	19.1	19.1	1	6	1976	22,900,000
Belgium	4.4	0.953	0.071	1980	44.2	3.3	1	0	1976	10,500,000

Country										
Senegal	4.4	0.464	0.074	1990	7.2	7.2	3	3	1976	11,900,000
Bolivia	4.3	0.729	0.071	1980	16.5	16.5	3	3	1976	9,500,000
Denmark	4.3	0.955	0.099	1980	43.5	1.2	1	0	1976	5,400,000
Gabon	4.3	0.755	0.008	1995	5.1	5.1	6	0	1976	1,400,000
Mozambique	4.2	0.402	0.071	1980	6.1	6.1	4	3	1976	21,900,000
Turkey	4.2	0.806	0.071	1980	20.4	1.7	3	-1	1976	73,000,000
Mauritania	4.1	0.52	0.025	2000	4.7	4.7	6	0	1976	3,100,000
Canada	4	0.966	0.071	1980	29.1	5	1	0	1976	32,900,000
Niger	4	0.34	0.081	2000	7.1	7.1	5	2	1976	14,100,000
Philippines	4	0.751	0.071	1980	22.8	22.8	4	1	1976	88,700,000
Colombia	3.9	0.807	0.099	1980	9.9	0	3	-1	1976	44,400,000
Hungary	3.9	0.879	0.083	1980	27	26.7	1	5	1976	10,000,000
Nepal	3.9	0.553	0.099	1980	17.7	17.7	4	2	1976	28,300,000
Norway	3.9	0.971	0.071	1980	38.6	3.4	1	0	1976	4,700,000
Togo	3.7	0.499	0.071	1980	10.2	10.2	5	2	1976	6,300,000
Gambia	3.6	0.456	0.006	2005	3.2	0.6	5	-3	1976	1,600,000
Czech Republic	3.5	0.903	0.056	1990	33.9	33.9	1	6	1993	10,300,000
Chile	3.3	0.878	0.071	1980	19.7	19.7	1	6	1976	16,600,000
Sweden	3.3	0.963	0.071	1980	40.1	2.2	1	0	1976	9,200,000
United Arab Emirates	3.3	0.903	0.083	1980	0	0	6	-1	1976	4,400,000
Chad	3.2	0.392	0.068	1995	10.7	10.7	7	0	1976	10,600,000
Spain	3.2	0.955	0.071	1980	35.6	35.6	1	4	1976	44,100,000
Malaysia	3.1	0.829	0.099	1980	11.4	4.3	4	-1	1976	26,600,000
Korea, Rep. of	3.1	0.937	0.099	1980	26.8	26.8	1	4	1976	48,000,000

(continued)

Country	Emigration Stock 2000–2002, %	HDI 2007	Change in HDI 1980–2006	Initial HDI Year	Level of Democracy 2006	Change in Democracy 1976–2006	Political Rights 2009	Change in Political Rights 1976–2009	Initial Political Rights Year	Population 2007
Yemen	3	0.575	0.088	1995	6.4	6.4	6	0	1990	22,300,000
Egypt	2.9	0.703	0.083	1980	2.3	-0.2	6	-1	1976	80,100,000
France	2.9	0.961	0.099	1980	31.1	-2.2	1	0	1976	61,700,000
Central African Republic	2.7	0.369	0.083	1980	7.6	7.6	5	2	1976	4,300,000
Liberia	2.7	0.442	0.071	1980	13.7	13.7	3	3	1976	3,600,000
Peru	2.7	0.806	0.083	1980	22.8	22.8	2	4	1976	28,500,000
Rwanda	2.7	0.46	0.071	1980	6.7	6.7	6	1	1976	9,500,000
Costa Rica	2.6	0.854	0.083	1980	19.8	-1.1	1	0	1976	4,500,000
Lesotho	2.6	0.514	-0.019	1980	8.6	8.6	3	2	1976	2,000,000
Timor-Leste	2.6	0.489	0.002	2005	13.5	0	3	3	1999	1,100,000
Syria	2.4	0.742	0.083	1980	6.6	6.5	7	-1	1976	20,500,000
Vietnam	2.4	0.725	0.163	1985	6.2	0	7	0	1976	86,100,000
Cambodia	2.3	0.593	0.078	2000	4	4	6	1	1976	14,300,000
Qatar	2.3	0.91	0.040	2000	0	0	6	-1	1976	1,100,000
Australia	2.2	0.97	0.099	1980	33.9	0.6	1	0	1976	20,900,000
Bhutan	2.2	0.619	0.017	2005	0	0	4	0	1976	700,000
Djibouti	2.2	0.52	0.007	2005	4.5	4.5	5	-2	1977	800,000
Pakistan	2.2	0.572	0.099	1980	5.7	-10.4	4	0	1976	173,000,000
Zambia	2.2	0.481	-0.014	1990	13.5	11.9	3	2	1976	12,300,000
Sierra Leone	2	0.365	0.015	2005	10.6	10.6	3	3	1976	5,400,000
Vanuatu	2	0.693	0.030	2000	23.4	9.5	2	0	1980	200,000

South Africa	1.7	0.683	1980	10.8	2	2	1976	49,200,000
Sudan	1.7	0.531	2000	0	7	−1	1976	40,400,000
Argentina	1.6	0.866	1980	35.8	2	4	1976	39,500,000
Congo, Dem. Rep.	1.5	0.389	2000	14.5	6	1	1976	62,500,000
Kenya	1.4	0.541	2000	9.4	4	1	1976	37,800,000
Libya	1.4	0.847	2000	0	7	0	1976	6,200,000
Venezuela	1.4	0.844	1980	16.1	5	−4	1976	27,700,000
Iran	1.3	0.782	1980	3	6	0	1976	72,400,000
Namibia	1.3	0.686	1990	10	2	2	1988	2,100,000
Thailand	1.3	0.783	1980	−3.8	5	1	1976	67,000,000
Malawi	1.2	0.493	1985	17.1	3	4	1976	14,400,000
Saudi Arabia	1.1	0.843	1990	0	7	−1	1976	24,700,000
Swaziland	1.1	0.572	1980	0	7	−1	1976	1,200,000
Cameroon	1	0.523	1980	6.6	6	1	1976	18,700,000
Côte d'Ivoire	1	0.484	1990	0	6	0	1976	20,100,000
Solomon Islands	1	0.61	2005	15.3	4	−2	1978	500,000
Botswana	0.9	0.694	1980	9.9	3	−1	1976	1,900,000
Indonesia	0.9	0.734	1980	24.6	2	3	1976	225,000,000
Madagascar	0.9	0.543	2000	9.3	6	0	1976	18,600,000
Papua New Guinea	0.9	0.541	1980	12.3	4	−2	1976	6,400,000
India	0.8	0.612	1980	10.6	2	0	1976	1,160,000,000
Nigeria	0.8	0.511	1990	12	5	1	1976	148,000,000
Tanzania	0.8	0.53	1990	2.8	4	2	1976	41,300,000

(*continued*)

Country	Emigration Stock 2000–2002, %	HDI 2007	Change in HDI 1980–2006	Initial HDI Year	Level of Democracy 2006	Change in Democracy 1976–2006	Political Rights 2009	Change in Political Rights 1976–2009	Initial Political Rights Year	Population 2007
United States	0.8	0.956	0.099	1980	34.5	9.6	1	0	1976	309,000,000
Japan	0.7	0.96	0.099	1980	32.8	3.6	1	1	1976	127,000,000
Myanmar	0.7	0.586	0.094	1985	0	0	7	−1	1976	49,100,000
Oman	0.7	0.846	0.010	2005	0	0	6	0	1976	2,700,000
Uganda	0.7	0.514	0.122	1990	10.9	10.9	5	2	1976	30,600,000
Brazil	0.5	0.813	0.083	1980	28.1	28.1	2	2	1976	190,000,000
China	0.5	0.772	0.071	1980	0	0	7	0	1976	1,330,000,000
Ethiopia	0.4	0.414	0.105	1995	11.8	11.8	5	2	1976	78,600,000
Maldives	0.4	0.771	0.087	1995	3.7	2.2	3	1	1976	300,000
Mongolia	0.3	0.727	0.050	2000	20.6	20.6	2	5	1976	2,600,000

Notes: Emigration stock figures are given as a percentage (%) of the home (sending) population. The Level of Democracy and Change in Democracy columns employ Vanhanen's indicators as described in the notes to Table 7.1. The HDI and population figures come from UNDP (2009). Change in HDI is the total change from the initial year of recording (listed in the next column) until the final recorded change in 2006. The Political Rights come from Freedom House (2010), where 1 is high and 7 is low. Change in Political Rights is the total change from the initial year of recording (listed in the next column) and the final recorded change in 2009.

Sources: UNDP (2009, 2010); Vanhanen (2007); Freedom House (2010).

Bibliography

Aarebrot, Frank H. and Stein Kuhnle 1976. "The Ecology of Exit-Voice: Economic Development and Political Response in an Early Phase of Nation-Building: 19th Century Norway." Paper presented at the Research Committee on Social Ecology, ISA World Congress, Toronto, August 19–24.

Abadan-Unat, Nermin 1995. "Turkish Emigration to Europe," in R. Cohen (ed.), pp. 279–84.

ABS 2008. [Australian Bureau of Statistics] "Table 10.1 Overseas arrivals and departures, sex and category of movement, year ended 31 December, 1925 onwards," http://www.abs.gov.au/AUSSTATS/subscriber.nsf/log?openagent& 310506500idsoo10_2008.xls&3105.0.65.001&Data%20Cubes&9CAEDEC 4F23AE10ECA25749B00177B7F&0&2008&05.08.2008&Latest.

Adler, Stephen 1985. "Emigration and Development in Algeria: Doubts and Dilemmas," in Rogers (ed.), pp. 263–84.

Allen, Robert C. 2009. *The British Industrial Revolution in a Global Perspective*. Cambridge: Cambridge University Press.

Almond, Gabriel A. and G. Bingham Powell, Jr. 1966. *Comparative Politics: A Developmental Approach*. Boston: Little, Brown.

Almond, Gabriel A. and Sidney Verba 1963. *The Civic Culture*. Boston: Little, Brown.

Alston, Lee J. and Joseph P. Ferrie 2007. "Shaping Welfare Policy: The Role of the South," in Fishback et al. (eds.), *Government and the American Economy: A New History*. Chicago: University of Chicago Press, pp. 490–506.

———— 1993. "Paternalism in Agricultural Labor Contracts in the U.S. South: Implications for the Growth of the Welfare State," *American Economic Review* 83 (September): 852–76.

Andersen, Arlow William 1990. *Rough Road to Glory. The Norwegian-American Press Speaks out on Public Affairs, 1875 to 1925*. Cranbury, NJ: Associated University Press.

———— 1975. *The Norwegian Americans*. Boston: Twayne Publishers.

Anderson, J. B. and J. Gerber 2007. "Data Appendix to Fifty Years of Change on the U.S.-Mexico Border: Growth, Development, and Quality of Life," http://latinamericanstudies.asdsu.edu/BorderData.html.

Anwar, Muhammad 1995. "New Commonwealth: Migration to the UK," in Cohen (ed.), pp. 274–8.

Armenia 2008. [National Statistical Service of the Republic of Armenia] "Population," *Statistical Yearbook of Armenia 2008:* 23–48, http://www.armstat.am/en/?nid=45.

Ascoli, Ugo 1985. "Migration of Workers and the Labor Market: Is Italy Becoming a Country of Immigration?" in Rogers (ed.), pp. 185–206.

Bairoch, Paul 1997. *Victories et déboires. Vol. II. Histoire économique et sociale du monde du XVIe siècle à nos jours.* Paris: Gallimard.

Ballard, R. 1987. "The Political Economy of Migration: Pakistan, Britain and the Middle East," in Eades (ed.) *Migrants, Workers and the Social Order.* London: Tavistock Publications, pp. 17–41.

Beck, Ulrich and Natan Sznaider 2006. "Unpacking Cosmopolitanism for the Social Sciences: A Research Agenda," *British Journal of Sociology* 57 (1): 1–23.

Beine, Michel, Frédéric Docquier, and Hillel Rapoport 2001. "Brain Drain and Economic Growth: Theory and Evidence Source," *Journal of Development Economics* 64 (1): 275–89.

Bell, Martin and Salut Muhidin 2009. "Cross-National Comparisons of Internal Migration," Human Development Research Paper 2009/30, July, UNDP.

Berlin, Isaiah 1969. "Two Concepts of Liberty," in Berlin *Four Essays on Liberty.* Oxford: Oxford University Press, pp. 118–72.

Bjørgum, Jorunn 1998. "Martin Tranmæl–Utdypning," *Norsk Biografisk Leksikon,* http://www.snl.no/.nbl_biografi/Martin_Tranm%C3%A6l/utdypning.

Blegen, Theodore C. 1958. *Amerikabrev.* Oslo: Aschehoug.

——— 1931. *Norwegian Migration to America: 1825–1860.* Northfield, MN: Norwegian-American Historical Association.

BMET 2009. [Bureau of Manpower, Employment and Training, Bangladesh] "Flow of Migration by Country of Employment," http://www.bmet.org.bd/Reports/Flow_Migration.htm.

Böhning, W. R. 1984. *Studies in International Labour Migration.* New York: St. Martin's.

——— 1975. "Some Thoughts on Emigration from the Mediterranean Basin," *International Labour Review* 3: 251–77.

Borchard, Edwin M. 1931. "Decadence of the American Doctrine of Voluntary Expatriation," *American Journal of International Law* 25: 312–16.

Borjas, George 1999. *Heaven's Door.* Princeton: Princeton University Press.

Borjas, George J. and Jeff Crisp (eds.) 2005. *Poverty, International Migration and Asylum.* Basingstoke: Palgrave.

BOS-Guyana 2009. [Guyana Bureau of Statistics] "Guyanese Emigrants from 1969–2006," e-mail exchange with Vanessa Profitt [Small], Statistician, Demography Dept., Bureau of Statistics (Guyana), July 20.

BOS-Nauru 2009. [Nauru Bureau of Statistics] "Migration Statistics – Emigration," e-mail exchange with Lindsay Thoma, July 6.

Brennan, G. and J. Buchanan 1980. *The Power to Tax: Analytical Foundation of a Fiscal Constitution*. Cambridge: Cambridge University Press.

Buchanan, J. M. 1975. *The Limits of Liberty: Between Anarchy and Leviathan*. Chicago: University of Chicago Press.

Bull, Edvard 1976. "Martin Tranmæl og ophavet til Trondheimsopposisjonen," *Tidsskrift for Arbeiderbevegelsenshistorie* 2: 75–147.

————— 1947. *Arbeiderklassen i Norsk Historie*. Oslo: Tiden Norsk.

Campbell, Rex R., Daniel M. Johnson, and Gary Stangler 1974. "Return Migration of Black People to the South," *Rural Sociology* 39 (4): 514–28.

Castles, Stephen and Godula Kosack 1973. *Immigrant Workers and Class Structure in Western Europe*. London: Oxford University Press.

CBS Aruba 2009. [Central Bureau of Statistics, Aruba] "Aa.1.2.1 Population Growth, 1972–2006," http://www.cbs.aw/cbs/readBlob.do?id=884. Updated through e-mail exchange with Monique Plaza Maduro at the CBS Aruba, June 21.

Cerase, Francesco P. 1974. "Expectations and Reality: A Case Study of Return Migration from the United States to Southern Italy," *International Migration Review* 8 (2): 245–62.

CFO Philippines 2009. [Commission on Filipinos Overseas] "Number of Registered Filipino Emigrants by Major Country of Destination: 1981–2008," http://www.cfo.gov.ph/Emigrant8108.pdf.

Chan, Kam Wing 2010. "Internal Migration in China: Trends, Geography and Policies," in United Nations Population Division, *Population Distribution, Urbanization, Internal Migration and Development: An International Perspective*. New York: United Nations, May 16.

————— 2001. "Recent Migration in China: Patterns, Trends, and Policies," *Asian Perspective* 25 (4): 127–55.

Chan, Kam Wing and Will Buckingham 2008. "Is China Abolishing the *Hukou* System?" *China Quarterly* 195 (September): 582–606.

Chan, Kam Wing and Man Wang 2008. "Remapping China's Regional Inequalities, 1990–2006: A New Assessment of *de facto* and *de jure* Population Data," *Eurasian Geography and Economics* 49 (1): 121–56.

Chau, Nancy H. and Oded Stark 1999. "Migration under Asymmetric Information and Human Capital Formation," *Review of International Economics* 7(3): 455–83.

Chernilo, Daniel 2006. "Social Theory's Methodological Nationalism: Myth and Reality," *European Journal of Social Theory* 9 (1): 5–22.

Chilton, Stephen 1991. *Grounding Political Development*. Boulder: Lynne Rienner.

————— 1988. *Defining Political Development*. Boulder: Lynne Rienner.

CIO Bahrain 2002. [Central Informatics Office, Bahrain] *Census 2001*, Part II, http://www.cio.gov.bh/en/default.asp?action=category&ID=67.

CIS 1996. [Committee for Statistics, International Center for Human Values, Moscow] "Emigrants from the Former USSR," in *The Statistical Handbook of Social and Economic Indicators for the Former Soviet Union 1980, 1990–92*. New York: Norman Ross, p. 46.

Clark, David A. 2005. "The Capability Approach: Its Development, Critiques and Recent Advances." Working Paper from the ESRC's Global Poverty Research Group, GPRG-WPS-032, http://www.gprg.org.

Cohen, Deborah 2011. *Braceros: Migrant Citizens and Transnational Subjects in Postwar United States and Mexico*. Chapel Hill: University of North Carolina Press.

———— 2006. "From Peasant to Worker: Migration, Masculinity, and the Making of Mexican Workers in the US," *International Labor and Working-Class History* 69: 81–103.

———— 2001. "Caught in the Middle: The Mexican State's Relationship with the United States and Its Own Citizen-Workers, 1942–54," *Journal of American Ethnic History* (Spring): 110–32.

Cohen, Robin (ed.) 1995. *The Cambridge Survey of World Migration*. Cambridge: Cambridge University Press.

Cohen, William 1991a. *At Freedom's Edge. Black Mobility and the Southern White Quest for Racial Control 1861–1915*. Baton Rouge: Louisiana State University Press.

———— 1991b. "The Great Migration as a Lever for Social Change," in Harrison (ed.), pp. 72–82.

Collier, Ruth Berins and David Collier 1991. *Shaping the Political Arena*. Princeton: Princeton University Press.

Córdova, Abby and Jonathan Hiskey 2009. "Migrant Networks and Democracy in Latin America," unpublished Working Paper, Nashville: Vanderbilt University.

COW 2002. [Correlates of War] "National Material Capabilities (v3.02)," http://www.correlatesofwar.org/COW2%20Data/Capabilities/nmc3–02.htm.

Crocker, David A. 1992. "Functioning and Capability: The Foundations of Sen's and Nussbaum's Development Ethic," *Political Theory* 20 (4): 584–612.

Cross, Harry E. and James A. Sandos 1981. *Across the Border: Rural Development in Mexico and Recent Migration to the United States*. Berkeley: Institute of Governmental Studies.

CSO 2008. [Central Statistics Office, Ireland] "Population and Migration Estimates. April 2008," http://www.cso.ie/releasespublications/documents/population/current/popmig.pdf.

CSO-Belize 2000. [Central Statistical Office, Belize] *Population Census 2000: Major Findings*. Belize: Central Statistical Office, Ministry of Budget Management, obtained through e-mail correspondence with Phillipa Rowley, Statistical Institute of Belize, June 22, 2009.

CSO-Mauritius 2000. [Central Statistical Office, Mauritius] "International Migration," *2000 Housing and Population Census*, chapter 3, http://www.gov.mu/portal/sites/ncb/cso/report/hpcenoo/census4/chap3.htm.

CSO-Poland 2008. [Central Statistical Office, Poland] *Demographic Yearbook of Poland 2008*, http://www.stat.gov.pl/cps/rde/xbcr/gus/PUBL_demographic_yearbook_2008.pdf.

CSP 2009. [Center for Systemic Peace] "Polity IV: Regime Authority Characteristics and Transitions Datasets," principal investigators Monty G. Marshall and Keith Jaggers, http://www.systemicpeace.org/inscr/inscr.htm.

Curran, Sara R. and Abigail C. Saguay 2001. "Migration and Cultural Change: A Role for Gender and Social Networks," *Journal of International Women's Studies* 2: 54–77.

CZSO 2007. [Czech Statistical Office] "International Migration: 1950–2007," *Czech Demographic Handbook 2007*, http://www.czso.cz/csu/2008edicniplan .nsf/engt/24003E060F/$File/4032080905.xls.

Daniel, Pete 1985. *Breaking the Land: The Transformation of Cotton, Tobacco and Rice Cultures since 1880.* Urbana: University of Illinois Press.

Danielsen, Rolf, Ståle Dyrvik, Tore Grønlie, Knut Helle, and Edgard Hovland 1995. *Norway: A History from the Vikings to Our Own Times.* Translated by Michael Drake. Oslo: Universitetsforlaget.

Davin, Delia 1999. *Internal Migration in Contemporary China.* New York: St. Martin's.

Davis, Dernoral 1991. "Toward a Socio-Historical and Demographic Portrait of Twentieth-Century African-Americans," in Harrison (ed.), pp. 1–19.

Davis, Kingsley 1951. *The Population of India and Pakistan.* Princeton: Princeton University Press.

de Haas, Hein 2005. "Morocco's Migration Transition: Trends, Determinants and Future Scenarios," *Global Migration Perspectives*, No. 28. Geneva: Global Commission on International Migration.

de Jong, Greta 2005. "Staying in Place: Black Migration, the Civil Rights Movement, and the War on Poverty in the Rural South," *Journal of African American History* 90 (4): 387–409.

Derry, T. K. 1973. *A History of Modern Norway, 1814–1972.* Oxford: Clarendon.

Deutsch, Karl W. 1966. *Nationalism and Social Communication: An Inquiry into the Foundations of Nationality.* 2nd edition. Cambridge: MIT Press.

DHS 2010. [U. S. Department of Homeland Security] "'509_final.pdf' and '403_final.pdf" files sent by John Simanski, Immigration Statistics Office, May 4.

——— 2009. "Table 2: Immigration by Region and Selected Country of Last Residence: Fiscal Years 1820 to 2007," personal e-mail correspondence with John Simanski, November 10.

——— 2008. "Table 2: Persons Obtaining Legal Permanent Resident Status by Region and Selected Country of Last Residence: Fiscal Years 1820 to 2008," *Immigration Statistics Yearbook 2008*, http://www.dhs.gov/xlibrary/ assets/statistics/yearbook/2008/table02.xls.

Diamond, Larry 1992. "Economic Development and Democracy Reconsidered," in Marks and Diamond (eds.), *Reexamining Democracy. Essays in Honor of Seymour Martin Lipset.* London: Sage, pp. 93–139.

Diaz-Cayeros, Alberto, Beatriz Magaloni, and Barry R. Weingast 2000. "Democratization and the Economy in Mexico: Equilibrium (PRI) Hegemony and its Demise," http://www.stanford.edu/class/polisci313/papers/demzo.07.06.pdf.

Dilorenzo, T. J. 1983. "Economic Competition and Political Competition: An Empirical Note," *Public Choice* 40: 203–9.

Donald, Henderson, H. 1921. "The Effects of the Negro Migration on the South," *Journal of Negro History* 6 (4): 421–33.

Doorenspleet, Renske 2000. "Reassessing the Three Waves of Democratization," *World Politics* 52 (April): 384–406.

Douglass, Frederick 1880. "Southern Questions," *Journal of Social Science* (May): 1–22.

Dowding, Keith, Peter John, and Stephen Biggs 1994. "Tiebout: A Survey of the Empirical Literature," *Urban Studies* 32 (4/5): 767–97.

Dowty, Alan 1987. *Closed Borders*. New Haven: Yale University Press.

DRC 2007. [Development Research Centre on Migration, Globalisation and Poverty] "Global Migrant Origin Database," March 2007 update, http://www.migrationdrc.org/research/typesofmigration/global_migrant_origin_database.html.

Drèze, Jean and Amartya Sen 1995. *India: Economic Development and Social Opportunity*. New York: Oxford University Press.

Du, Yang, Albert Park, and Sangui Wang 2005. "Migration and Rural Poverty in China," *Journal of Comparative Economics* 33 (4): 688–709.

Du Bois, W. E. B. 1977 [1935]. *Black Reconstruction in America 1860–1880*. New York: Kraus International.

Durand, Jorge, Douglas S. Massey, and Emilio A. Parrado 1999. "The New Era of Mexican Migration to the United States," *Journal of American History* 86 (2): 518–36.

Durand, Jorge, Douglas S. Massey, and Rene M. Zenteno 2001. "Mexican Immigration to the United States: Continuities and Changes," *Latin American Research Review* 36 (1): 107–27.

Ebiri, Kutlay 1985. "Impact of Labor Migration on the Turkish Economy," in Rogers (ed.), pp. 207–30.

Ebony 1971. "The South Today," 26 (10): 64–5.

Eisenstadt, S. N. 1963. "Bureaucracy and Political Development," in LaPalombara (ed.), *Bureaucracy and Political Development*. Princeton: Princeton University Press, pp. 96–119.

Ekiert, Grzegorz 1996. *The State against Society. Political Crises and Their Aftermath in East Central Europe*. Princeton: Princeton University Press.

Eldridge, Hope T. and Dorothy S. Thomas 1964. *Population Redistribution and Economic Growth, United States, 1870–1950, Vol. III: Demographic Analyses and Interrelations*. Philadelphia: American Philosophical Society.

Emerson, Rupert 1963. *Political Modernization: The Single-Party System*. Denver: University of Denver.

Epple, D. and Z. Zelenitz 1981. "The Implication of Competition among Jurisdictions: Does Tiebout Need Politics?" *Journal of Political Economy* 89: 1197–217.

EUROSTAT 2009. "Emigration by Sex and Citizenship," Online Data Explorer: http://epp.eurostat.ec.europa.eu/portal/page/portal/population/data/database.

Evans, Peter 1979. *Dependent Development: The Alliance of Multinational, State and Local Capital in Brazil*. Princeton: Princeton University Press.

Fargues, Philippe 2004. "Arab Migration to Europe: Trends and Policies," *International Migration Review* 38 (4): 1348–72.

Ferenczi, I. and W. F. Willcox 1929. *International Migrations*, Volume I. New York: National Bureau of Economics Research.

FIBS 2009. [Fiji Island Bureau of Statistics] E-mail correspondence with Susana B. Saumaka, June 18.

Fischel, William 2006. "Footloose at Fifty: An Introduction to the Tiebout Anniversary Essays," in Fischel (ed.), *The Tiebout Model at Fifty: Essays in Public Economics in Honor of Wallace Oates*. Cambridge, MA: Lincoln Institute of Land Policy, http://papers.ssrn.com/sol3/Delivery.cfm/SSRN_ID895609_code184559.pdf?abstractid=895609&mirid=5.

Fite, Gilbert C. 1950. "Recent Changes in the Mechanization of Cotton Production in the United States," *Agricultural History* 24 (1): 19–28.

Fitzgerald, David 2006. "Inside the Sending State: The Politics of Mexican Emigration Control," *International Migration Review* 40 (2): 259–93.

Freedom House 2010. "Freedom in the World Country Ratings 1972–2009," http://www.freedomhouse.org/images/File/FIW%20All%20Scores,%20Countries,%201973–2010.xls.

——— 2008. "Country Reports," http://www.freedomhouse.org/template.cfm?page=21&year=2008.

——— 2000. "Democracy's Century," www.freedomhouse.org/reports/century.html.

FSSS-Russia 2009. [Russian Federal State Statistics Service] "Indicators of International Migration," *Статистическое обозрение – 2009*, http://www.gks.ru/bgd/regl/b09_06/IssWWW.exe/Stg/1/01–03.htm.

——— 2008. "Table 5.9: International Migration," *Russia in Figures 2008*, http://www.gks.ru/bgd/regl/b08_12/IssWWW.exe/stg/d01/05–09.htm.

Gabrielsen, Bjørn 1959. *Martin Tranmæl ser tilbake*. Oslo: Tiden.

Galenson, Walter 1949. *Labor in Norway*. Cambridge, MA: Harvard University Press.

Gamio, Manuel 1930. *Mexican Immigration to the United States: A Study of Human Migration and Adjustment*. Chicago: University of Chicago Press.

García y Griego, Larry Manuel 1988. "The Bracero Policy Experiment: U.S.-Mexican Responses to Mexican Labor Migration, 1942–1955," doctoral dissertation submitted to Dept. of History, University of California, Los Angeles.

Gjerde, Jon 2007. "Echoes of Freedom: The Norwegian Encounter with America," in Østrem (ed.), *Fiksjon, Fakta og Forskning*. Stavanger: University of Stavanger, pp. 48–60.

Godkin, E. L. 1867. "The Labor Crisis," *North American Review*, CX (July): 177–9.

Goldstone, Jack A. (ed.) 1999. *Who's Who in Political Revolutions. Seventy-Three Men and Women Who Changed the World*. Washington DC: Congressional Quarterly, Inc.

——— (ed.) 1998. *The Encyclopedia of Political Revolutions*. Washington DC: Congressional Quarterly, Inc.

Gordy, Eric 1999. *The Culture of Power in Serbia*. University Park, PA: Penn State University Press.

Gottlieb, Peter 1987. *Making Their Own Way: Southern Blacks' Migration to Pittsburgh, 1916–30*. Urbana: University of Illinois Press.

Green, Nancy L. 2005. "The Politics of Exit: Reversing the Immigration Paradigm," *Journal of Modern History* 77 (2): 263–89.

Green, Nancy L. and Francois Weil 2007. *Citizenship and Those Who Leave: The Politics of Emigration and Expatriation*. Urbana: University of Illinois Press.

Gregory, James N. 2005. *The Southern Diaspora. How the Great Migrations of Black and White Southerners Transformed America*. Chapel Hill: University of North Carolina Press.

Grossman, James R. 1991. "Black Labor Is the Best Labor: Southern White Reactions to the Great Migration," in Harrison (ed.), pp. 51–71.

———— 1989. *Land of Hope: Chicago, Black Southerners, and the Great Migration*. Chicago: University of Chicago Press.

Guiraudon, Virginie and Gallya Lahav 2000. "A Reappraisal of the State Sovereignty Debate. The Case of Migration Control," *Comparative Political Studies* 33 (2): 163–95.

Gunatilleke, Godfrey 1998. "Macroeconomic Implications of International Migration from Sri Lanka," in Appleyard (ed.), *Emigration Dynamics in Developing Countries. Volume 2: South Asia*. Aldershot: Ashgate, pp. 113–46.

Ha, Wei, Junjian Yi, and Junsen Zhang 2009. "Inequality and Internal Migration in China: Evidence from Village Panel Data," Human Development Research Paper 2009/27 (July), UNDP.

Haarstad, Kjell 1978. "Utvandrerne fra bygdene–Presset eller Lokket?" in Engen (ed.) *Utvandringa–det stora oppbrotet*. Oslo: Det Norske Samlaget, pp. 38–58.

Haggard, Stephan and Beth A. Simmons 1987. "Theories of International Regimes," *International Organization* 41 (3): 491–517.

Hahn, Steven 2003. *A Nation under Our Feet: Black Political Struggles in the Rural South from Slavery to the Great Migration*. Cambridge, MA: Belknap.

Halperin, Sandra 2004. *War and Social Change in Modern Europe*. Cambridge: Cambridge University Press.

Harris, J. R. and M. P. Todaro 1970. "Migration, Unemployment and Development: A Two-Sector Analysis," *American Economic Review* 60: 126–42.

Harrison, Alferdteen (ed.) 1991. *Black Exodus. The Great Migration from the American South*. Jackson: University Press of Mississippi.

Hatton, Timothy and Jeffrey G. Williamson 1998. *The Age of Mass Migration*. New York: Oxford University Press.

Hayter, Teresa 2004. *Open Borders: The Case against Immigration Controls*. 2nd edition. London: Pluto.

HDR China 2007. *Access for all. Basic Services for 1.3 Billion People*. Human Development Report China 2007/08. UNDP China.

Heisler, Barbara Schmitter 1985. "Sending Countries and the Politics of Emigration and Destination," *International Migration Review* 19 (3): 469–84.

Henri, Florette 1975. *Black Migration: Movement North, 1900–1920*. Garden City: Anchor Press/Doubleday.

HIAS 2009. [Hebrew Immigrant Aid Society] "Timeline," http://timeline.hias.org/programs/let-my-people-go-timeline/en/first/timeline.htm.

Hicks, Norman and Paul Streeten 1979. "Indicators of Development: The Search for a Basic Needs Yardstick," *World Development* 7: 567–80.

Hirschman, Albert O. 1993. "Exit, Voice, and the Fate of the German Democratic Republic. An Essay in Conceptual History," *World Politics* 45 (January): 173–202.

———— 1992. "Abwanderung, Wiederspruch und das Shicksal der Deutschen Demokratischen Republik," *Leviathan* 20: 39–58.

———— 1978. "Exit, Voice, and the State," *World Politics* 31 (1): 90–107.

———— 1970. *Exit, Voice, and Loyalty*. Cambridge, MA: Harvard University Press.

Hiskey, Jonathan and Damarys Canache 2005. "The Demise of One-Party Politics in Mexican Municipal Elections," *British Journal of Political Science* 35: 257–84.

Hobbes, Thomas 1998 [1651]. *On the Citizen*. Edited and translated by Richard Tuck and Michael Silverthorne. Cambridge: Cambridge University Press.

Hodne, Fritz 1975. *An Economic History of Norway 1815–1970*. Trondheim: Tapir.

Holley, Donald 2000. *The Second Great Emancipation. The Mechanical Cotton Picker, Black Migration, and How They Shaped the Modern South*. Fayetteville: University of Arkansas Press.

Hollifield, James F. 1992a. *Immigrants, Markets and States*. Cambridge, MA: Harvard University Press.

———— 1992b. "Migration and International Relations: Conflict and Control in the European Community," *International Migration Review* 25: 568–95.

Honig, Bonnie 2001. *Democracy and the Foreigner*. Princeton: Princeton University Press.

Hovde, B. J. 1934. "Notes on the Effects of Emigration upon Scandinavia," *Journal of Modern History* 6 (3): 253–79.

Huntington, Samuel P. 2004. *Who Are We? The Challenges to America's National Identity*. New York: Simon and Schuster.

———— 1991. *The Third Wave: Democratization in the Late Twentieth Century*. Norman: University of Oklahoma Press.

———— 1965. "Political Development and Political Decay," *World Politics* 17 (3): 386–430.

ILO 2009. [International Labour Office] "Outflows of Nationals by Sex and Country," Table MB, LABORSTA database, http://laborsta.ilo.org/STP/guest.

———— 1976. *Employment Growth and Basic Needs: A One-World Problem*. Report of the Director-General of the International Labour Office. Geneva: ILO.

IMF 2003. [International Monetary Fund] *IMF Direction of Trade Statistics*, http://fisher.lib.virginia.edu/collections/stats/dot/.

INEC 2009. [Instituto Nacional de Estadistica y Censos, Ecuador] "Entradas y Salidas de Ecuatorianos y Extranjeros Período: 2003 – 2008," http://www.inec.gov.ec/c/document_library/get_file?folderId=2470869&name=DLFE-22532.pdf.

———— 2004. "Separata Estadística: Migracion Internacional," http://www.inec.gov.ec/c/document_library/get_file?folderId=78158&name=DLFE-3808.pdf.

INEC-Nicaragua 1994. [National Institute of Statistics and Census, Nicaragua] "Table 11.2.14: Migracion externa por ano (1989–1993)," *Compendio Estadistico 1991–1993*, p. 84. Copy by e-mail from Fátima Pérez, 8 July 2009.

INEI-Peru 2008. [El Instituto Nacional de Estadística e Informática, Peru] *Perú: Estadísticas de la Migración Internacional de Peruanos, 1990–2007.* 2nd edition (February), http://www1.inei.gob.pe/biblioineipub/bancopub/est/libo758/libro.pdf.

INE-Spain 2009. [Instituto Nacional de Estadística, Spain] *Anuarios Estadísticos.* Various Years, http://www.ine.es/inebaseweb/libros.do?tntp=25687(1858–1997); after 1997 http://www.ine.es/en/prodyser/pubweb/anuarios_mnu_en.htm.

Inglés, José D. 1963. *Study of Discrimination in Respect of the Right of Everyone to Leave Any Country, Including His Own, and to Return to His Country* E/CN.4/Sub. 2/229/Rev.1. New York: United Nations, Economic and Social Council, Commission on Human Rights, Subcommission on Prevention of Discrimination and Protection of Minorities.

INSEE 2005. [Institut National de la Statisque et de Etudes Economiques] "Comparative Population Projections for France, Hungary and Slovakia," F0504, May, www.insee.fr/fr/publications-et-services/docs_doc_travail/f0504.pdf.

Iregui, Ana María 2005. "Efficiency Gains from the Elimination of Global Restrictions on Labour Mobility: An Analysis using a Multiregional CGE Model," in Borjas and Crisp (eds.), pp. 211–40.

ISTAT 2009. [Instituto nazionale di statistica, Italy] "Demographic Balance Tables, 2002–2007," http://demo.istat.it/index_e.html.

Jackson, Bylden 1991. "Introduction: A Street of Dreams," in Harrison (ed.), pp. xi–xviii.

Johnston, Oscar 1947. "Will the Machine Ruin the South?" *Saturday Evening Post,* 219 (48): 36–7, 94–8.

Joppke, Christian 2000. *Immigration and the Nation State: The United States, Germany and Great Britain.* Oxford: Oxford University Press.

———— (ed.) 1998. *Challenge to the Nation-State: Immigration in Western Europe and the United States.* Oxford: Oxford University Press.

JSY 2009. [Japan Statistical Yearbook] "Population and Households," *Japan Statistical Yearbook 2009.* Chapter 2, http://www.stat.go.jp/data/nenkan/pdf/yhyou02.pdf.

———— 2005. "Table 2:13: Japanese Living Abroad by Status of Residence (Permanent, Long-term) and Countries (1955–2003)," http://www.stat.go.jp/data/chouki/zuhyou/02-13.xls.

Kapur, Devesh and John McHale 2005. *Give Us Your Best and Brightest.* Washington, DC: Center for Global Development.

Karpat, Nemal H. 1972. "Developments in Turkey, 1950–70," *Middle Eastern Studies* 8 (3): 349–75.

Key, V. O. Jr. 1984 [1949]. *Southern Politics in State and Nation. A New Edition.* Knoxville: University of Tennessee Press.

Kindleberger, Charles P. 1967. *Europe's Postwar Growth: The Role of Labor Supply.* Cambridge, MA: Harvard University Press.

———— 1951. "Group Behavior and International Trade," *Journal of Political Economy* 59 (1): 30–46.

King, Russell 1985. *Return Migration and Regional Economic Problems.* London: Croom Helm.

King, Russell, Jill Mortimer, and Alan Strachan 1984. "Return Migration and Tertiary Development: A Calabrian Case Study," *Anthropological Quarterly* 57: 112–23.

Koht, Halvdan 1939. *Det Norske Arbeiderpartis Historie 1887–1937.* Volume 2. Oslo: Det norske Arbeiderpartis Forlag.

Kokkvoll, Arne 1979. "Martin Tranmæl–en biografi," *Tidsskrift for arbeiderbevegelsens historie* 2: 11–32.

Krasner, Stephen D. 1983. "Structural Causes and Regime Consequences: Regimes as Intervening Variables," in Krasner (ed.), *International Regimes.* Ithaca, NY: Cornell University Press, pp. 1–22.

Kritz, M., C. B. Keely, and S. M. Tomasi (eds.) 1981. *Global Trends in Migration: Theory and Research on International Population Movements.* Staten Island, NY: Center for Migration Studies.

Kuhnle, Stein 1981. "Emigration, Democratization and the Rise of European Welfare States," in Torsvik (ed.), *Mobilization, Center-Periphery Structures and Nation-Building.* Oslo: Universitetsforlaget, pp. 501–24.

———— 1972. "Stemmeretten i 1814. Beregninger over antall stemmerettskvalifiserte etter Grunnloven," *Historisk Tidskrift* 51: 373–91.

Lahmeyer, Jan 2003a. "India: Historical Demographical Data of the Whole Country," http://www.populstat.info/Asia/indiac.htm.

———— 2003b. "Ireland: Historical Demographical Data of the Whole Country," http://www.populstat.info/Europe/irelandc.htm.

Laing, Samuel 1851. *Journal of a Resident in Norway during the Years 1834, 1835 and 1836.* London: Longman, Brown, Green, and Longmans.

Landman, Todd 2003. "Economic Development and Democracy," in Landman, *Issues and Methods in Comparative Politics: An Introduction.* London: Routledge, pp. 99–129.

Langholm, Sivert and Francis Sejersted (eds.) 1980. *Vandringer. Festskrift til Ingrid Semmingsen på 70-årsdagen.* Oslo: Aschehoug.

Lary, Diana 1999. "The 'Static' Decades: Inter-Provincial Migration in Pre-Reform China," in Pieke and Mallee (eds.), *Internal and International Migration. Chinese Perspectives.* Surrey: Curzon, pp. 29–48.

Latvijas Statistika 2009. "International Long-Term Migration of Population," e-mail exchange with Sandra Vitola, July 8.

Lee, Everett Spurgeon 1957. "Methodological Considerations and Reference Tables," in Kuznets, Miller, and Easterlin (eds.), *Population Redistribution and Economic Growth, United States, 1870–1950,* Volume 1. Philadelphia: American Philosophical Society.

Legrain, Phillipe 2006. *Immigrants: Your Country Needs Them.* London: Little Brown.

Lemann, Nicholas 1991. *The Promised Land: The Great Black Migration and How It Changed America.* New York: Alfred A. Knopf.

Lerner, Daniel 1958. *The Passing of Traditional Society: Modernizing the Middle East.* Glencoe, IL: The Free Press.

Levitt, Peggy 2005. "Social Remittances – Culture as a Development Tool." Paper presented to the International Forum on Remittances, Washington,

DC, June 30, 2005. July 20 draft, http://www.un-instraw.org/en/images/stories/remmitances/documents/Forum/peggy_levitt.pdf.

Lewis, W. Arthur 1958. "Unlimited Labour: Further Notes," *Manchester School* 26 (1): 1–32.

——— 1954. "Economic Development with Unlimited Supplies of Labour," *Manchester School* 22 (2): 139–91.

Lie, Håkon 1991. *Martin Tranmæl. Veiviseren.* Oslo: Tiden.

——— 1988. *Martin Tranmæl: et bål av vilje.* Oslo: Tiden.

Lipset, Seymour M. 1959. "Some Social Requisites of Democracy: Economic Development and Political Legitimacy," *American Political Science Review* 53 (March): 69–105.

Locke, John 1690. *Essay Concerning Human Understanding,* http://oregonstate.edu/instruct/phl302/texts/locke/locke1/Essay_contents.html.

Long, Larry H. and Kristin A. Hansen 1975. "Trends in Return Migration to the South," *Demography* 12 (4): 601–14.

Lorenz, Einhart 1972. *Arbeiderbevegelsenshistorie. 1. del: 1789–1930.* Oslo: Pax.

Lowell, Briant Lindsay 1987. *Scandinavian Exodus. Demography and Social Development of 19th-Century Rural Communities.* Boulder: Westview.

Lucas, R. 1981 "International Migration: Economic Causes, Consequences and Evaluation," in Kritz et al. (eds.), pp. 84–109.

Malme, Arnfinn 1979. "Trygve Bull: 'Opprører til sine siste dager,'" *Tidsskrift for arbeiderbevegelsens historie* 2: 87–94.

Mandle, Jay R. 1978. *The Roots of Black Poverty: The Southern Plantation Economy after the Civil War.* Durham: Duke University Press.

Manning, Scott 2007. "World Population Estimates Interpolated and Averaged," http://www.digitalsurvivors.com/archives/World%20Population%20Estimates%20Interpolated%20and%20Averaged.pdf.

Marks, Carole 1991. "The Social and Economic Life of Southern Blacks during the Migration," in Harrison (ed.), pp. 36–50.

——— 1989. *Farewell. We're Good and Gone.* Bloomington: Indiana University Press.

Martin, Philip L. and Mark J. Miller 1980. "Guestworkers: Lessons from Western Europe," *Industrial and Labor Relations Review* 33 (3): 315–30.

Massey, Douglas, S. 1990. "Social Structure, Household Strategies, and the Cumulative Causation of Migration," *Population Index* 56 (1): 3–26.

Massey, Douglas S. and F. Garcia-España 1987. "The Social Process of Migration," *Science* 237: 733–8.

Massey, Douglas S. and R. Zenteno 1999. "The Dynamics of Mass Migration," *Proceedings of the National Academy of Science (USA)* 96: 5328–35.

Maurseth, Per 1979. "Martin Tranmæl 1879–1979," *Tidsskrift for arbeiderbevegelsens historie* 2: 3–10.

McHugh, Kevin E. 1987. "Black Migration Reversal in the United States," *Geographical Review* 77 (2): 171–82.

McKenzie, David 2007. "Paper Walls Are Easier to Tear Down: Passport Costs and Legal Barriers to Emigration," *World Development* 35 (11): 2026–39.

McKeown, Adam M. 2010. "Chinese Emigration in Global Context, 1850–1940," *Journal of Global History* 5: 95–124.

——— 2009. E-mail exchange, October 8.

McMillen, Neil R. 1991. "The Migration and Black Protest in Jim Crow Mississippi," in Harrison (ed.), pp. 83–99.

Measuringworth.com 2010. "GDP Deflator 1850–2005," http://www.measuringworth.com/datasets/usgdp/result.php.

Mellbye, Johan E. 1909. "Utvandringen," in Selskapet til Emigrationens Indskrænkning (ed.), *Mot Emigrationen*. Kristiania: Det Mallingske Bogtrykkeri, pp. 1–18.

Meyer, Michael 2009. *The Year That Changed the World. The Untold Story behind the Fall of the Berlin Wall*. New York: Scribner.

Ministry of Labour 2003. [Government of India] "Report of the Committee to Study the Operation and Long-Term Relevance of the Emigration Act, 1983 and Functioning of the Office of the Protector General of Emigrants," August.

Ministry of Labour and Employment 2004. [India] "Economic Emigration," *Annual Report 2003–4*, Chapter 13, http://labour.nic.in/annrep/annrepo304/english/Chapter13.pdf.

Ministry of Overseas Indian Affairs 2009. *Annual Report 2007–8*, http://moia.gov.in/writereaddata/pdf/Annual_Report_2007-08.pdf.

Mitchell, B. R. 2007. *International Historical Statistics. The Americas 1750–2005*. 6th edition. Basingstoke: Palgrave.

———— 2003a. *International Historical Statistics. Africa, Asia & Oceania 1750–2000*. 4th edition. Basingstoke: Palgrave.

———— 2003b. *International Historical Statistics. Europe 1750–2000*. 5th edition. Basingstoke: Palgrave.

Monaco 2008. "Table 4.3: Individus resident en 2000 dans un pays etranger, suivant le sexe, par annee d'immigration," in *Le recensement pour l'année 2008*, chapter 4, http://www.monaco.gouv.mc/devwww/wwwnew.nsf/e89a6190e96cbd1fc1256f7foo5dbe6e/d82fdob8468157e2c12575a8002860d9/$FILE/Recensement2008_Ch4.pdf.

Money, Jeannette 1999. *Fences and Neighbors: The Political Geography of Immigration Control*. Ithaca, NY: Cornell University Press.

———— 1998. "No Vacancy: The Political Geography of Immigration Control in Advanced Industrial Countries," *International Organization* 51: 685–720.

Moore, Truman 1965. *The Slaves We Rent*. New York: Random House.

Mørkhagen, Sverre 2009. *Farvel Norge. Utvandring til Amerika 1825–1975*. Oslo: Gyldendal.

Moses, Jonathon W. 2011a. "Introducing EMIG 1.2: A Global Time-Series of Annual Emigration Flows, unpublished working paper, January 20 draft.

———— 2011b. "Migration in Europe," in Tiersky, Jones, and van Genugten (eds.), *Europe Today*. 4th edition. Lanham, MD: Rowman & Littlefield, pp. 371–97.

———— 2011c. "Schengen," in Jones, Menon, and Weatherhill (eds.), *Oxford Handbook of the European Union*. Oxford: Oxford University Press.

———— 2009. "The American Century? Migration and the Voluntary Social Contract," *Politics and Society* 37 (3): 454–76.

———— 2006. *International Migration: Globalization's Last Frontier*. London: Zed.

_____ 2005a. "Exit, Voice and Sovereignty: Migration, States and Globalization," *Review of International Political Economy* 12 (1): 53–77.

_____ 2005b. "Home Alone: Integration and Influence in National Contexts," in Jones and Verdun (eds.), *The Political Economy of European Integration: Theory and Analysis.* London: Routledge, pp. 71–87.

_____ 2005c. *Norwegian Catch-Up: Development and Globalization before World War II.* Aldershot: Ashgate.

_____ 2003. "Two (Short) Moral Arguments for Free Migration," in Thorseth (ed.), *Anvendt etikk ved NTNU* 2: 25–30.

Moses, Jonathon W. and Bjørn Letnes 2005. "If People Were Money: Estimating the Gains and Scope of Free Migration," in Borjas and Crisp (eds.), pp. 188–210.

_____ 2004. "The Economic Costs to International Labor Restrictions: Revisiting the Empirical Discussion," *World Development* 32 (10): 1609–26.

Mountford, Andrew 1997. "Can a Brain Drain Be Good for Growth in the Source Economy?" *Journal of Development Economics* 53(2): 287–303.

MPI 2009. [Migration Policy Institute] MPI Data hub: http://www .migrationinformation.org/datahub/.

MTICDA 2009. [Ministry of Trade, Industry, Consumer and Diaspora Affairs, Dominica] E-mail exchange with MTICDA, June 23.

Murphy, Rachel (ed.) 2009. *Labour Migration and Social Development in Contemporary China.* London: Routledge.

_____ 2002. *How Migrant Labor Is Changing Rural China.* Cambridge: Cambridge University Press.

Musgrave, Richard A. 1959. *The Theory of Public Finance.* New York: McGraw-Hill.

_____. 1939. "The Voluntary Exchange Theory of Public Economy," *Quarterly Journal of Economics* LII (February): 213–17.

National Statistics-UK 2009. "Total International Migration (TIM) Tables: 1991–Latest," http://www.statistics.gov.uk/downloads/theme_population/2_ series_(TIM_calendar_year).zip.

Needler, Martin C. 1961. "The Political Development of Mexico," *American Political Science Review* 55 (2): 308–12.

NOS 1921. [Norges Offisielle Statistikk, Norway] *Utvandringsstatistikk.* No. 25. Kristiania: Departementet for Sociale Saker.

Novak, Daniel A. 1978. *The Wheel of Servitude: Black Forced Labor after Slavery.* Lexington: University of Kentucky Press.

NSB-Seychelles 2009. [National Bureau of Statistics, Seychelles] "Migration and Tourism Statistics, 2008," http://www.nsb.gov.sc/Documents/Publications/ Migration%20&%20Tourism%202008.pdf.

NSS-Armenia 2002. [National Statistical Service, Armenia] "Population," *Statistical Yearbook of Armenia, 2002,* http://www.armstat.am/file/doc/650.pdf.

NSSG 2009. [National Statistical Service of Greece] "Emigration transocéanique de la Grèce aux années 1821–1930" and "Emigrants from Greece, by Sex: 1961–1977," personal e-mail correspondence with Katerina Nasiakou, June 15–16.

Nussbaum, Martha 2005. "Women's Bodies: Violence, Security, Capabilities," *Journal of Human Development* 6 (2): 167–83.

———— 2003. "Capabilities as Fundamental Entitlement: Sen and Social Justice," *Feminist Economics* 9 (2–3): 33–59.

———— 2000. *Women and Human Development: The Capabilities Approach.* Cambridge: Cambridge University Press.

———— 1995. "Human Capabilities, Female Human Beings," in Nussbaum and Glover (eds.), *Women, Culture and Development.* Oxford: Clarendon Press, pp. 61–104.

———— 1990. "Aristotelian Social Democracy," in Douglas, Mara, and Richardson (eds.), *Liberalism and the Good.* New York: Routledge, pp. 203–52.

———— 1988. "Nature, Function and Capability: Aristotle on Political Distribution," *Oxford Studies in Ancient Philosophy* 145: 84.

Oates, Wallace 2005. "The Many Faces of the Tiebout Model," http://www.economia.unict.it/web/MatDid_vecchio/Anno2005–2006/imazza/Materiale_Didattico/e2_economia_pubblica/Oates-tiebout.fin.095.pdf.

O'Brien, Kevin J. and Lianjiang Li 2000. "Accommodating 'Democracy' in a One-Party State: Introducing Village Elections in China," *China Quarterly* 162, Special Issue: Elections and Democracy in Greater China (June): 465–89.

O'Donnell, Guillermo 1973. *Modernization and Bureaucratic Authoritarianism: Studies in South American Politics.* Berkeley: Institute of International Studies.

OECD 1975. [Organization for Economic Cooperation and Development] *The OECD and International Migration.* Paris: OECD.

Oen, Arvid 1980. "Politisk Klima, Thranittere og Emigrasjon," Department of History, University of Trondheim, Spring.

Offe, Claus 1996. *Varieties of Transition. The East European and East German Experience.* London: Polity Press.

Olsen, Bjørn Gunnar 1991. *Martin Tranmæl og hans menn.* Oslo: Aschehoug.

Özden, Çaglar and Maurice Schiff (eds.) 2007a. *International Migration, Economic Development and Policy.* Washington, DC: World Bank and Palgrave.

———— 2007b. "Overview," in Özden and Schiff (eds.), pp. 1–16.

———— 2006. *International Migration, Remittances and the Brain Drain.* Washington, DC: World Bank and Palgrave.

Pajo, Erind 2008. *International Migration, Social Demotion, and Imagined Advancement: An Ethnography of Socioglobal Mobility.* New York: Springer.

Papademetriou, Demetrios G. 1978. "European Labor Migration: Consequences for the Countries of Worker Origin," *International Studies Quarterly* 22 (3): 377–408.

Park, Han S. 1984. *Human Needs and Political Development.* Cambridge, MA: Schenkman.

Pasquino, Gianfranco 2009. "The Theory of Political Development." Paper presented to the International Political Science Association, Santiago, July, 12–16.

Piore, Michael J. 1979. *Birds of Passage: Migrant Labor in Industrial Societies.* Cambridge: Cambridge University Press.

Pritchett, Lant 2006. *Let Their People Come. Breaking the Gridlock on Global Labor Mobility.* Washington, DC: Center for Global Development.

Pryser, Tore 1980. "Gesell og rebel?" in Langholm and Sejersted (eds.), pp. 211–34.

Przeworski, Adam, Michael E. Alvarez, José Antonio Cheibub, and Fernando Limongi 2001. "What Makes Democracies Endure?" in Diamond and Plattner (eds.), *The Global Divergence of Democracies*. Baltimore: Johns Hopkins University Press, pp. 167–84.

————— 2000. *Democracy and Development: Political Institutions and Well-Being in the World, 1950–1990*. Cambridge: Cambridge University Press.

Pye, Lucian W. 1966. *Aspects of Political Development*. Boston: Little, Brown.

————— (ed.) 1963. *Communications and Political Development*. Princeton: Princeton University Press.

Ransom, Roger L. and Richard Sutch 1977. *One Kind of Freedom: The Economic Consequences of Emancipation*. New York: Cambridge University Press.

Reich, Gary 2002. "Categorizing Political Regimes. New Data for Old Problems," *Democratization* 9 (4): 1–24.

Reiersen, Johan Reinert 1981 [1844]. *Pathfinder for Norwegian Emigrants*. Translated by Frank G. Nelson. Northfield, MN: Norwegian-American Historical Association.

Rejai, Mostafa and Kay Phillips 1979. *Leaders of Revolution*. Beverly Hills: Sage.

Republic of Cyprus 2009. *Demographic Report 2007*, http://www.mof.gov.cy/mof/cystat/statistics.nsf/All/1A87FF0C4E254CC1C22571FE002D4AD4/$FILE/DEMOGRAPHIC_REPORT-2007.pdf?OpenElement.

Rhoades, R. E. 1978. "Intra-European Migration and Rural Development: Lessons from the Spanish Case," *Human Organisation* 14: 324–42.

Riggs, Fred 1981. "The Rise and Fall of 'Political Development,'" in Long (ed.), *The Handbook of Political Behavior*, Volume 4. New York: Plenum Press, pp. 289–347.

Riley, Jason L. 2008. *Let Them In: The Case for Open Borders*. New York: Gotham Books.

Ringen, Stein 2007. *What Democracy Is For: On Freedom and Moral Government*. Princeton: Princeton University Press.

Rogers, Rosemarie (ed.) 1985a. *Guests Come to Stay. The Effects of European Labor Migration on Sending and Receiving Countries*. Boulder: Westview.

————— 1985b. "Post-World War II European Labor Migration: An Introduction to the Issues," in Rogers (ed.), pp. 1–28.

Rokkan, Stein 1967. "Geography, Religion, and Social Class: Crosscutting Cleavages in Norwegian Politics," in Lipset and Rokkan (eds.), *Party Systems and Voter Alignments: Cross-National Perspectives*. New York: Free Press, pp. 367–444.

Rustow, Dankwart A. and Robert E. Ward 1964. "Introduction," in Ward and Rustow (eds.), *Political Modernization in Japan and Turkey*. Princeton: Princeton University Press, pp. 3–13.

Samuelson, Paul A. 1955. "Diagramatic Exposition of a Pure Theory of Public Expenditures," *Review of Economics and Statistics* 37 (4): 350–6.

————— 1954. "The Pure Theory of Public Expenditure," *Review of Economics and Statistics* 36 (4): 387–9.

Sánchez, Oscar Arias 2000. "The Legacy of Human Development: A Tribute to Mahbub ul Haq," *Journal of Human Development* 1 (1): 9–16.

Sandos, James A. and Harry E. Cross 1983. "National Development and International Labour Migration: Mexico 1940–1965," *Journal of Contemporary History* 18 (1): 43–60.

Sassen, Saskia 1996. *Losing Control? Sovereignty in an Age of Globalization.* New York: Columbia University Press.

SB-Hong Kong 2009. [Security Bureau of the Hong Kong Special Administrative Region] E-mail exchange with Ms F. Y. Li (SSO(D): Demographic Statistics Section). Ref: CENST/4513/1, July 5.

SBD 2009. [Statisches Bundesamt Deutschland, Germany] "Migration between Germany and Foreign Countries 1991 to 2007," http://www .destatis.de/jetspeed/portal/cms/Sites/destatis/Internet/EN/Content/Statistics/ Bevoelkerung/Wanderungen/Tabellen/Content50/WanderungenInsgesamt, templateId=renderPrint.psml.

SCB-Sweden 2009. [Statistiska centralbyrån, Sweden] "Befolkningsutveck-lingen i riket. År 1749–2008," http://www.ssd.scb.se/databaser/makro/ Visavar.asp?xu=C9233001&yp=tansss&inl=&prodid=BE0101&preskat= O&omradekod=BE&omradetext=Befolkning&tabelltext=Befolkning sutvecklingen ± i ± riket%2E ± %C5r&huvudtabell=BefUtv1749&starttid= 1749&stopptid=2008&langdb=&lang=1&fromSok=Sok&innehall= Doda&deltabell=%20&deltabellnamn=Befolkningsutvecklingen%20i% 20riket.%20%C5r.

Schierup, Carl-Urik 1995. "Former Yugoslavia: Long Waves of International Migration," in Cohen (ed.), pp. 285–8.

Scott, Emmett J. 1919. "Additional Letters of Negro Migrants of 1916–1918," *Journal of Negro History* 4 (October): 412–75.

Scott, Franklin D. 1952. "Søren Jaabæk, Americanizer in Norway: A Study in Cultural Interchange," *Norwegian-American Studies and Records* 17: 84–107.

Seip, Jens Arup 1963. *Fra embedsmannsstat til ettpartistat og andre essays.* Oslo: Universitetsforlaget.

Selskapet til Emigrationens Indskrænkning 1910. "Beretning om virksomheten fra dannelsen til og med aaret 1909," *Mot Emigrationen* No. 6. Kristiania: Selskapet til Emigrationens Indskrænkning.

Semmingsen, Ingrid 1978. *Norway to America: A History of the Migration.* Minneapolis: University of Minnesota Press.

———— 1960. "Norwegian Emigration in the Nineteenth Century," *Scandinavian Economic History Review* 3 (1): 150–60.

———— 1950. *Veien mot Vest. Utvandringen fra Norge 1865–1915.* Volume II. Oslo: Aschehoug.

———— 1941. *Veien mot Vest. Utvandringen fra Norge til Amerika 1825–1865.* Volume I. Oslo: Aschehoug.

Sen, Amartya 2000. "A Decade of Human Development," *Journal of Human Development* 1(1): 17–23.

———— 1999. *Development as Freedom.* Oxford: Oxford University Press.

———— 1985. *Commodities and Capabilities*. Amsterdam: North Holland.

———— 1984. *Resources, Values and Development*. Cambridge, MA: Harvard University Press.

———— 1979. "Equality of What?" Tanner Lecture delivered to Stanford University on May 22, http://home.sandiego.edu/~baber/globalethics/senequalityofwhat.pdf.

Simon, Julian L. 1989. *The Economic Consequences of Immigration*. Oxford: Basil Blackwell.

SLBFE 2009. [Sri Lankan Bureau of Foreign Employment] "Migration for Foreign Employment and Labour Force 1992–2006," http://www.statistics.gov.lk/NCMS/RepNTab/Tables/SLBFE/Table19.pdf.

Slov-Stat 2009. [Slovak Republic] "Movement of Population: Emigration," http://www.statistics.sk/pls/elisw/casovy_Rad.procDlg.

Smith, James P. and Barry Edmonston (eds.) 1997. *The New Americans: Economic, Demographic and Fiscal Effects of Immigration*. Washington, DC: National Academy Press.

Smith, Michael Peter and Matt Bakker 2008. *Citizenship across Borders. The Political Transnationalism of El Migrante*. Ithaca, NY: Cornell University Press.

Snodgrass, Michael n.d. "Patronage and Progress: The Bracero Program from the Perspective of Mexico," http://www.iusd.iupui.edu/BiCCHEC_Site/_ppt/Patronage_and_Progress.pdf. Forthcoming in Fink et al., (eds.) *Workers across the Americas: The Transnational Turn in Labor History*. Oxford: Oxford University Press.

SORS 2009. [Statistical Office Republic of Slovenia] "International Migration by Citizenship, Slovenia, Annually," http://www.stat.si/pxweb/Dialog/Saveshow.asp.

Soysal, Yasemin Nuhoglu 1994. *Limits of Citizenship: Migrants and Postnational Membership in Europe*. Chicago: University of Chicago.

Spencer, Ian R. G. 1997. *British Immigration Policy since 1939: The Making of Multi-Racial Britain*. London: Routledge.

SSB 2009a. [Statistical Bureau of Norway] "Tabell 1: Innvandring og utvandring 1951–2008," http://www.ssb.no/innvutv/tab-2009-05-07-01.html.

———— 2009b. "Befolkning. Tabell 3.13. Folkemengde, fødte, døde, ekteskap, flyttinger og folketilvekst," http://www.ssb.no/emner/historisk_statistikk/tabeller/3-3-13t.txt.

———— 1965. "Ekteskap, Fødsler og Vandringer i Norge 1865–1960," *Samfunnsøkonomiske Studier* Nr. 13. Oslo: SSB.

Stark, Oded 2003. "Rethinking the Brain Drain," *World Development* 32 (1): 15–22.

STATEC 2009 [Luxembourg] "Arrivées et départs et excédents des arrivées sur les départs 1967 – 2008," http://www.statistiques.public.lu/stat/TableViewer/tableView.aspx?ReportId=592&IF_Language=fra&MainTheme=2&FldrName=4.

Statistics Austria 2009. "International Migration to and from Austria by Citizenship 1961 bis 2008," compiled May 27, 2009, http://www.statistik.at/web_en/static/results_overview_migration_immigration_and_emigration__028953.xls.

Statistics Belgium 2009. "Mouvement de la population de la Belgique – Hommes et Femmes (Belgique): Emigrations externs," http://statbel.fgov.be/figures/t26/MvtBelg_fr.xls.

Statistics Canada 2009. "Table 051–0037 – International Migration Components, Canada, Provinces and Territories, Quarterly (Persons)," CANSIM database, http://cansim2.statcan.gc.ca/cgi-win/cnsmcgi.exe?Lang=E&CNSM-Fi=CII/CII_1-eng.htm.

Statistics Denmark 2009. "Summary Vital Statistics: Number Emigrated," http://www.statistikbanken.dk/statbank5a/default.asp?w=1680.

Statistics Estonia 2009. E-mail exchange with Marje Asper, July 1.

Statistics Finland 2009. "Vital Statistics and Population 1749–2008, Whole Country: Emigration," http://pxweb2.stat.fi/Dialog/varval.asp?ma=070_muutl_tau_202_en&ti=Vital + statistics + and + population + 1749 + - + 2008%2C + whole + country&path=../Database/StatFin/vrm/muutl/&lang=1&multilang=en.

Statistics Iceland 2009. "External Migration by Sex and Citizenship 1961–2009," http://www.statice.is/?PageID=1171&src=/temp_en/Dialog/varval.asp?ma=MAN01400%26ti=External ± migration ± by ± sex ± and ± citizenship ± 1961–2009 ± ± ± %26path=../Database/mannfjoldi/Buferlaflutningar/%26lang=1%26units=Number.

Statistics Netherlands 2009. "External Migration; Sex, Age (31 Dec), Marital Status and Country of Birth," *CBS Statline*, http://statline.cbs.nl/StatWeb/publication/default.aspx?DM=SLEN&PA=03742ENG&D1=1–2&D2=0&D3=0&D4=0&D5=0&D6=a&LA=EN&HDR=T&STB=G1%2cG2%2cG3%2cG4%2cG5&VW=D.

Statistics New Zealand 2009. "International Travel and Migration: May 2009 (Table 1)," http://www.stats.govt.nz/NR/rdonlyres/7EE3FDFB-3029–4CF2–9700-7C6AA6C1812E/41864/itmmay09alltables.xls.

Statistics Portugal 2007a. "Emigrants (Series 1970–1988 – No.) by Sex and Type of Emigration," http://www.ine.pt/xportal/xmain?xpid=INE&xpgid=ine_indicadores&indOcorrCod=0001269&selTab=tab2.

———— 2007b. "Emigrants (No.) by Sex and Type of Emigration," http://www.ine.pt/xportal/xmain?xpid=INE&xpgid=ine_indicadores&indOcorrCod=0001270&selTab=tab2.

Statistics South Africa 2009. E-mail exchange with Kenneth Chatindiara, reference number REQ-05248–658ZSF, June 11.

Statistikos Departmentas 2009a. [Lithuania] "Emigration," http://db1.stat.gov.lt/statbank/default.asp?w=1680.

———— 2009b. "Table 4.2: International Long-Term Migration," Centralas statistikas parvaldes datubazes [on-line database], http://data.csb.gov.lv/Dialog/varval.asp?ma=04–02&ti=4–2. ± INTERNATIONAL ± LONG-TERM ± MIGRATION&path=../DATABASEEN/Iedzsoc/Short%20term%20statistical%20data/04.%20Population/&lang=1.

Stokes, Gale 1993. *The Walls Came Tumbling Down. The Collapse of Communism in Eastern Europe*. Oxford: Oxford University Press.

Storthingstidende 1873a. *Forhandlinger i Storthinget*, April 28, No. 54. Kristiania/Oslo: Storting.

————— 1873b. *Forhandlinger i Storthinget*, May 1, No. 65. Kristiania/Oslo: Storting.

Stortings Forhandlinger 1845. "Angaaende Udvandringer til fremmede Verdensdele," Vol. I, No. 6 (Kristiania): 1–60.

Sundbärg, Gustav 1913. *Emigrationsutredningen: Betänkande i utvandringsfrågan och därmed sammanhängande spörsmål.* Stockholm: Nordiska. http://www.ub.gu.se/sok/ebok/egna/textarkiv/emigrationsutredningen/pdf/oo_ betankande.pdf.

Svalestuen, Andres A. 1980. "Professor Ingrid Semmingsen- emigrasjonshistorikeren," in Langholm and Sejersted (eds.), pp. 9–42.

Swiss Statistics 2009. "Components of Population Change – Migrations," http://www.bfs.admin.ch/bfs/portal/en/index/themen/o1/o6/blank/key/o8.html.

Tiebout, Charles M. 1956. "A Pure Theory of Local Expenditures," *Journal of Political Economy* 64 (5): 416–24.

Tolnay, Steward Emory and Elwood Meredith Beck 1995. *A Festival of Violence: An Analysis of Southern Lynchings, 1882–1930.* Urbana: University of Illinois Press.

————— 1991. "Rethinking the Role of Racial Violence in the Great Migration," in Harrison (ed.), pp. 20–35.

————— 1990. "Black Flight: Lethal Violence and the Great Migration, 1900 to 1930," *Social Science History* 14 (Fall): 347–70.

Torado, Michael P. 1986. *Economic Development in the Third World.* New York: Longman.

————— 1969. "A Model of Labor Migration and Urban Unemployment in Less Developed Countries," *American Economic Review* 59: 138–49.

Torpey, John 2000. *The Invention of the Passport: Surveillance, Citizenship and the State.* Cambridge: Cambridge University Press.

Tranmæl, Martin 1975 [1912]. "Faglige organisationsformer," in Lurås and Riise (eds.), *Det tyvende aarhundre: analyse og registrering av artiklene 1901–1965.* Oslo: Statens bibliotekskole, pp. 49–50.

Turgot, Anne-Robert-Jacques, Baron de Laune 1778. "Letter to Richard Price of 22 March 1778," *Oeuvres.* 1810, Vol. 9, Paris: Delance.

Tveite, Stein 1980. "'Overbefolkning,' 'Befolkningspress' og 'Vandring,'" in Langholm and Sejersted (eds.), pp. 43–52.

UN 2009. "Net Migration (Per Year), Both Sexes Combined (Thousands)," Population Division of the Department of Economic and Social Affairs of the United Nations Secretariat, *World Population Prospects: The 2008 Revision,* http://esa.un.org/unpp.

————— 2006. "UN Statistics Show Migration as a Dynamic and Diversifying Force in Global Development," press release: September 12, http://www .un.org/migration/presskit/pressrelease12sept.pdf.

————— 1979. "Trends and Characteristics of International Migration since 1950," *Department of Economic and Social Affairs. Demographic Studies* No. 64.

————— 1958. "Economic Characteristics of International Migrants: Statistics for Selected Countries, 1918–1954," United Nations Population Studies, No. 12. New York: UN Department of Economic and Social Affairs.

UN Demographic Yearbooks various years. New York: Department of International Economic and Social Affairs.

UNDATA 2010. "World Development Indicators," http://data.un.org/Data .aspx?q=gdp&d=WDI&f=Indicator_Code%3aNY.GDP.MKTP.CD.

UNDP 2010. [United Nations Development Programme] "HDI Trends and Indicators (1980–2007)," http://hdr.undp.org/en/media/HDI_trends_ components_2009_rev.xls.

———— 2009. *Overcoming Barriers: Human Mobility and Development.* Human Development Report 2009. New York: Oxford University Press.

———— 2008. *Access for All: Basic Public Services for 1.3 Billion People.* China Human Development Report 2007/08. Beijing: China Publishing Group Corporation.

———— 2002. *Deepening Democracy in a Fragmented World.* Human Development Report 2002. New York: Oxford University Press.

———— 1997. *Human Development and Poverty Alleviation.* China Human Development Report. Beijing: UNDP.

———— 1990. *Human Development Report 1990.* New York: Oxford University Press.

UNPOP 2008. [United Nations Population Division] "World Population Prospects: The 2008 Revision," Population Division of the Department of Economic and Social Affairs of the United Nations Secretariat, http://esa.un.org/unpp.

UPECEDS-San Marino 2009. [Ufficio Programmazione Economica e Centro Elaborazione Dati e Statistica, San Marino] *Bollettino di Statistica,* http://www .upeceds.sm/eng/pubblicazioni.html.

U.S. Department of Commerce 1965. *Statistical Abstract of the United States: 1965.* Washington, DC: U.S. Government Printing Office, Bureau of the Census.

U.S. Department of Labor 1989. *The Effects of Immigration on the US Economy and Labor Market,* Immigration Policy and Research Report 1. Washington, DC: U.S. Department of Labor.

USDA 1974. [U.S. Dept. of Agriculture] "Statistics on Cotton and Related Data, 1920–1973," *Statistical Bulletin No. 535.* Washington, DC: Economic Research Service USDA.

Utvandringskomiteen 1912–13 1915a. *Indstilling II.* "Lov om utvandring m.v." Kristiania: Departementet for Sociale Saker, Handel, Industri og Fiskeri.

———— 1915b. *Indstilling III.* "Om foranstaltninger til at lette nordmaend at flytte hjem til Norge." Kristiania: Departementet for Sociale Saker, Handel, Industri og Fiskeri.

Vanhanen, Tatu 2007. "Measures of Democracy 1810–2006," FSD1289, version 3.0 (2007-11-15). Tampere: Finnish Social Science Data Archive, http://www.fsd.uta.fi/english/data/catalogue/FSD1289/meF1289e.html.

———— 2003. *Democratization: A Comparative Analysis of 170 States.* London: Routledge.

Vickery, William Edward 1977. *The Economics of the Negro Migration, 1900–1960.* New York: Arno Press.

Villarreal, René 1977. 'The Policy of Import-Substituting Industrialization, 1929–1975," in Reyna and Weinert (eds.) *Authoritarianism in Mexico.* Philadelphia: Institute for the Study of Human Issues, pp. 67–104.

284

Bibliography

Weiner, Myron 1995. *The Global Migration Crisis*. New York: HarperCollins.
Wergeland, Agnes Mathilde 1906. "Hvorfor folk udvandrer?" *Nylænde* (June): 167–74; 188–95.
Wergeland, Henrik 1837. "Om Udvandring til Amerika." *Statsborgeren*, April 16, http://www.dokpro.uio.no/wergeland/WIII3/WIII3085.html.
Wickramasekera, Piyasiri 2002. "Asian Labour Migration: Issues and Challenges in an Era of Globalization," International Migration Papers, No. 57. Geneva: ILO, http://www.ilo.org/public/english/protection/migrant/download/imp/imp57e.pdf.
Wilkie, James W. 1971. "New Hypotheses for Statistical Research in Recent Modern History," *Latin American Research Review* 6 (2): 3–17.
Wimmer, Andreas and Nina Glick Schiller 2003. "Methodological Nationalism, the Social Sciences, and the Study of Migration: An Essay in Historical Epistemology," *International Migration Review* 37 (3): 576–610.
———— 2002a. "Methodological Nationalism and Beyond: Nation-State Building, Migration and the Social Sciences," *Global Networks* 2 (4): 301–34.
———— 2002b. "Methodological Nationalism and the Study of Migration," *European Journal of Sociology* 43 (2): 217–40.
Winters, L. A. 2002. "The Economic Implications of Liberalising Mode 4 Trade." Paper prepared for the Joint WTO-World Bank Symposium on "The Movement of Natural Persons (Mode 4) under the GATS," Geneva, April 11–12, preliminary (April 8) draft, http://www.tessproject.com/guide/pubs/mode4/Economic_Implications_of%20Lib_Mode4_Trade.pdf.
Woodson, Carter G. 2008 [1918]. "The Migration of the Talented Tenth," in Woodson (ed.), *A Century of Negro Migration*, http://www.caraf.camdenlinks.org.uk/pdf/century-negro-migration%5B1%5D.pdf.
World Bank 2006. *Global Economic Prospects. Economic Implications of Remittances and Migration 2006*. Washington, DC: World Bank.
Wyman, Mark 1993. *Round-Trip to America. The Immigrants Return to Europe, 1880–1930*. Ithaca: Cornell University Press.
Zachariassen, Aksel 1939. *Martin Tranmæl*. Oslo: Tiden.
Zangrando, Robert L. 1980. *The NAACP Crusade against Lynching, 1909–1950*. Philadelphia: Temple University Press.
Zhu, Nong and Xubei Luo 2008. "The Impact on Rural Poverty and Inequality in China," World Bank Policy Research Working Paper No. 4637.
Zodrow, George R (ed.) 1983. *Local Provision of Public Services: The Tiebout Model after Twenty-Five Years*. New York: Academic Press.
Zolberg, Aristide R. 1981. "International Migrations in Political Perspective," in Kritz et al., (eds.), pp. 15–51.

Index

For EU product safety concerns, contact us at Calle de José Abascal, 56–1°,
28003 Madrid, Spain or eugpsr@cambridge.org.

www.ingramcontent.com/pod-product-compliance
Ingram Content Group UK Ltd.
Pitfield, Milton Keynes, MK11 3LW, UK
UKHW042153130625
459647UK00011B/1313